Managing School Time

Brian Knight

In association with
The National Association of Head Teachers

Published by Longman Group UK Limited
6th Floor, Westgate House, The High, Harlow, Essex CM20 1YR
Telephone (0279) 442601
Fax (0279) 444501

First published 1989
Reprinted 1990

British Library Cataloguing in Publication Data
Knight, Brian
    Managing school time.
    1. Schools. Curriculum. Planning
    1. Title
    375'.001

ISBN 0-582-03085-4

ISBN 0-582-03085-4

Printed and bound in Great Britain by
Biddles Ltd, Guildford and King's Lynn

Contents

Dedication

I would like to dedicate this book to the memory of Barry Taylor, the most humane and thoughtful of Chief Education Officers. It was he who first encouraged me to write about school time. I hope that he would approve.

* * * * *

'I want to establish a school where the clock will be stopped from morning to midnight. I want the age limit for admission lifted and the classes so organised that a boy or girl working ... who has an hour or two to spare, may come to school. I know I will be laughed at, but what of it? I already have a name for that school. It is Opportunity.'

Emily Griffith self-educated rustic schoolteacher and founder in 1916 of the Public Opportunity School, Denver, Colorado.

List of Tables

List of diagrams

Foreword

This book has only been made possible by the kindness and help of many people. I owe a great debt of gratitude to all who have answered my enquiries so patiently and helped in so many other ways.

For information on the use of school time in the United Kingdom I received detailed information from the following schools, for which I am most grateful: Ansford School, Castle Cary, Somerset; Banbury School, Wiltshire; Blyth Tynedale High School, Northumberland; Deans Community High School, West Lothian; Ernesford Grange School and Community College, Coventry; Greendown Community School, Swindon, Wiltshire; John Bentley School, Calne, Wiltshire; the former Kinghurst School, Birmingham; Light Hill School, Solihull; North Area College, Stockport; Park School, Rayleigh, Essex; Pike Deans Community High School, Livingstone, East Lothian; Stantonbury Campus, Milton Keynes, Buckinghamshire; Sutton Centre, Sutton-in-Ashfield; Tudor Grange School, Solihull; Whitesmore School, Birmingham.

I have received particular help from the following: Tim Brighouse, Professor of Education at Keele University and formerly Chief Education Officer of Oxfordshire; Susan Fey, Executive Director of the City Technology Colleges Trust; Sarah Draper, Brook School (now part of Handsworth Grange School), Sheffield; Margaret Hayward, Headmistress of Sydenham School, Bridgwater; A. P. Gelsthorpe, Principal, Thomas Estley Community College, Broughton Astley, Leicestershire; Robin Lunn, Headmaster of Archway School, Stroud, Gloucestershire; E. McConnell, Headmaster, Marlborough School, Woodstock, Oxfordshire; Ken Shorey, Headmaster of Court Moor School, Fleet, Hampshire; Ken Saxby, Headmaster of Tideway School, Newhaven; Chris Stark, Deputy Head, Devizes School, Wiltshire; Squadron Leader L. W. Ward of the Service Children's Education Authority, Ministry of Defence.

I would also like to thank sincerely my former colleagues at Holyrood School, Chard, who wrestled with different forms of the school day for so long, and the present Head, Roland Chant.

I would like to acknowledge considerable help from the Local Education Authorities of Avon, Coventry, Dorset, Northumberland, Oxfordshire, Somerset and Surrey, as well as from several branches of the Department of Education and Science.

For Scotland I was very fortunate to obtain detailed advice and help from Bill Ritchie, formerly HM Depute Senior Chief Inspector, Scottish

Education Department; A. G. Robertson, Regional Timetabling Unit, Strathclyde; and Frank Pignatelli, Depute Director of Education, Strathclyde. For Northern Ireland the Education Department, Bangor, kindly provided information.

For information on the use of school time in independent schools, I was greatly assisted by the heads of the following: Bancrofts School; Bedales School; Clifton High School for Girls; City of London School; Eton College; Gordstonstoun School; Harrow School; King Edward's School, Bath; Ladies College, Cheltenham; Manchester Grammar School; Marlborough College; Merchant Taylors School; Millfield School; Nottingham High School; Paragon School, Bath; Plymouth College; Queens College, Taunton; Roedean School; Wellington School and Wells Cathedral School.

I received particularly valuable assistance from S. M. Andrews, Headmaster, and David Goodland, formerly Senior Master, Clifton College; T. B. Wheare, Headmaster of Bryanston School; and Alan Quilter, South West Regional Director of ISIS.

For the use of school time in Europe I am most grateful for detailed assistance from Mr. John Richardson of the Eurydice European Unit of the EC. For information on individual countries I am indebted to the London Embassies of Belgium, Denmark, the Federal Republic of Germany, France, the German Democratic Republic, Greece, Hungary, the Republic of Ireland, Netherlands, Norway, Spain and Switzerland; the Austrian Institute and Italian Cultural Institute; and the Ministries or Boards of Education in Finland, Luxembourg, Portugal and Sweden.

In the USA I received helpful information from the Departments of Education in Minnesota and Wyoming and the Montana Office of Public Institutions. I am very grateful for the help and advice of the following: Frank Hutchings of the Mid-Continent Regional Educational Laboratory, Colorado; Professor Raymond Gilbert, Northwestern State University, Louisiana and Vancell Stovall, Caddo Parish School Board, Shreveport; The Los Angeles Unified School District; Sally McIntosh and Herbert Weinfield, Office of Federal Projects Administration, Dade County Public Schools Board, Florida; Richard Miller, Executive Director of the American Association of School Administrators; Prudence Opperman, New York City Board of Education; Sam Pantleo, Principal of Central High School, Pueblo, Colorado; Thomas Shannon, Executive Director of the National School Boards Association; Edwin Steinbrecher, Assistant Superintendent, Jefferson County Schools, Colorado; S. C. L. Stiverson, Colorado Department of Education.

For Canada I benefitted from help from the Ontario Department of Education and J. E. Brooks, Principal of Tilbury District High School, and detailed information from Marion Nelles of Brantford, Ontario.

I am particularly grateful to Dr. Clive Dimmock of the Department of Education, University of Western Australia for help and advice on school time developments in Australia. I received most helpful information from the Education Departments of New South Wales, the Northern Territory, Queensland, South Australia, Tasmania, Victoria and the office of the Australia Capital Territory Schools Authority.

For New Zealand I am most grateful for the detailed advice from Murray Jaspers, Education Officer in the New Zealand Department of Education.

I have also been fortunate to receive considerable assistance from the London Embassies of Colombia, Pakistan and South Africa; the Indian High Commission in London; and the Ministry of Education and Culture in Israel. I am also indebted to the following for their kind assistance: Tao Ximing, Director of the Beijing Municipal Education Bureau; Miss Selina Love, Deputy Head of Labone Secondary School, Accra; Mr. Laoki Murata, First Secretary at the Japanese Information Centre, London; Miss Violet Loo of the Singapore High Commission in London; and the Headmaster of St. Paul's British School, S. Paulo, Brazil.

I would also like to thank a number of people and organisations who have all helped in different ways: R. E. Born, Principal Psychologist of the Dorset LEA, for use of his paper on arousal theories; Dr. Robert Burns, Senior Research Scientist, Far West Laboratory for Educational Research and Development, San Francisco; Professor John Carroll of the University of North Carolina; David Hargreaves, Professor of Education, Cambridge University; Dr. Jim Hough of Loughborough University of Technology School of Education; Keith Palmer, formerly Deputy Head of Banbury School; Graham Parker, Principal Architect of the Architects and Building Branch of the Department of Education and Science; and Philip Waterhouse, formerly Director of the NCET Supported Self Study Project. I am also grateful for the encouragement and support of Professor Richard Pring of the University of Exeter School of Education, and of his colleague Dr. Michael Golby who also kindly read a draft of the book. I would like to express my gratitude to the staff of the School of Education library for all their assistance. I have also received great help from the library of the National Union of Teachers and the data-base of the National Development Centre for Management Training, Bristol.

I would like to thank particularly Tim Simkins, Senior Lecturer, Centre for Educational Management, City Polytechnic, Sheffield, who kindly read and commented on a considerable portion of the book, and Dr. Audrey Stenner, Head of Buckden Primary School, Cambridgeshire, who read a full draft and commented upon it. Their help has been invaluable.

Finally, this book would not have been possible without the help and support of my dear wife Joan. Apart from dealing totally with the word processing and correspondence and helping in innumerable other ways, she has also endured for years my own fixation with the use of school time. To her I owe more than I can say.

Acknowledgements

We are grateful to the following for permission to reproduce copyright material:

The Australian Council for Educational Research Ltd for an extract & Fig 1.5 adapted from C. Power 'Initio Ad Finem: Dr Who and Alternative Ways of Organising Time in Education' in *Alternative Ways of Organising Time in Education'* (1980), (c) Australian Schools Commission; the Author, Professor F. Coulter for Fig 9.3 from his article 'Homework — a neglected research area' in *British Educational Research Journal* 5.(1) 1979. Carfax Publishing Co; Professor J. Carroll for Fig 8.1 developed from 'A Model of School Learning' in *Teachers College Record* 64(8) 1963; Devizes School for Fig 3.2 from *Devizes School Flexi-time leaflet;* Embassy of Japan for Table 6.2 (adapted) from p7 in *Education in Japan: A Brief Outline* (1986). Ministry of Education, Science and Culture, Japan; the Controller of Her Majesty's Stationery Office for Table 3.2 after Table 21 in *HMI Survey of Primary Education in England* (1978). McCutchan Publishing Corporation for Tables 8.1 (after), 8.2 (adapted) from Tables 6.1 & 6.2 by Penelope Peterson & Herbert Walberg pp 127 & 128 *Research on Teaching.* (c) 1979 by McCutchan Pubg. Corp. Berkley, CA 94702; The Mid-continent Regional Educational Laboratory (McREL) for Fig 8.4 from *Achieving Excellence* (1988); Panorama DDR for Table 6.1 from Table p 62 in *Education in the GDR* (1987); John Wiley Inc for Fig 8.2 adapted from Fig p5266 *International Encyclopaedia of Education* ed. T. Husen & T. Postlethwaite.

Glossary

ALT	Academic learning time (see chapter eight)
BTEC	Business and Technician Education Council
BTES	Beginning Teacher Evaluation Study (see chapter eight)
CDT	Craft, design and technology
CGLI	City and Guilds of London Institute
CIPFA	Chartered Institute of Public Finance and Accountancy
CPVE	Certificate of Pre-Vocational Education
DES	Department of Education and Science
FE	Further Education
GCSE	General Certificate of Secondary Education
HMI	Her Majesty's Inspectorate
ILEA	Inner London Education Authority
INSET	In-service Training
MSC	Manpower Services Commission (now renamed The Training Agency)
NCET	National Centre for Educational Technology (formerly CET)
NUT	National Union of Teachers
PTR	Pupil – teacher ratio
SCOTVEC	Scottish Vocational Education Council
SSS	Supported Self Study
TVEI	Technical and Vocational Education Initiative

Timetabling: commonly referred to in North America as scheduling.

1 Time as a resource

The use of time pervades every aspect of a school. The head in his or her study, the teacher in the classroom, the student at homework, the parent helper and the adult user — all are deeply affected by it. The timetable and the bell, the systems and the structures and even more our unquestioned assumptions about school time and the forces that shape it, rule our educational lives.

Throughout this book four ideas constantly recur:

1. Time is a very important resource, affecting fundamentally almost every aspect of a school.
2. The use of this resource can and should be systematically analysed and studied.
3. Time structures and systems should be planned and designed, not just allowed to grow.
4. The existing structures and systems, evolved largely in the last century, are ill-suited to the last years of this century and the beginning of the next. In the schools that serve the 'Information Society' new time systems will be needed.

Time then is an ever-present, all-pervading resource in schools, affecting in one way or another virtually everything we do. But if it is an essential resource it is also a very odd one.

It cannot be seen, heard or touched, and is almost impossible to define. Yet it can be described, measured, structured and managed. It is twenty-four hours finite: it cannot be compressed or expanded. It cannot be transferred or stored, and has to be spent. Yet it is inexhaustible. And all financial resources in schools have to be converted into units of time before they can be used.

The role of time as a resource

Financial resources have to be transmuted twice before they actually affect the classroom process. First, money has to be converted into physical resources: staff, premises, goods and services. But these physical resources have to be made available in units of time (resource hours) for actual use. The process looks simple enough (see Fig. 1.1).

The two conversions are quite different. The first mainly determines the mix and selection of physical resources. Once the mix has been decided the quantities of various resources are fixed, apart from minor improvements from wise purchasing.

1

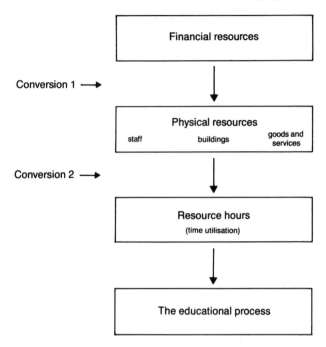

Figure 1.1 – Conversion of financial resources for use in the educational process

Example
If an additional £1,000 is granted to a school, the chosen mix of
resources will decide whether say £100 of it is spent on specific
textbooks. Once this allocation is decided, the quantity of books
is virtually determined, (although a discount could produce a small
increase).

The second conversion, into resource hours, is quite different. At
this stage there can be no alteration in the mix, quality or quantity
of the resources themselves. The conversion impacts not on the
resources but on their use. The quality of use can be affected —
teaching on Friday afternoon may be less effective than Monday
morning. But the dramatic effect is on quantity. In the case of staffing
the effect is more restricted, because salaries can only bring a limited
number of hours, depending on contract or custom and practice. Even
here there can be considerable scope for increased contact-time. For
example the Audit Commission (1985: 30 – 33) highlighted substantial
scope for improvements in 'lecturer productivity' in further education.
But the greatest variation is in the use of premises and goods. Here
time usage can vary from nil to a theoretical maximum of 24 hours

per day, 365 days per year. As the use of new educational technology and community demand for use of premises grows, this aspect of conversion into resource hours will become increasingly important.

Example
If £1,000 is allocated to school A and school B and in each school half is spent on staffing and half on a computer, the mix is 1:1 in cash terms, the same for both schools. But while this finance will buy the same amount/grade of teaching hours in each school, if school A locks the computer in a cupboard and school B runs it from dawn to dusk, the 'computer hours' in school B will be vastly different from school A, and its ratio of computer resources : staffing resources is greatly increased in use terms (though not in cash terms).

The simple conversion model now looks rather more complicated (see Fig. 1.2).

There is an additional complication. Not all time use in schools is derived from financial resources. A considerable amount is donated — by students, who choose whether to attend in class or do homework, and by volunteer helpers (and in this category we could include teacher out-of-school activities). Of course it can be argued that such resources are really paid for by the opportunities foregone by the donors. However they are 'free' for the school and are a very substantial element in the total time resource available. So they are shown as an additional stage in the conversion process at the bottom of Fig. 1.2.

There are other aspects of the conversion process to consider. The first conversion involves managers in active decision-making on recruitment and deployment of staff, development of premises and purchase of goods and services. The second operates more in a 'black box' mode. The school sets up time structures and time management policies, and these determine quantities of resource hours almost automatically — so many lessons for Mr. Smith, so much homework for Jenny Brown, so much usage for Room 99 and so on. For this conversion the school's managers take a more passive role, partly because the system takes over and partly because once the structures and policies have been set up they tend not to change, for reasons outlined in the next chapter.

Time structures

School time is organised in structures which fall into three categories:

1. Macro-structures: the school year, school week and the framework of the school day. These are determined at least in part by external forces,

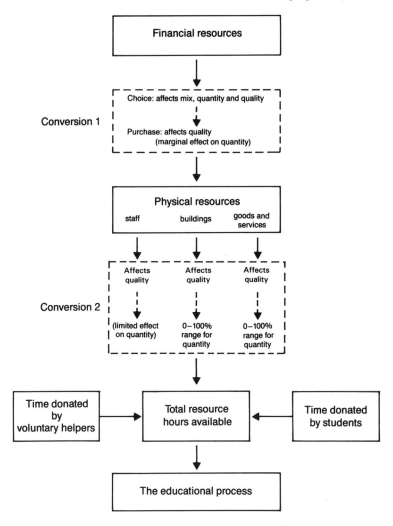

Figure 1.2 – Conversion of financial resources into resource hours

and affect not just the school but other schools, agencies, and transport as well as parents and the community.

2. Micro-structures: the timetable; lesson, course and activity lengths; modules and units; special events; extension of school (such as out-of-school activities), etc. These micro-structures are internal to the school and closely related to the curriculum.

3. Individual time patterns: teachers, non-teaching staff and pupils will have their own patterns of time use determined partly by need and habit but also by the macro- and micro-structures.

These individual patterns fall into three groups:

  (a) Time directing other people, e.g. a teacher managing his or her class, the head or senior teacher managing staff.
  (b) Time cooperating with other people, e.g. team-teaching, the operation of departments, groups of children in class or in teams, community education activities.
  (c) Individual centred activities, e.g. school or department administration; teacher preparing lessons, assessing work etc; teacher or student engaged in individual study, at school or at home.

Inherent in individual time patterns are priorities for the use of time, whether explicit or implicit.

Structures of any kind support an activity and reflect it. But they also limit it and determine what it can be used for. The layout of a kitchen limits and even determines what can be cooked in it; the structure of a building influences its use; the structure of our language affects our ideas. Time structures in a school limit and to some extent determine its curriculum, its pastoral arrangements, its ethos and its relationship with the local community, as well as the activities and life of its staff and students. If they were visible this would be patently obvious. Significantly, when they do take a physical form — the timetable on the wall, the school bell — they are only too apparent.

School time structures are not predetermined. We create them, by decision or default. For any one purpose there is always a wide range of structures available — much wider than we commonly recognise — with many different characteristics:

rigid	— flexible
formal	— informal
uniform	— varied
regular	— irregular
group-based	— individualised
age-related	— non age-related
linear	— modular
coarse grained	— fine grained
compartmented	— integrated
prescriptive	— spontaneous
branching/spiral	— repetitive

Time structures do not just affect the content of school activity: they also affect its quantity and quality.

Time use: quantity

The most striking thing about the quantity of school time is the lack of it. Typically, schools are closed for almost half the days of the year. On the days that they are open, excluding lunch-breaks they are only in session for about 40 per cent of the time from 8 a.m. to 10 p.m.,

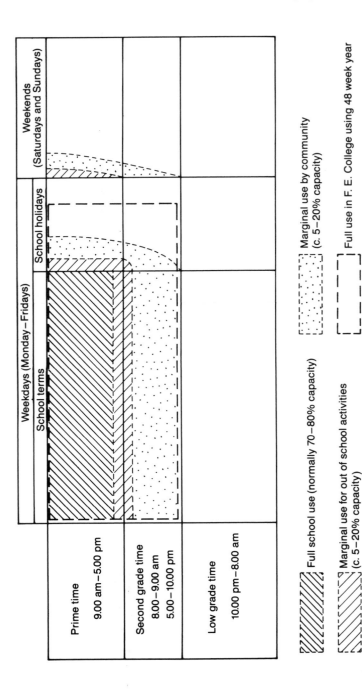

Figure 1.3 – The proportion of time in a calendar year used by a school in England and Wales

with some marginal addition for out-of-school and community activities, and only 60 per cent of the time from 9 a.m. to 6 p.m. If we look at actual lesson-time the percentages are lower still: 33 and 50 per cent respectively.

Fig.1.3 shows the proportion of the time in a calendar year (365 twenty-four hour days) which is typically utilised by English schools. Time available has been divided into three zones. (The actual times of these zones would need adjusting slightly for other countries. However the pattern will be broadly similar.)

1. Prime time, 9 a.m. – 5 p.m.: daylight, warmer and related to normal working hours.
2. Second grade time, 8 – 9 a.m. and 5 – 10 p.m.: usable 'working time'. Conventionally little used for children's education in England, but the evening time is heavily used for adult education and leisure for all ages.
3. Low grade time, 10 p.m. – 8 a.m.: largely dark, colder, mainly used for sleeping and ablutions.

Of course the situation varies slightly from school to school. Some schools have extensive community use (although its percentage utilisation of available space will still be quite small.) Schools outside the state system tend to have slightly greater utilisation, with more out-of-school activities and often Saturday morning or late afternoon lessons, and obviously more if they are boarding schools. The situation varies from country to country, particularly for those with hot climates, although surprisingly little in terms of total percentage utilisation. But overall, schools are very poor users of the potential time available. They compare badly with further education colleges, particularly those operating a 48 week year. This is illustrated by the area enclosed by a broken line on Fig.1.3.

The fact that this low time utilisation by schools occurs worldwide suggests there may be compelling reasons for it: the economics of transport, timetabling considerations, social control factors, family and community pressures etc. And obviously the paid staffing resources of a school can only provide a given number of hours. So if the hatched education area of Fig.1.3 is extended it will only spread lesson time more thinly, unless expenditure increases to expand teaching resources.

However, although extending school hours does not in itself expand the quantity of education, it would increase both the extent of access time and the utilisation of the plant. Fig. 1.4 illustrates this. Let the number of teachers in a school be t and the minimum number of hours per day for them to provide their teaching commitment be h. Then the school's total teacher hours will be th. Two extreme models can be constructed. Model A compresses the duration of the school day into the minimum hours possible; model B doubles its duration (but halves the number of teachers and students present at any one time).

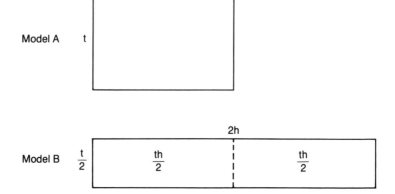

Key: t = number of teachers

      h = minimum hours of a teachers daily commitment

Figure 1.4 – Alternative models of school time utilisation

Both models provide the same quantity of education per week, expressed in teacher hours (*th*). But in model B the school is open for twice as many hours. So a particular room or piece of equipment is available for twice as much use, and students and staff have, at least in theory, twice the access to school facilities.

This simple example illustrates how different time structures alter the use of time and the availability of resources. Although theoretical, it is a perfectly feasible model. If $h = 5.5$ hours daily (a typical duration for a school day excluding lunch), then $2h = 11$ hours, well within the 14 hours of prime and second grade time available each day.) An actual example is explored in chapter twelve.

It is worth noting that model B also affects the quality of time, and indeed the following other aspects of education:

1. The number of students and staff on campus at any one time is halved, on average.
2. School facilities (but only half of them) are available for community use for twice the hours each week.
3. Staff and student commitments are spread over a wider timespan (unless the time is split between two half-school shifts).
4. More choice of activity and more flexibility for course provision can be provided.
5. Communication between staff (and students) will be more difficult.
6. Additional heating and lighting, and possibly transport costs will be incurred.
7. There is accommodation available throughout for additional pupils and staff. Were these to be enrolled, premises and equipment overheads would be spread more thinly and so unit costs would fall.

Time use: quality

In our everyday life we are very aware of the quality of time: 'I get more done before breakfast' 'only come awake after midnight', 'need a deadline to work to', 'just as I was getting interested', 'there are so many interruptions', 'a Friday afternoon car', and so on.

Quality of time in school is affected by a range of factors including:

1. Extent, illustrated in Fig.1.4.
2. Time of day. Traditionally the best working time is first thing in the morning, although current research questions this (see chapter two). Time of week or time of term effects are similar.
3. Duration. The length of an activity affects student motivation, course objectives and content, learning methods.
4. Flexibility. The ability to shorten or lengthen the activity as the learning situation requires.
5. Management. The teacher's effectiveness in managing time in his or her lessons and decisions on time priorities and timetabling have an obvious effect on the quality of time.
6. Student control of time. This can lead to considerable increase in student motivation — but can also lead to a lack of useful activity!

These issues are explored throughout this book.

Time for change

Whatever the quantity and quality of time available, the actual time that we use still lies at that thin edge which unrolls between the past and the future. We cannot change the past; we can only plan to change the future; actual change only occurs in the present.

Unfortunately school time structures are by their nature hostile to change. Major changes in schools, and even many minor changes, can often only be implemented through that narrow window at the start of the first day of the school year. Changes of any consequence in organisation, curriculum, learning methods, timetable, or use of resources commonly need to be introduced then. This is particularly true of secondary schools and colleges. Primary schools can and do change timetables in mid-year, for example in running whole-school projects or for short-term activities, but despite their greater flexibility they too tend to concentrate major change at the start of the year.

Schools have acquired a skeleton of time structures which often allows major change and growth only once a year. This could be the flexibility of a dinosaur! For it is quite possible that once-a-year change will not be enough to allow schools to adjust to accelerating change in society and technology. (This is explored more fully in chapter twelve.) Yet there is nothing inherent about education, as opposed to schools, to create such inflexibility. Community education, for example, can launch major developments in a matter of weeks. So can some of the educational media, and some of the less traditional agencies concerned with education — the Training Agency (TA), formerly the Manpower Services Commission (MSC), for example. Individualised learning can adapt almost instantly. So if schools accept that flexibility for change is important, they will need to adapt their systems to allow for it.

The economics of time

If economics is about decisions in allocating scarce resources that have alternative uses, then it is very much concerned with time. Indeed time features prominently in economic thinking.

Clifford Sharp (1981) provides a useful introduction to the literature and the main theories. He argues that 'the fundamental issue is to consider how time can be allocated between all available activities so that maximum utility can be obtained... the marginal utility from the last unit of time allocated to one of the chosen activities must be greater than that which could be obtained from any excluded activity.' However, this allocation is complicated because many activities have financial as well as time costs. The opportunity costs of the alternative uses to which time can be allocated cannot be separated from the opportunity costs of the finance required for those uses.

This sort of economic analysis is useful for sharpening insight into school time, but it is not very practical. Economists have long puzzled over schools as organisations. If a school is a productive enterprise which produces education, how and why does a change in the input of resources (e.g. time) affect outcomes (e.g. student achievements)? The problem has been to see how the process actually operates, i.e. how resources are allocated to and affect an individual student. In a primary school classroom, for example, we can see the teacher making frequent decisions on the allocation of his or her time to individual students, and the students making frequent individual decisions about how they will use their own time. Some economists have gone so far as to think of students as customers, choosing to buy or not to buy the resources of the school with their time. This links with the idea that education is the accumulation of human capital, partly paid for with the alternative uses of time, and even earnings, which the student foregoes by attending school. This growing emphasis on the micro-economics of the classroom and its relation to teachers' and students' use of time is examined more fully in chapter eight.

Time is sometimes described as 'the school currency'. For example, Colin Power (1980):

> ...time is the coin of the realm in education. Education is a process which takes time, and which can and does occur at points in time other than those which happen to be convenient to an educational institution and its administrators. What educational administrators, teachers, and

students choose to spend their time on is a measure of what they really value in life and in education. Time is what teachers must give if they are to help others to learn. Time is what learners must spend if they are to 'buy' the education they want.

This is a useful metaphor, but it does not fully describe the situation. A currency is a medium of exchange. Time, in its school context, is a measure of the extent to which a good can be utilised. It is best regarded as an enabling or transmuting resource, making other resources accessible and available and affecting their quality and quantity in use.

Some ideas about school time

Because there has been relatively little study of the use of school time, its theory and concepts are underdeveloped. So the most important concept, accepted by most teachers and affecting most schools, is not normally articulated:

'Seat-time'

As I have suggested elsewhere (Knight 1983:101):

> Seat-time is a basic feature of our school economy — as characteristic and as obstructive of change as slavery or strip-farming in other economies. Seat-time decrees that all students of the same age shall sit in their place for the same amount of time, whether they need it or not, whether they benefit or not, whether they progress or not. A student may be doing no more than keeping his/her seat warm. He or she still has to be provided with his or her daily dose of seat-time.

'Seat-time' implicitly underlies the time organisation of most schools. It also leads to a corollary....

The time-ration

If seat-time is fixed and a student cannot have less, then like Oliver Twist he cannot have more. Yet it is self evident that students learn at different rates and need different amounts of time to reach the same standard. However it is the exception for students to receive different amounts of time in relation to their learning needs. There is little logical justification for this situation persisting, although there are historical and perhaps economic reasons for it. It is a classic example of the organisation of an institution determining its method of operation, instead of the opposite.

These fixed time notions were attacked by John Carroll (1963) whose 'Model of School Learning' suggested that under such conditions differences in aptitude are simply translated into differences of achievement, while under non-fixed time conditions they are translated into the amount of time required to master the same task.

These ideas were taken further by Benjamin Bloom (1968) who, in his strategy of mastery learning, suggested that given sufficient time and the right learning conditions, most people could learn most tasks. In theory, anyone could master anything if the amount of learning time available is infinite. (This is improbable at the extremes, but acceptable. Unmusical as I am, I could probably learn to play a Beethoven concerto if my life depended on it — though it might take many years!)

Time as a container
In the same family of fixed time ideas is the concept that time is a container of fixed capacity to hold the curriculum. Popularly this is expressed as the problem of 'getting the quart into the pint pot'. The desirable curriculum, with ever increasing demands for new knowledge, understanding and skills, is seen as much larger than the time available. But quite apart from the possibilities of increasing the time available by extending the school day or using it more effectively, or increasing students' learning at home or at a distance, or by extending the period of education (lifelong?), the answer to the riddle is quite simple:

Q. 'How can we get the quart into the pint pot?'
A. 'By filling the pint pot twice as fast.'

The metaphor breaks down at this point because it suggests throwing out the first pint from the pot to make way for the second. But conceptually it contains an important truth. If learning can be achieved twice as fast, the student can learn twice as much. This emphasis on the accelerated use of time to increase efficiency will become important once the new educational technology makes its full impact. After all, much new technology is labour-saving — and labour-saving is a synonym for time-saving. Shops speed the turnover of goods; factories reduce the production time for their products; hospitals can complete more operations because patients are moved out more quickly. In schools it is not clear that the learning process has yet become much, if at all, faster.

Criterion-referencing
This is related to mastery learning. Simply stated it is the idea that learning should be related to criteria of achievement, not to a norm for the expected average achievement of a group. The example often quoted is the driving test, taken by the learner when ready, whether after learning for ten days or ten years. So in theory at least it discounts failure and uses flexible use of time to allow students to meet the criteria.

This too is a powerful concept, but putting it into practice has proved elusive. In England and Wales the General Certificate of Secondary

Education (GCSE), the new secondary school examination, is finding criterion-referencing very difficult to implement, largely because the criteria become very complex. Criterion referencing has been more successful in graded tests for foreign languages which are not age- or stage-related and are taken when students are ready to achieve them.

Disposable time and 'time-pools'

The idea of disposable income is familiar. Disposable time is similar — that quantity of 'free' time left after necessary time has been committed to essential work, sleep, eating, ablutions and household chores.

In a school a teacher or student may allocate some of this disposable time to extend his or her school activities. It is very unlikely that he or she will be willing to allocate all of it, because of other demands. So we can visualise each teacher or student as having a limited 'pool' of time which he or she proposes to devote to education. The pool will at any one time have a maximum size, which will be increased by involvement, motivation and interest. It will also have a minimum, often established in theory by statute, contract or custom but likely to be further reduced in practice by demotivation, disaffection and boredom.

Time as a variable in educational provision

A very useful insight into the use of time as a variable in producing alternative educational provision for different clients was developed by Power (1980). He saw education as being largely equated since the 19th century with schools, whereas an analysis of client groups and programmes to meet their needs could suggest many alternative forms of provision.

To assist this analysis, Power sees provision as a three dimensional matrix with clients, programmes and time as the three dimensions (see Fig. 1.5).

He suggests that it is helpful to identify existing client/programmes and describe them in terms of current time arrangements. By modifying the time variable, and considering other possible time arrangements, alternative or improved programmes and/or access for additional clients can be identified.

Example

Basic literacy skills programmes for children with special needs are normally provided within the school day and school term, usually at set times on a regular weekly basis and often continuing indefinitely.

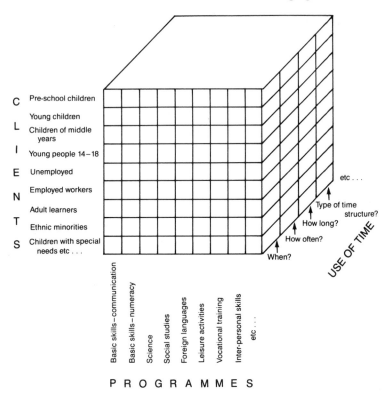

Source: Adapted from Power C (1980: 102)

Figure 1.5 – Using time as a variable to create educational alternatives

If we consider different time arrangements we may uncover alternatives. Similar programmes for adult literacy, for example, are informal in structure and suited in timing, frequency and duration to the preference of the client. Clearly this is one alternative method of provision. A further alternative might be to combine adult and juvenile literacy programmes. A third could lie in extended day programmes, before or after school, or in holiday programmes. A fourth could be pre-school advancement programmes, and a fifth 'intensive burst' programmes offering total immersion in this skill area. A sixth could be informal but timetabled individual counselling sessions and so on.

This example illustrates the value of this matrix concept for broadening thinking about time arrangements and so leading to alternative provision.

The costs of school time

Time costs money, and school time in a labour intensive industry is expensive.

Unit costs

As can be seen from Table 1.1, educating a primary pupil in England and Wales in 1988 – 89 cost approximately 1.8p a minute, £1.08 an hour, £5.76 a day and £1,095 a year. Educating a secondary student cost 2.8p a minute, £1.67p an hour, £9.19p a day and £1,747 a year.

Such figures are useful for highlighting the cost of school time but they don't much help the manager. They are broad national averages and will differ considerably between Local Education Authorities (LEAs), schools, classes and activities. The pupil-teacher ratio will be the main determinant of such variation. However, they could be more useful when costings for alternative learning approaches become available, e.g. a comparison of classroom, computer assisted and distance learning costs for similar learning activities.

Time as a cost factor

School time is in various ways a determinant of school costs. The most significant aspect is the ratio of teachers' contact : non-contact time, i.e. the proportion of their school time spent in front of a class. The Audit Commission (1986) found that for all secondary teachers in England and Wales this averaged 78.3 per cent for shire counties, 77.2 for metropolitan districts and 73.2 for London LEAs, with an average of 77.4. The variations between individual LEAs were even wider, from 69.3 per cent in ILEA to 81.8 in the Isle of Wight. Variations between and within secondary schools will obviously be greater still. Contact ratios in primary schools are higher. The average for maintained primary school teachers in England, January 1986, was 91.4. This included heads and deputies so the average contact time for a classroom teacher time would be higher still.

Such variations substantially affect classroom unit costs and may affect the value for money achieved, particularly through the pupil-teacher ratio (PTR), and with it average class size and the number of lessons provided. Higher contact ratios can either improve provision or reduce expenditure. However non-contact time provides time for servicing classroom activity as well as for management, professional development and pastoral work. So reducing it too severely may not be cost effective.

Other aspects of school time management also affect expenditure. Different patterns of school day, school week and school year can have an effect upon the cost of:

Table 1.1 Average school time unit costs in England and Wales 1988 – 89

		Primary			Secondary	
Cost of educating one pupil						
For one minute			1.8p			2.8p
For one 35-minute period			63	p		98	p
For one hour	£	1.08		£	1.67	
For a school day	£	5.76		£	9.19	
For a school week	£	28.82		£	45.97	
For a school year	£	1,095.30		£	1,747.00	
For 4 × 35-minute periods per week for a year (typical course)				£	148.00	
For 4 periods per week for 5 years (typical 5 year course, eg French)				£	741.00	

Cost of educating one class of average size						
(taken as 24.25 primary, 20.43 secondary)						
For one minute			44	p		57	p
For one 35-minute period	£	15.29		£	19.92	
For one hour	£	26.21		£	34.15	
For 4 periods (eg a week's science)	£	61.16		£	79.69	
For one period per week for a year	£	581.00		£	757.00	
For 4 periods per week for 1 year (a typical course)	£	2,324.00		£	3,028.00	
For 4 periods per week for 5 years (eg a 5-year science course)	£	11,620.00		£	15,142.00	
For one school day (eg a primary class)	£	140.00		£	188.00	
For one school week	£	699.00		£	939.00	
For a school year	£	26,561.00		£	35,691.00	

Cost of one school					
(Primary 200 pupils, secondary 800 pupils)					
For one hour	£	216.00	£	1,337.00
For one day	£	1,153.00	£	7,356.00
For one school week	£	5,764.00	£	36,778.00
For one school year	£	219,060.00	£	1,397,600.00

Note: These costs exclude debt charges and school meals but include central LEA administration, transport and aid to pupils.

Source: CIPFA Education Statistics 1988 – 89, net expenditure per pupil pp 57 and 62.

- teaching salaries
- non-teaching salaries
- wear and tear on premises
- heating, lighting and water charges
- school meals, and free school meals
- transport from home to school
- community education costs

The spread of local management of schools, arising in England and Wales from the 1988 Education Reform Act, and from similar developments in Australia, the USA and Canada, and in Europe, will lead to a growing awareness of the interrelation between school time and school finances. Looking further to the future, the growth of individualised use of time, as opposed to class-orientated time, is likely to lead both to increased and reduced expenditures — at present it is not clear where the balance will lie (this is explored in chapter nine).

The impact of time as a resource

I suspect that many readers, as well as the author, will still be baffled about the real nature of time. What actually is it? And what sort of resource is it? And how does it operate?

Four features of school time stand out:

1. It is essentially an enabling resource.
   It makes other physical resources available and manageable.
2. It is normally used in a structured form. The range of these structures, and their effects, is both extensive and underestimated.
3. The management, active or passive, of school time affects virtually every aspect of education — the effective quantity and quality of its resources; the curriculum, learning methods, pastoral care and ethos, community education... and costs.
4. Because time affects each of us every second of the day, we are very sensitive about any change in its management. So the context of time management needs to be fully understood, and this will be examined in the next chapter.

* * * * *

Mr. Smith arrives early at his school. He spent two hours yesterday preparing new maths cards and wishes to set these out before the children's arrival. The children enter, and soon the bell rings.

After he has finished the register and found time to deal with some pupils' pastoral problems, he takes his class of ten year olds to morning assembly. It runs on a little, and so his morning lesson begins late — a pity, since there is a lot to do.

This week Mr. Smith is emphasising maths — his headteacher has suggested that his class should concentrate on that area. She doesn't seem to realise that all the new curriculum activities leave less time for maths. Mr. Smith begins the lesson with firm, clear directions, so the class settle quickly to various activities. Of course they are always fresh early in the morning. He decides to help one group who had difficulties yesterday, and puts off other eager petitioners until later. One of the group has taken his project home and obviously spent much time on it — probably with his family, judging by its content.

By ten o'clock the volunteer aide has appeared, and the pressure on the teacher lessens. Some pupils are flagging and need some of the teacher's time. Others are working purposefully on their own. The cut and thrust of classroom activity continues. 'Helen — stop wasting your time!' 'Johnny, if you've finished, can you help James?' 'Just wait a minute until I've finished this.'

One of the pupils is using a computer. Mr. Smith wonders, has he grasped fractions more quickly than with another method? Will the learning be as lasting? He senses that the class tempo is slowing, and ends the lesson early with some rounding off remarks. But one pupil is looking anxious — she always works more slowly and needs more time. In fact she works on after the bell until she is ushered out.

During the staffroom breaktime, snatches of conversation can be heard. 'Union is raising the four-term year again' '...not obliged to do this within our contract hours'.

After break Mr. Smith is timetabled with a twelve-year old group. He introduces some tasks on costs of various items and uses information from the school management system. 'If this school costs £440 an hour to run, and there are 400 pupils...' After thirty minutes the class breaks off to watch a television broadcast (the video recorder has broken down, so it can't be watched at a more convenient time). On their return work continues. The headteacher comes in and takes up some of Mr. Smith's time while his queue of pupils lengthens. She is thinking of starting the school day earlier — what does he think? It's risky in a community which doesn't like its habits disturbed. As she leaves, she mentions that the room will be used by a community group this evening.

The demand for use of the computer has not been satisfied, and Mr. Smith has agreed to let one group work in his lunch hour...

2 The context: forces at work

School time systems are not invented out of thin air. In fact on the whole they are not invented at all. Usually they evolve, emerge, or just exist.

Where school time systems are not actually designed they are the product of a whole range of powerful social, educational, technical and financial forces. And where they are specifically designed they can only be set up within the parameters which those forces allow (although it may be possible to move the parameters). In either case, the greatest single force — if it can be termed a force — is inertia.

This chapter attempts a systematic analysis of these forces, and so underpins the remaining chapters. Four of these forces — historical, social, financial and organisational — create the general environment in which school time systems operate. They press from the outside and make their main impact on time macro-structures, although this pressure proceeds to affect micro-structures and individual time use (see Fig.2.1). On the whole they are conservative forces, resisting change in time use but rapidly consolidating it if it occurs. The remaining factors — educational, physiological and psychological, technological and management — operate largely from within the school system and on the whole are forces for change.

Historical forces

In the developed world virtually all citizens have been through school. So they have a memory of what school should be like from their impressionable years — and this is even true of those who disliked it.

This image of what school should be like applies particularly to the school day, and to a lesser extent to the school week and year, so it creates a strong, natural resistance to change. It does not extend much to the micro-structures of school time — the memory of those is more hazy and less fundamental — and not at all to individual time use. So it is relatively easy to change individual time use without conflicting with historical preconceptions, but virtually impossible to change macro-structures without doing so. Yet changing the former may need change of the latter.

If a change is made in a school's time structure, the new system rapidly becomes the historical one. Once established it is soon accepted

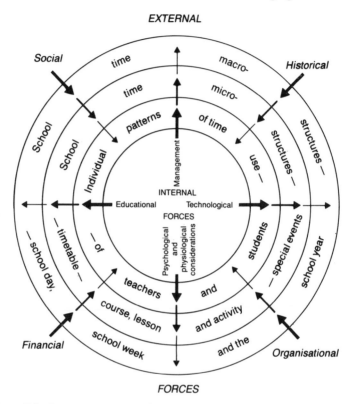

Figure 2.1 – Forces operating on school time systems

as part of the school's history by students, parents and teachers. So this force of history discourages change back as much as further change forward.

Social forces

The social forces affecting school time structures are powerful and extensive. Again, they mainly affect the macro-structures. Once children are safely enfolded inside their school, the internal time arrangements make little impact on society outside. And again, inertia is a crucial factor. The existing time-structures, however unsatisfactory, do exist and so do the social arrangements that support them. Any kind of change will, at least initially, disrupt these arrangements.

Daily routine

Getting up times can vary considerably between families. But almost all families establish a routine, and this has to take account of schools' starting times. A change in school time changes the life of most families with children. Some will welcome it — silently. Others will resist it — vocally. Occupational factors are important. Farmers are accustomed to early rising, but office workers may not welcome it!

Mealtimes are much less important. Most families will adjust these quite easily, and in any case it may often be necessary to feed different members of the family at different times. However it is interesting that the gastronomic French have unusually long school lunch-hours.

Shopping arrangements and domestic chores are less important still. For most families they can be easily adjusted, though they will present difficulties for some. They are easier where food shops have long or late opening hours.

Work

If only one parent of a two parent family works, a change in school hours will create fewer problems, apart possibly from mealtimes or holidays. But if both parents or the sole parent work then much more difficult problems can arise, particularly over supervision and care of children out of school. But the stereotype of the 'working mother' resisting any change in school hours is misleading. Such parents have to be well organised anyway to look after the children in the holidays and often early mornings or late afternoons, so they are often better able to adjust than some non-working mothers or fathers.

Transport

Many families have complicated daily travel arrangements to school and to work, often integrated with other families or working colleagues. A change in the school day is likely to upset these. However, there is often no intrinsic reason why the new times should fit work travel less well. Some families will be gainers, some losers, and once a pattern is re-established the new arrangements will usually be accepted. Already many parents will devise travel arrangements for out of school activities or for children who enter reception classes part time.

Other members of the family

Problems can arise where older children take younger siblings to school or pick them up, or assist older members of the family, or where a parent takes children to two different schools at the same time. A change in school hours can create problems, although eventually new arrangements will be sorted out.

Home conditions

These mainly affect individual time patterns. In under-privileged areas schools may be more reluctant to create extensive home-learning arrangements (in England such schools have sometimes created

optional homework facilities within the school at the end of the day.)
In the future in such areas there could be problems in creating distance
learning arrangements or expanding individualised learning.

Leisure

In the developed world leisure is becoming a potential force *for* change
in the school day. As the leisure hours of the working population
increase, and as people retire earlier and stay fit and healthy longer,
so there will be increasing pressure for school day arrangements to
open up school facilities for the benefit of the community.

An important leisure aspect relating to school time is parents'
holidays. There is an increasing tendency for parents to take children
on holiday during term time, and this leads to greater questioning of
the traditional terms. However in England the traditional holiday
pattern on the whole has been a major factor of resistance to the four-
term year, although it does not seem to have operated so strongly
in the USA against different school year patterns, or in Australia.
Family evening and weekend leisure is not likely to conflict much with
school time. However one can speculate on the furore if an English
state school proposed Saturday, or Saturday morning, working. Yet
this pattern is happily accepted in many independent schools, and
in some European countries.

Safety and security

There will be resistance to any arrangements which appear to risk
children's safety. So starting earlier in the morning will be resisted in
some areas because in winter children will be travelling in the dark,
with a greater risk of accidents (although with less at night). Equally
there is likely to be resistance to arrangements which cause children
to come home at irregular times, particularly if the times are not always
predictable. However, much depends on custom. The French for
example fully accept the idea of older children coming home from
school during the day if they do not have a class. Much depends on
the age of children concerned. Generally parents seem to accept such
arrangements for children over thirteen or fourteen.

Social order

Society may also be disturbed if it feels that the school system is
loosened excessively by new time structures. It sees schools as having
a custodial or socialising role. If a new system appears to be too loose
and to create opportunity for pupils to get into mischief, concerns for
social order will arise.

The ethos of a society

Some societies seem to embrace change of any kind more readily than
others. The USA seems generally quicker to embrace innovation than

the UK (although even in the US there are communities which are very resistant to certain types of change). Education is deeply interwoven with the whole culture of a society, and changing the time arrangements for education may strike deep at the unarticulated beliefs of that culture.

In Germany education is felt to be an integral part of home life, and so it is considered important for children to be at home in the afternoons to be educated. Similarly in Denmark children start school at seven, and then only for limited hours, for similar reasons. But the ethos of a society can also work for change in the use of school time — as it has in Japan in the development of extra evening coaching.

Concern for education

The catalogue of social pressures above, mostly resistant to change in school time arrangements, is daunting. But most parents are concerned that their children should benefit fully from school and be happy there, so if they and the community can be persuaded that a planned change is for the good of their children, they will go along with it and adjust their personal and family lives. Of course they will grumble — and rationalise their personal objections as educational ones! But there are many examples to show that they can and will change if properly prepared and consulted. Social arrangements can be compared to a drainage system. It flows happily for years without disturbance, but when the landscape is altered the drainage is disturbed. However given time it re-establishes new channels and flows smoothly again.

Financial factors

The school time systems that exist are by definition already financed. The funding for them is already established and is seen as 'normal.' So, barring some strong force for retrenchment, the assumption is likely to be made that such systems should continue to be financed (regardless of whether they are effective or not).

Finance, then, is a strongly conservative force in relation to school time, particularly in relation to the macro-structures. Any new system which requires substantial additional funds is likely to be resisted, however commendable it may be. An excellent example of this is the fate of the Newsom Report (1963) recommendation that schools in England and Wales should introduce a third session of additional activities at the end of the school day. At the time it was hailed as an imaginative step — but it did not recognise the financial pressures from increasing the quantity of educational time, leading to additional teacher salary costs, as well as increased transport and some catering and premises costs. It was introduced on a pilot basis in a number of authorities but rapidly withered away.

Different school days, weeks and years may not be so strongly resisted if they just rearrange the same quantity of education. A change which increases the *extent* but not the quantity of education within the school day (as in model B, Fig. 1.4) would lead to some additional heating, lighting and transport costs, and possibly some others, but these would be much more modest and so easier to justify. A more extensive school week — a six-day week — would, however, be much more costly.

In one respect financial considerations can be a force for change. Just as they resist increased expenditure, so they encourage changes which reduce it. In recent years in the United Kingdom financial pressures have driven LEAs to lengthen Christmas and shorten summer holidays to save fuel. A more complex example is school lunch-hours. These create costs for heating and lighting, wear and tear of buildings, and supervisory salaries. They may also affect the profit or loss on school meals. Here again LEAs have encouraged shorter lunch-hours (although the problems of supervision have been the greatest factor for change), and some have even accepted the so-called 'continental day' (see chapter three).

This regard for cost-efficiency in the use of school time will be encouraged by the development of local management of schools. Logically one could expect this to work in favour of compressing the school day to the minimum duration, or reducing the school week to four days and so reducing the number of days in the school year, to reduce premises-related or transport costs. However this pressure conflicts with current trends towards loosening and extending the school day and developing community education on the grounds of greater effectiveness. Indeed compressing school time structures has inherent contradictions: it is more cost-efficient (reduces running costs), but less effective in the use of plant (idle for an even greater part of the year).

The financial implications of changes in school time micro-structures are marginal. On the whole these micro-structures are a sealed system, so while changes in the timetable, lesson lengths, course lengths and structures, and special activities may affect the use of staff or buildings they need not affect appreciably the expenditure on them. However they can have some effect on the need for support staff, books, equipment and materials, examination/assessment costs, and in-service training. But these will be marginal in relation to the whole school budget.

The cost implications of changes in individual time use are much more problematical. In the use of teachers' time, the most important is any change in average contact time. For students' time, the most important is the trend towards supported self-study and individualised and distance learning. This could reduce expenditure on teaching but increase it on tutoring, counselling and non-teaching support salaries.

It is likely to involve additional expenditure on hardware and adaptation of premises, and on software and learning resources (this is discussed in chapter nine).

The financial implications of changes in school time structures are set out in Table 2.1. Column 2 shows the percentage distribution of school costs (secondary schools in England and Wales 1986 – 87, but primary schools are broadly similar), while columns 3 – 6 indicate those items likely to change if time structures are altered, as discussed above.

Organisational factors

Laws, regulations and policies

Every school system has laws and regulations which affect the macro- and micro-structures of school time. Some only affect school time indirectly, e.g. those relating to daily pupil registration. Even independent schools have regulations or at least policies. In theory regulations only reflect the other forces described in this chapter. In practice they acquire a force — an inertial force — of their own. For regulations, and even more legislation, are not revised every year; they remain until it is clear they need revision. And even then it will often be easier to amend particular items than to review the whole.

One can question whether detailed central regulations about school time should be made at all. Would it not be more sensible for central government or local authorities to prescribe the minimum annual quantity of education and leave the governors and heads of schools free to manage the time, including decisions on the actual hours and number of days needed to provide it? The 1988 Education Reform Act is inconsistent: it delegates authority to governors to fix the times and duration of the school day, but not the number of days in the school year.

Types of schools

Just as school types affect curricular or management structures, so they affect time structures.

PRIMARY/SECONDARY

Primary school days tend to be slightly shorter than secondary — often with a shorter day still for the youngest children. Primary timetables are less complex and less structured. Interestingly when middle schools are created for pupils ages 9 – 13, the timetable of the 11 – 13 groups tends to maintain some primary features. So the type of school clearly affects the timetable of these children compared with their secondary school counterparts.

Table 2.1   The financial implications of changes in school time structures (England and Wales, 1986–87)

	2	3	4	5	6
1 Areas of expenditure	Percentage of all expenditure, Secondary Schools (a) 1986–87	Effect on expenditure of changes in time structures			(see key)
		Macro Structures		Micro structures	Individual use of time
		Quantity (b)	Extent (c)		
Teaching and establishment					
Teaching salaries	55.2	/			?
Non-teaching support and clerical salaries	3.7	/	(/) (d)	?	/(e)
Books, stationery, equipment, materials	3.5	(/)		?	/
Other supplies and services; establishment expenses	1.8				
Premises					
Salaries	4.2		?		
Repairs, maintenance and grounds	4.2	(/) (f)	(/) (f)		
Fuel, light, cleaning materials and water	3.5	(/)	/		?
Furniture and fittings	0.2				
Rent/rates	3.3				
Debt charges	5.6				?(g)
School meals (all costs less income, excluding value of pupil free meals)	3.0		?		?
Transport					
Home to School	2.3		?		?
Other	0.3				
Aid to pupils					
(mainly free meals)	1.7				
Community Education	N/A(h)	?	?		
LEA overheads, including inspection and special services	6.1				
Inservice Training	1.2			?	?

Key: /   =   Substantial increase or decrease
      (/)   =   marginal increase or decrease
      ?   =   possible increase or decrease
Notes: (a)   =   Primary school percentages are broadly similar
        (b)   =   Total teacher hours of education provided
        (c)   =   Number of hours in a year over which (b) is provided
        (d)   =   Offices open for longer
        (e)   =   More ancillary support staff required
        (f)   =   More wear and tear
        (g)   =   Modification to premises
        (h)   =   Figures not available
Source of col. 2: CIPFA Education Statistics Estimates 1986–87.

SELECTIVE/COMPREHENSIVE

The comprehensive organisation of schools in England and Wales showed in an interesting way the effect of school type on time structures. Originally most grammar schools operated a 7 x 40 minute period teaching day, and secondary modern schools tended to copy them. When such schools combined this pattern was often retained. Only later was it realised that this did not suit the new type of school and needed changing, often to 8 x 35 minutes. The seven period pattern only allowed three double periods a day — so utilisation of laboratories, workshops and other specialist spaces was 25 per cent less. Also it only provided thirty-five periods in the week, whereas forty made it easier to mount the broader curriculum of the comprehensives.

More recently comprehensive schooling has led to some more imaginative and varied approaches to the school day, outlined in the next chapter.

SMALL/LARGE

Larger schools have greater problems over circulation of students, and may need to adapt a different type of day to allow for this. So large comprehensives often adopt a 5 x 55 minute pattern to reduce the number of lesson changes. They are more likely to timetable time for class movement. Large schools may also have problems over feeding students if the lunch hour is short. Split site schools have particular timetable problems, since allowance has to be made for movement between sites. In addition this movement time eats into the 'time pools' of the teachers.

Size of school could have an important bearing in the future on the use of time for individualised learning. Large schools may find this more difficult to organise, because of the numbers involved, but will be better able to assemble the necessary resources, staffing and accommodation.

RURAL/URBAN

Rural schools have particular constraints, apart from contract transport. Fewer children can leave school in the lunch hour. Use of facilities after school is more difficult to organise (some rural schools even put a 'clubs' session within the normal day to compensate). Urban schools on the other hand can if they wish fit in extra lessons before morning school or after the end of the afternoon.

Changes in enrolments

When student numbers rise beyond the capacity of their buildings, various expedients may be adopted. The simplest is a staggered lunch hour to allow some extra use of specialist accommodation. A more extreme solution is the 'all-year' school introduced in parts of the USA. More extreme still is the shift system which is still used in many countries — in some cases three or even four shifts per day.

The 'open enrolment' provision of the 1988 Education Reform Act in England and Wales is likely to increase pressures from changing enrolment. Popular schools, oversubscribed, will tend to look at such devices to prevent overcrowding and increase utilisation of plant. More sophisticated versions of a shift system could be quite feasible and acceptable, although they have hardly been explored. (All of these features are discussed further in the next chapter.)

Falling rolls may also have some effect on school time. Schools may find they are not large enough to form a viable group in certain subjects and so resort to classes outside the main school day, perhaps with combined age-groups and/or consortium arrangements with neighbouring schools. There is a trend at present for such consortia to develop in England for this reason, particularly in urban areas.

Free or fee-paying

Schools charging fees have more options available for time management, partly because they can augment their total of teacher-hours by charging for extra activities, and partly because their volunteer clients will be willing and often able to make their own transport arrangements. So independent day schools have more varied patterns of school day (as well as the possible use of Saturdays) than their state counterparts. With the development of grant-maintained schools opting out of LEAs and the City Technology Colleges (CTCs), wider school day options may spread to the state sector. It is significant that the CTCs have adopted somewhat different, longer patterns of school day (see chapter three).

The same principle operates in community education, where it is easy to mount additional activities to meet market demand, with fees paying for the additional tutor and other costs — even early morning, late night or weekend sessions.

State schools face a dilemma. Are they to stay rationed in the amount and structure of time they can provide to students of compulsory school age? Or should they acknowledge that once that ration is supplied for all their students, extra time can be provided on a paying basis — for private coaching, extra activities, parent consultations? On the one hand, equality of misery; or the other, differentiation by purse and privilege. To some extent the problem already exists, where students buy into a school residential trip, or in some LEAs pay fees for an evening class. The problem won't go away — in fact with increasing leisure and rising incomes the arguments for this sort of development will strengthen.

Transport

Schools which depend heavily on contract transport are obviously much more constrained in their school day options, particularly if some of the transport is shared with other schools. But urban schools too will often have some transport constraints. The times of local buses or trains may limit possible starting times. In fact transport is almost the first factor to be considered in school day design.

Links with other organisations

A less important factor. Some schools have time arrangements tied in with other schools, for example consortium arrangements for teaching specialist subjects. Others share facilities, for example playing fields or swimming pools. Normally these are not a permanent constraint. However there may be more rigid links with outside organisations, such as external examination boards, which place firm constraints on a short period of the school year.

Community education

This covers a wide range of activities, including:

- adult education classes
- youth or adult vocational training programmes
- community and youth activities
- holiday play schemes
- lettings of school premises to the community usually sporting but also arts, library, etc.
- 'joint use' of facilities, (where two or more authorities have jointly funded capital provision)
- 'dual use' (where a school is adapted and managed to open its facilities to the public)
- networks, linking people or groups of similar interests
- provision for individual study, often with tutorial support
- promoting of community development or welfare

During the school day such activities will probably only use the slack in school accommodation by grace and favour, unless there are areas specifically set aside for them. This school day use need not affect time-structures, but if it flourishes it is likely to create a less formal atmosphere in which new approaches to school time are encouraged.

Outside of the school day community education creates its own timetable. Unlike school timetables this will be very flexible, altering from day to day and week to week as needs require. In many ways it is an ideal but difficult model for future school timetables. It also provides informal extension of the school day, since school students can participate in it and it provides management and supervision which can support school activities as well.

Where community education flourishes it is likely to be a force for change in the use of school time.

Security, cleaning and maintenance arrangements

In some areas school supervision can be a problem. This can inhibit development of less rigid timetable structures unless specific provision is made. The Dukeries Complex at Ollerton in Nottinghamshire for example has a team of caretakers working a seven-day, all year, day and evening shift system for this purpose.

Cleaning can conflict with extended use of school time, though the problem is surmountable. Major maintenance and spring-cleaning programmes do not suit full 52-week use.

The forces described above create the environment for the management of school time, and mainly work from the outside. The remaining forces, however work outward from the centre of the school, from the staff and the individual student or class.

Education theory and practice

In primary schools

In primary schools the use of time has been substantially altered by changes in the curriculum. The original class based routine of English, maths and a very limited curriculum has diversified with physical education, science, art, light craft, and audio-visual aids, and currently with technology and use of computers. Some of these developments require specialist areas, and all of them specialist equipment. So there has been a clear trend for the primary timetable, although still class based, to become more complex and diverse. The actual distribution of activities has remained pragmatic, with some support still for the traditional view that English and maths are best learned in the morning.

Greater changes come from new learning approaches, rooted in new theories. Holistic and heuristic approaches were the parents of the 'integrated day', the most important conceptual contribution from the primary field to the management of school time. Currently this approach is less popular, perhaps because it is more difficult to manage. A strong emphasis on individual and group work has however continued, strengthened by increasing use of volunteer parents. Further trends could arise with the impact of new technology and community education and activities.

In secondary schools

CURRICULUM PRESSURES

Here the curriculum has diversified in a similar way to primary schools. Previous specialist activities like physical education, art, music and domestic crafts have been augmented by increased practical work in science, the growth of craft, design and technology (CDT), drama and the appearance of computing. One consequence has been an increased demand for long or double periods, and the shift towards 40 or 25 period weeks (see chapter three).

At the same time the curriculum became stuffed with more content — new humanities courses, business studies, electronics and computing, various applications of CDT, health and environmental education, personal, social, moral and citizenship education, consumer education…. One reaction in England and Wales was to try and stretch curriculum time by increasing the number of weekly periods, and even the oddity of the six day timetable where Day 1 moved back by one day each week.

Another expedient, almost universally adopted, was to introduce options for 14—16 year olds, and sometimes for younger ages. However, as the demand for additional items continued, these options became overcomplex. The new national curriculum in England and Wales will simplify this and so will probably lead to simpler time-structures. Indeed, it has thrown up all manner of issues about the allocation and use of time. These are examined more fully in the chapter on the curriculum (chapter six).

An interesting example of ideas altering time-structures is the case of equal opportunities. When it became illegal for boys only to work with wood and metal and girls with fabric and food, it became clear that each sex could only spend half the previous time on its traditional material. So 'carousels' were invented to move students through a sequence of different disciplines in the same weekly slot.

Finally, community education has led to the community curriculum — involving students studying, helping and working with their local community, and encouraging adults to come into school and help them in the process. The former aspect, with the need for small-group local visits doesn't fit well into normal period patterns.

NEW LEARNING METHODS

Simultaneously interest has grown in the process rather than the content of the curriculum — in essence the development of skills, attitudes and understanding rather than knowledge. Initially this did not normally require new approaches to the use of time. It could often be developed within the existing structures. However the emphasis on 'process' in the GCSE introduced in 1986 has enlarged the role of projects and fieldwork, neither of which fit very happily into the traditional pattern.

At the same time supported self study has gained momentum — a more coherent approach to individualised study with the vital ingredient of tutorial support. This has been seen as valuable in its own right by teaching study skills, and useful for solving minority subject problems and meeting the needs of gifted children and other special groups. It too fits uneasily into the traditional timetable pattern. (This is explored more fully in chapter nine.)

PREVOCATIONAL EDUCATION

The attempt to make education more relevant to the world of work and more effective at providing the skills required for it is perhaps the best example of new educational thinking affecting the use of school time. It originated in England and Wales with the thinking of the Further Education Unit (e.g. in 'A Basis for Choice' 1979), the work of the Manpower Services Commission (MSC), particularly its Technical and Vocational Education Initiative (TVEI), and the work in schools of the City and Guilds of London Institute (CGLI) and the Business and Technician Education Council (BTEC). Stress was laid on a number of new features, mainly for students 14 – 18, such as:

- – experience based learning
- – problem solving
- – project work*
- – cross-curricular assignments*
- – inter-personal and group skills
- – personal and social development
- – profiles and records of achievement*
- – guidance and counselling*
- – negotiation of the curriculum*
- – work experience*
- – residential experience*

Those marked * do not fit at all well into the traditional timetable, and the others will often feel uncomfortable. To meet these new demands, various devices have been used: work-experience, activity or residential weeks; carousels and options; inter-school and college consortia for courses; team-teaching and blocked time; 'withdrawal' arrangements for guidance and profiling; and modular curricula.

The most interesting use of time for prevocational education has occurred in courses for 16 + students leading to the Certificate for Pre-Vocational Education (CPVE). Here students commonly begin with starter modules but proceed to negotiate their curriculum and its actual structure. The curriculum contains most of the features listed above. However this flexibility is much easier in the 16 + context with students above the compulsory school age and in smaller groups.

MODULAR APPROACHES

These are a very interesting recent phenomenon in schools in the UK, although they have been extensively used in other countries. Modules are important for the curriculum but they also affect school time micro-structures. They make these much more flexible, make possible the development of non age-related courses, and affect the quality of time.

They have produced the key timetabling concept of 'time-slots' and are examined more fully in chapter seven.

It is difficult to draw general conclusions about the effect of educational thinking and practice on school time. It is clear that there is a close connection. It is also clear that when a new educational development emerges, its ideal time use often does not fit well into existing structures. Usually its momentum is not sufficent to change these, and so some device or expedient has to be invented. In the past ten years a much greater number of these non-conforming developments has appeared; if we extrapolate this we can expect existing time structures to come under growing pressure.

Physiological and psychological considerations

Both affect school time, though they are seldom made explicit.

For the former there seems to be a general assumption that school time structures should pay regard to the health and physical well-being of students. There are a number of manifestations: a slightly shorter day for the youngest children; school days normally limited to not more than 6 hours; time for physical recreation — particularly marked in independent schools, which often break up the week with games afternoons, and also French schools which have a games session on Wednesday afternoons.

The notion of fatigue in school needs careful examination. It is not clear that mental fatigue is a physiological problem at all but rather a subjective experience in the form of boredom. If a student changes to new mental work, recovery can be immediate. Postural fatigue does seem to occur, although it is markedly different from fatigue from heavy physical work with its build-up of toxic materials in the muscles. Overall it looks as if traditional school day patterns with a variety of activities, short work-sessions, periodic breaks, playtime and physical exercise are a sound practical solution to the fatigue and boredom problem.

However, school arrangements are not altogether consistent. For example there is evidence that long terms cause a falling-off in performance (and attendance) from teachers and students, yet almost all countries still operate them. Logically there is a case for reducing the less effective learning time on Friday afternoons by closing earlier — yet few schools do so. It would be logical to reduce school time slightly in the first year of secondary education, when the pressures of a new school and subjects, homework and greater travelling make children tired. Yet this is not commonly done. Indeed, the distribution of school time between different ages in England and Wales does not look very logical at all, particularly when compared with a country such as Denmark (see Fig.2.2).

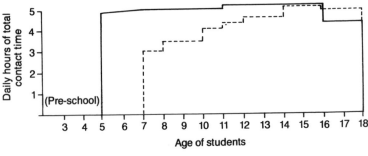

Key: ——— School students, England & Wales, daily total contact time

— — — — School students, Denmark, daily contact (class) time
(maximum allowed, may be less)

Note: Schools in Denmark are open for 5 per cent more days p.a.

Figure 2.2 – Allocation of total daily contact time for different age students in England and Wales, and Denmark

Further, the variation between countries outlined in chapter four, with some systems providing equal length days for children of all ages, some shortening the day for younger children and some even lengthening it, defies logic.

Recent research on time of day effects on learning and memory has produced some interesting if unsettling conclusions. Here I am very indebted to the following paper written by Mr. R. E. Born, Principal County Psychologist for the Dorset LEA, who made use of the advice and work of Dr. Simon Folkard of the MRC Perceptual and Cognitive Performance Unit, University of Sussex:

> In the first quarter of this century there was considerable interest in the optimal scheduling of different subjects within the school day. Freeman and Hovland (1934) reviewed this work and concluded that 'the balance of evidence apparently favours an afternoon superiority for sensory and motor performance, but there is little agreement as to the time when complicated mental work can be done most efficiently'. Earlier Gates (1916) had concluded 'in general the forenoon is the best time for strictly mental work…while the afternoon may best be taken up with school subjects in which the motor factors are predominant.' Gates' conclusion is drawn from the fact that tasks involving a large short term memory component were performed best in the morning and he postulated mental fatigue as being responsible. The results of this early work remain today enshrined in the idea that academic work is best in the morning. Unfortunately, recent evidence throws doubt on this viewpoint.
>
> In those early days much work was concerned with short term memory. This was usually found to decrease during the day. The assumption, not unreasonable at the time, was that long term memory

and other functions also decrease during the day. Unfortunately, this was an incorrect assumption.

Arousal theory had its roots in those early days but did not come to prominence until the 1960s and there has followed a period of work on human functioning due to this theory. Arousal theory experimentation shows a twenty-four hour cycle in the level of arousal with a low point of 4 a.m. and a high point at 8 p.m. with some evidence of a post lunch decrement (due to a time of day effect, not due to lunch itself — there are no similar dips after breakfast or evening meal). This circadian rhythm shows itself in the performance efficiency of a number of tasks. For instance, Blake (1967) showed efficiency improving during the day on sorting, vigilance, letter cancelling and simple addition. Simple reaction time showed some improvement as well but digit span, a short term memory function, got worse. A lot of this kind of work has been of interest to industry, in particular the effects of shift working, and the circadian rhythm is now a well established concept.

The evidence therefore suggests that a lot of human functioning is better in the afternoon and early evening than in the morning. It would predict that children are more aroused in the afternoon and therefore will react quicker, be prone to make less mistakes, be less prone to simple error, and generally livelier and more difficult to control. Arousal theory will also predict the superiority of short term memory in the morning and it has been found that short term memory worsens during the day although the results are not entirely consistent. For strings of digits, it peaks at 10.30 a.m. For word lists, a similar pattern is found except for the most recent items in the list. For meaningful prose it appears to drop from 8 a.m. 'Working Memory' which is evidenced in simple arithmetical tasks, such as multiplication or addition, peaks at about midday. Folkard (1975) has argued that this midday peak represents a 'trade off' between decreasing immediate memory ability and increasing information processing speed over the day.

Arousal theory, however, predicts that long term memory should increase during the day. Work in this area has shown more consistency than the immediate memory results. A good example for us is Folkard (1977) who looked at long term memory for information presented in prose form to comprehensive school children. The children who learnt at the 3 p.m. session were superior in performance to those who learnt at 9 a.m. This sort of effect has been replicated under various conditions with similar results i.e. superior long term memory performance in the afternoon and evening. With adults, it probably peaks at about 8 p.m.

Further work in this area on the mechanisms behind the various types of memory functioning throws some doubt on a unitary arousal theory but from a practical point of view produces some interesting results. With meaningful material, the morning superiority of short term memory seems limited to less important items. The important items do not show the same time of day effect. Linked with this is evidence that different processes are spontaneously used in the morning as opposed to the afternoon. Remembering in the morning is dominated by a rehearsal/maintenance strategy whilst in the afternoon a semantic/elaborative strategy is used. Therefore, the use of meaning is more apparent in the afternoon.

To summarise the present state of memory findings we can say that short term memory for less meaningful material is best in the morning peaking at about 10.30 a.m. but this is less true for important material. As far as long term storage is concerned, afternoon and evening learning produces the best results. Also, at this time the method of storage appears to use meaning rather than (sound) rehearsal.

Circadian rhythms underly many immediate processing functions and memory functions. Travel between time zones indicates that in a relatively short period these rhythms change to the new zone time. There is a fairly general finding that phase shift occurs if external surroundings change in step. Therefore, if the habits of a nation changed then the circadian rhythms would probably change as well in the main. This occurs twice a year in this country at present [connected with British Summer Time]. However, there are possible complications with long term memory in that some evidence shows that even when some basic bodily rhythms have changed and short term memory peaks at the new time, long term memory remains linked still to the same time of day. This suggests that it is linked to a different circadian rhythm (possibly linked to the light/dark cycle).

The only other point worth making regarding circadian rhythms and arousal is that the effects of loss of sleep are greater in the morning (low arousal) than in the afternoon (high arousal) and this would cause problems if children got up earlier in the morning but still maintained the same bedtime.

This research appears to conflict with teachers' received wisdom, reflecting Gates quoted above, that mornings are the best time for learning and that the last part of the afternoon is the worst. However there may not be a conflict. Teachers' perceptions may be correct — that in the morning children are less tired, more keen and more amenable. This may offset the greater learning efficiency, in the more limited sense, of the afternoons (the percentage gains suggested are in the order of 15 per cent or less). However, Davis (1987) reports research on a balanced sample of first grade children in California, half in classes which worked on reading in the first period of the day and half in the last period. He concluded: 'Last period instruction was generally more beneficial than first period instruction; the difference between the two groups' adjusted means represents in excess of one year of reading achievement difference...' This is the first classroom finding of time of day effects on learning. Also, apart from class learning, the implications of this theory for individualised learning are considerable, and suggest that this should be concentrated in the afternoon.

There is clearly a need for further research. There are also other questions. To what extent do individual students have optimum learning times, as popular belief suggests (the 'larks' and 'owls' syndrome)? Do time of day effects influence the learning of skills, or development of understanding, or abstract thinking....?

Technological developments

The school slate does not need a complex time system. Technology in schools has remained relatively primitive — largely still chalk, paper and talk. Where advanced technology has appeared — audio-visual aids, television broadcasts, specialised science and workshop equipment, computers — it has still been used largely in a class context. Its main effect has been to increase specialist facilities which require more complicated timetables in secondary schools, and more fixed points in the primary school day. A neat example of the impact of technology on school time has been the effect of the video recorder in removing fixed points for educational broadcasts and so increasing their use. There have however been some advances in technology which have encouraged individual student activity. The spread of cheap textbooks has increased homework; computers have been partly used for individualised learning. In the future it seems likely that the main impact of technology will be in this direction. If so, this will throw up much more serious demands for new time structures, often conflicting with those which have previously existed. This prospect is explored more fully in chapter nine on individual learning time.

If investment in educational technology becomes substantial, it will create pressures to maximise this investment by extending the time in which it is used. This too has radical implications for school time.

School management

School management has always existed but has only comparatively recently been analysed. The conceptualising of the role of the head actually changes the role. He or she thinks consciously instead of intuitively about it, about planning, allocating resources, and evaluating.

This process will eventually trickle down to school time management. Heads and senior staff will see planning, allocating and evaluating the use of time as one of their functions, just as they increasingly see the school budget as a proper area to manage. Indeed the development of local management of schools will focus attention both on the costs of school time and the effectiveness of time structures and policies.

So in this sense school management, theory and practice, is becoming a force for change with school time. But not without reservations. For one aspect of management involves control of the organisation, and in school terms that can imply regular routine, formal structures and predictable systems. Individualised timetables will not fit easily into a tight ship.

* * * * *

Throughout this analysis, inertia has often seemed the prevailing factor. Individual use of time is constrained by school time micro-structures, which are constrained by the macro-structures, which are held in place by powerful historical, social, financial and organisational forces, most of which support the existing system. Yet within schools new forces are creating turbulence — new educational developments, theories and management attitudes, and above all the looming impact of new technology. At present the inertial forces are stronger, but eventually the new pressures may become too strong. The system will then break and re-establish itself in a new form. This possibility is examined in chapter twelve.

3 The school day in the United Kingdom

Definitions

School days differ a good deal in detail and different terms are often used for the same feature. The following definitions are used throughout this book.

The most important are:

Class contact time
Lesson time, with a teacher or team of teachers (sometimes called 'instructional time'). This also includes tutorial time for supported self study.

Other contact time
Registration, assemblies, and any timetabled pastoral time which is informal and unstructured in nature (i.e. not a lesson). Some of this involves learning, but it cannot conveniently be counted as class contact.

Total contact time
Class contact plus other contact, and also self study in school. In other words, all timetabled school time when students are in contact with teachers and/or with learning resources. So this *excludes breaks*.

School time
All time between the starting bell and the finishing bell of the school day, including breaks, but *excluding the lunch break*.

School day span
All time between the starting bell and the finishing bell of the school day, including lunch time.

Other terms which are necessary for complete description are:

Self study in school
Supervised or unsupervised individual study, normally in school time, not in a taught class and excluding homework.
(This is not an important feature in most schools at present, but is likely to become more prominent.)

School learning time
Class contact and self study in school time, combined.

Break time
All breaks (excluding lunch) and timetabled circulation (class movement) time.

Lunch time
The whole of the break in which lunch occurs.

Out of school activities
Any voluntary organised school activity outside the school day, i.e. before
or after school, in lunch or other breaks, weekends or holidays. Activities
which are supervised/taught *and* obligatory (such as compulsory games
or required involvement in an activity) should be counted as class contact.
In practice the distinction between class contact time and out of school
activities can be blurred, particularly in independent schools.

Out of school study
Individual study outside the school day i.e. before or after school or in
lunch breaks. Mainly this will comprise 'homework', but increasingly it may
involve voluntary individual study or group activities at school and distance
learning, either at home or school.

Total educational time
All time spent on educational activity in the broadest sense, including class
contact, other contact, self study in school, out of school activities and
out of school study. (It excludes break time and lunch time.)

Fig. 3.1 sets out all these defined activities and shows their
inter-relationship.
Note: Some school day activities may occur off campus although
organised by the school (e.g. educational visits, activities in a sports
centre or another school/college).

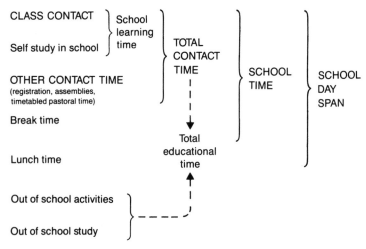

Note: Definitions in capitals are those most frequently used in the text

Figure 3.1 – Definitions of activities in the school day

The present school day in the United Kingdom

Regulations

The underlying regulations for the school day in England and Wales have been contained within the Education (Schools and Further Education) Regulations 1981, regulation 10. These imposed three requirements:

1. A minimum of at least three hours 'secular instruction' (a nice whiff of the nineteenth century here!) for pupils mainly under the age of eight, and four hours for older pupils.
2. The division of each school day into two sessions separated by a break in the middle of the day unless exceptional circumstances make this undesirable (except that a school with a six day week may provide a single session on two days).
3. A school year of 380 sessions (normally 190 days) — see chapter five.

These minima were often extended by LEAs, for example requiring secondary schools to be open for five and a half hours per day. Many LEAs tightened up their regulations after the Education (Schoolteachers' Pay and Conditions of Employment) Order 1987, which required teachers to be available for duties for 1,265 hours per year.

The 1988 Education Reform Act marks a significant change. It makes it the duty of the governing body of each school to determine the beginning and end times of each school session within the regulations. (In practice this has often been the 'de facto' position.) For any change in times, consultation has to be made with the LEA, and with parents at a meeting. Changes can only take place at the beginning of the school year and with three months notice to parents.

As a result LEA regulation of the school day will be weakened. LEAs can give advice for minimum and maximum lengths and breaks, and seek standardisation to create economies in transport. However governors will not be obliged to follow it — although ingenious LEAs will devise schemes for Local Management of Schools which will allow them to charge schools for any additional expense.

An important change occurred in May 1989 when the Secretary of State issued a draft circular of guidance for governing bodies. This was the first occasion when the Department of Education and Science provided positive guidance about the school day. The circular seems to have been driven by concern about the problems of delivering the national curriculum within the time available (discussed later in chapter six). It sees review of the time allocation for teaching as an integral part of curriculum planning, and suggests:

> Schools which use the time available to them less effectively will find themselves at a disadvantage in the curricular opportunities they can

offer pupils while also making adequate provision for religious education and the range of foundation subjects. The lower the number of taught hours the greater the pressure that will be placed on pupils as they try to complete programmes of study, and the less scope there will be for pupils to follow options outside the National Curriculum.

Two sets of statistics are used to support the argument. One (Annex A) suggests that schools vary considerably in the balance between taught lessons and registration/assemblies/breaks/before and after school supervision. This isolation of class contact time is important, but the argument is confused by the inclusion of supervision occurring outside the school day. The other appears to show considerable variations in class contact time for both primary and secondary schools (but the variation appears to be accentuated considerably by the range of types of schools included, see below).

The circular proposes to revoke the existing ineffective minima. It does not replace them — though the way is left open — but lays down 'as a general guide to good practice' minimum teaching per week:

(a) 21 hours for 5 – 7 year olds
(b) 23.5 hours for 8 – 13 year olds
(c) 25 hours for 14 – 15 year olds

In practice (b) represents about an additional hour per week for primary and middle schools, and (c) typically an extra 1 hour 40 minutes for students aged 14 – 16. Younger students in secondary schools could have 1 hour 40 minutes less than their 14 – 16 counterparts, although the circular suggests that schools may wish to consider otherwise.

As a document the draft circular is interesting. It is clearly anxious to increase the quantity of class contact time (by 4.5 per cent primary, 7 per cent secondary). The rationale for this is not coherently advanced, and we are left with that riddle discussed at the end of chapter five. Does more time really make a difference? In this particular case, for reasons discussed below the effect of the change is likely to be imperceptible in terms of pupil outcomes. The circular does not address the problems of quality of time discussed throughout this book, and its advice to governing bodies of considerations to be taken into account is only superficial. (Of course the final circular may be improved – it will appear after this book goes to press.)

However, the importance of the circular should not be underestimated. The Department at last is involving itself with school time — and so the long term implications may be profound.

The regulations in Scotland and Ireland are very similar to the English 1981 regulations, though in practice school days in secondary schools there have tended to be longer.

Primary schools in the United Kingdom

Unlike secondary schools, primary schools use a simple but very flexible school day structure. The outline of the day is more uniform, with fewer variations and less experimentation.

A full account was given in Hilsum & Cane (1971). They described the typical day in sixty-six Surrey primary schools in 1969. This is set out in the Appendix, Example 1. The same format for school days is used throughout the Appendix to allow easy analysis.

The great majority of schools started at 8.55 or 9.00 a.m., the earliest at 8.50. Only one started later than 9.15, though some schools started 15 – 35 minutes later in winter. Seven of the schools closed 3.15/3.20 p.m., the bulk at 3.30 – 3.45, and the latest at 4 p.m. School day span ranged from 375 – 430 minutes.

Within the day mean total contact time (including assemblies, excluding breaks) was 288 minutes, but with significant variation (see Table 3.1). Variation between the extremes was considerable, amounting to over 40 minutes a day and equivalent to more than three hours per week. This is equivalent to over 125 hours per year or 25 days extra. (However it is possible that some of the shorter days were operated by infant schools.) Mean time for lunch was 83 minutes. Nearly a quarter of the schools had 15 minutes shorter lunch hour, which the authors saw as an important loss of time for out-of-school activities.

Until recently there has been little similar research. However Mortimore et al (1988) in a sample of 50 ILEA primary schools in 1980 – 84 found very similar starting times (about half 9.00 a.m.) and closing times, and a similar 40 minute spread of total contact time between schools. However the mean total contact time was about ten minutes more (see Table 3.1). This is broadly consonant with the DES 1989 circular statistics which suggest average primary school *class* contact time of 270 minutes. The circular expresses concern about variations – 'over half of primary schools provide 23 or more hours of teaching and about 15 per cent provide 25 or more. But over a quarter offer fewer than 22 hours, with 10 per cent or so offering only 20 or fewer hours'. However it is likely that the inclusion of infant schools at one end and middle schools deemed primary at the other exaggerate the variation.

It appears that the primary day has changed little since 1970. There has not been the severity of supervision problems to force extensive reduction in lunch hours, and there have not been curricular or other changes requiring school day adjustment. There has been some tendency to shorten lunch-hours and a slight trend to earlier starting times and to eliminate the afternoon break. (Dorset LEA has three schools with lunch-hours of 30 – 40 minutes, and eighteen with 45 – 50 minutes — of a total of 190 — although the withdrawal of

Table 3.1   Variation in total contact time in English primary schools, 1969 and 1980

No. of Minutes	Surrey 1969 No. of schools	ILEA 1980 – 84 No. of schools
265	1	
270	4	
275	7	
280	9	1
285	11	2
290	14	6
295	5	9
300	3	16
305	6 (305 minutes or more)	10
310		4
315		0
320		2
Mean total contact time in minutes (excludes breaks)	288	299

Source: Hilsum and Cane (1971), Mortimore *et al.* (1988)

school meals has influenced this.) Recent developments are tending to standardise the primary day in England and Wales. The new teachers' pay and conditions of service arrangements have made LEAs examine teacher and therefore school hours more carefully. Many have recommended or directed schools to provide specified hours. Surrey, for example, has recommended the following:

	Class contact time	Total contact time
First schools (5 – 7, 5 – 9 or 5 – 11)	250 minutes	290 minutes
Middle schools (9 – 13)	280 minutes	324 minutes
Secondary schools (11 + or 13 +)	280 minutes	340 minutes

The figures for first schools are virtually identical to those found by Hilson and Cane in the same county 20 years earlier. (The figures for children 7 – 11 and 14 – 16 are below those now recommended by the DES.)

The primary school day in Scotland and Northern Ireland is similar to that of England and Wales. In Scotland the new national conditions of service of 1986 lay down a 'maximum class contact time' (including assemblies) of 25 hours per week. That is similar to most English primary schools, but would prune the few examples of longer days found in the research above. In Northern Ireland five hours of total contact are normal. Schools start slightly earlier in Scotland, normally by 9.00 a.m., and slightly later in Northern Ireland, 9.00 a.m. – 9.30 a.m.

The school day in primary schools is quite different from that in secondary schools in an important respect. It is only partially as opposed to totally timetabled, i.e., for only part of the week are teachers other than class-teachers timetabled with classes. This partial timetabling is flexible and can be altered easily and almost immediately.

The HMI survey of primary education in England (1978) found that over three quarters of its sample classes were taught for part of the week by teachers other than their class-teachers, typically for about two hours per week and with only a small proportion exceeding five hours (see Table 3.2). This timetabling occurred mainly for music, PE, English and art and craft. It is likely to increase in the future with the inclusion of science and technology in the national curriculum.

Generally there does not seem to have been experimentation in compressed and flexible day patterns in primary schools. Probably given their existing flexibility and the limitations of younger children there is no demand. However a fundamental examination of the use of time could bring benefits. For example, four and five year olds *could* be brought into school for half the present length of day in shifts with the same amount of staffing used to halve the pupil-teacher ratio. A shortening of the day by say 15 minutes could provide time for individual tutoring of individual students under non-class conditions. Or such a shortening of the day in a large primary school could provide staffing for an optional third session for special projects, supported self study and use of new educational technology. A compressed day could encourage the growth of community led activities in the afternoons. A model for such developments is explored in chapter 12.

Table 3.2   Percentage of primary school classes taught by teachers other than their own class teachers, England 1975 – 77

Numbers of hours per week taught by teachers other than own class teacher	Classes		
	7 year old	9 year old	11 year old
None (i.e. class teacher only)	26	14	10
Up to 2 hours	45	35	27
2 – 5 hours	25	42	46
5 – 10 hours	3	7	13
10 or more hours	1	2	4
TOTAL %	100	100	100

Source: After HMI Survey of Primary Education in England (1978), Table 21.

Secondary schools in England and Wales

A TYPICAL CURRENT SCHOOL DAY
Example 2 in the Appendix represents the most common type of day
in current use in England and Wales, although there are many minor
variations.

Starting time
This usually falls between 8.45 and 9.05 a.m. Earlier starts occur
mainly where schools wish to adopt a 'longer morning' or a
'compressed day' pattern (see below). Start times can be determined
by external factors like availability of or shared transport, road
congestion, or links with other schools. There seems to be growing
anecdotal evidence on the value of an earlier start — providing a more
positive opening to the day, the possibility of a long morning/short
afternoon and an earlier finish leaving more daylight for activities and
leisure and more time for meetings or INSET.

Registration
This is normally taken in tutor/form rooms at the start of the morning
and afternoon session. A few schools hold a registration period during
or at the end of the day. The occasional school registers pupils in a
teaching class rather than pastoral group — a system widely used in
US high schools.

Assemblies/tutor-time
This is a good example of a feature which evolved in response to
system changes. So it lacked proper design and often had
unsatisfactory aspects.

Forty years ago secondary schools normally began every day with
registration and then class movement to an assembly. Minimum
duration for both was 15 minutes, maximum 30 – 35, with 20 or 25
minutes the norm. As schools became larger, holding daily assemblies
for the whole school became difficult and so smaller assemblies were
held, only on two or three days of the week. On other days classes
stayed with their tutor for tutor-time. This extra pastoral time was
initially welcomed but in practice was unsatisfactory. Tutor-time was
tied to the length of the assembly — too long to do nothing in, too
short to do anything worthwhile. Many schools failed to solve the
problem (some managed to make 25 minute tutor-time effective, but
they are the minority).

A number of devices could be used including: (a) extending the
period following assembly and allowing the assembly to bite into it

for the year group(s) concerned (this implies assembly is taken by staff free in that period); (b) combining assembly/tutor-time with personal, social and moral education; (c) blocking time across a year-group and including assembly as part of the block; (d) providing two or more assemblies for the whole school at the same time (only possible where spaces are available).

The 1988 Education Reform Act has altered the situation by reinstating daily assemblies. Apart from the problems of lack of suitable spaces, this will now often squeeze out the tutor-time described above, and so may provide less time for pastoral care. Tutor-time can be timetabled elsewhere, perhaps as part of personal and social education, but since that is not a foundation subject of the national curriculum it is itself under pressure.

Compulsory daily assemblies raise another issue, that of cost. If we assume that an average assembly, with associated movement, takes 20 minutes, then its costs on average are as follows:

	Secondary Schools		Primary Schools	
	per pupil	per school of 800 pupils	per pupil	per school of 200 pupils
per day	56p.	£ 446	36p.	£ 72
per week	£ 2.78	£ 2,228	£ 1.80	£ 360
per year	£105.82	£84,659	£68.40	£13,680

(Derived from net expenditure per pupil, CIPFA Education Estimates 1988 – 89)

Are the outcomes worth the cost, and is this the best use of the time and finance involved?

In some schools assembly and tutor-time occurs later in the morning or in the afternoon (sometimes at the end of the day).

Breaks and circulation-time

The minimum length of breaks is determined mainly by the layout of the school, particularly the time needed by staff to reach the staffroom from outlying classrooms, and the maximum by the problems of student supervision. Twenty minutes is typical. A few schools have afternoon breaks, although these have tended to disappear.

Circulation time is often timetabled, particularly in larger schools. It acts an an unsupervised mini-break, and allows access to lockers, lavatories, etc. It probably takes more time from the school day than allowing circulation to be stolen from the next lesson, but creates a more regular and organised day. Smaller schools do not normally use it.

Lunch breaks

Because of supervision problems during recent teachers' industrial action, and to a lesser extent a desire to reduce fuel costs or shorten the school day, lunch-hours have tended to shrink in the last few years. The shortest lunch-hours are now 40 and occasionally only 30 minutes, usually linked to a 'compressed day'.

Actual lengths of lunch-hours depend on a range of factors, including:

(a) the minimum time for feeding students requiring school dinner
(b) the minimum time necessary for students who wish to go home for lunch
(c) the minimum time required for lunch-time activities, particularly sports
(d) supervision problems
(e) preparation for afternoon lessons, particularly science equipment.

There is a trade-off between these. Reducing the lunch-hour may improve (d) but create problems under (b), (c), (e) and even (a).

Some schools run staggered lunch breaks. In effect lunch becomes a 'period.' So the school day could be modified as in Table 3.3. A is the simplest model; B has two lunch sessions but uses the intervening break to extend each into a full lunch-hour; C is more complex, with three lunch sessions (this pattern is common in North America). An actual example from a large comprehensive school, the Park School, Rayleigh, which has operated for 11 years is given in Appendix 1, Example 3. More complex versions are possible, sometimes including registration.

Staggered lunch hours offer considerable advantages. They can:

 – increase the number of period slots in the day, and so maximise use of accommodation. In table 3.3 the potential use of every room in the school is increased by 12.5%

Table 3.3   Example of staggered lunch-break arrangements

A*		B		C*
11.30 Lesson 4	(35)	11.30 Lesson 4	(35)	11.30 Lesson 4 (35)
12.05 Lunch 1/Lesson 5	(35)	12.05 Lunch 1/Lesson 5	(35)	12.05 Lunch 1/ (35) Lesson 5
12.40 Lesson 5/Lunch 2	(35)	12.40 Break	(30)	12.40 Lunch 2/ (35) Lesson 5/6
1.15 Lesson 6	(35)	1.10 Lesson 5/Lunch 2	(35)	1.15 Lunch 3/ (35) Lesson 5/6
1.50 Lesson 7	(35)	1.45 Lesson 6	(35)	1.50 Lesson 7 (35)

Note: * Length of school day span is reduced by thirty minutes

- shorten lunch-breaks (models A and C in Table 3.3) and reduce numbers at lunch at any one time, and so reduce supervision problems and improve the school's ethos
- shorten the span of the day (models A and C), ending school earlier (also reducing heating bills).

They do however have disadvantages:

- timetabling is more complex
- some double-periods 5 – 6 may be undesirably split into singles
- lunch-time activities are complicated (B) or eliminated (A) and (C)
- inter-staff communication and meetings is made more difficult
- time for staff and student relaxation and staff preparation for afternoon lessons is reduced in models (A) and (C)
- fewer students can go home to lunch in models (A) and (C)
- noise from students circulating after their lunch can distract lessons
- afternoon registration can cause difficulties, although it can be inserted between the two lunch breaks or before period 7 in the example.

My impression is that most English schools consider that the disadvantages outweigh the advantages unless pressure on accommodation is acute. The assessment is very much affected by their individual situation — the geography of the buildings, separateness of dining accommodation and recreational areas, number of lunch time activities and meetings, etc. However, the system is well established in some schools and common in North America, so it would probably pay many schools to examine the possibilities much more fully. This is another example of a school time feature evolving or continuing, rather than being designed.

MAIN VARIATIONS IN THE CURRENT SECONDARY SCHOOL DAY

Two initial points needs to be made. First, innumerable variations are possible. School days can be classified into species and subspecies, but there are countless minor mutations — far more than appear at first sight. Second, and more important, even five minutes variation can often make a significant difference, edging a school day from one type to another.

In the example below, as the start of the school day is pushed five minutes earlier in each model A – E, the start of the lunch hour advances too. A breakpoint is reached at which it becomes too early, e.g. 11.40 a.m. in model F1. To avoid this, periods 5 – 6 are brought before lunch, and lunch put back to 12.50 in model F2. So at that critical point just five minutes change topples the school day from a 4 + 4 period pattern into a 6 + 2 pattern. The impact of small changes at critical points is a key factor of school day design, and is discussed further in chapter thirteen.

Example

	A	B	C	D	E	F1	F2
Start of school	9.00	8.55	8.50	8.45	8.40	8.35	8.35
Start of lunch break	12.05	12.00	11.55	11.50	11.45	11.40	12.50
Afternoon registration	1.10	1.05	1.00	12.55	12.50	12.45	1.55
Lesson 5	1.15	1.10	1.05	1.00	12.55	12.50	2.00 (Lesson 7)
End of school	3.40	3.35	3.30	3.25	3.20	3.15	3.10

Length of day

Over the last few years there has been national publicity for suggestions that there are extreme variations between the days operated by different schools in England and Wales. The DES 1989 draft circular suggests that 30 per cent of secondary schools in 1988 offered 25 hours teaching or more, about half 23 or less, with 5 per cent 22 hours or less. However, the picture is misleading, as almost certainly the bulk of the schools below 23 hours 20 minutes per week (i.e. 280 minutes per day) would be middle schools deemed secondary. This is illustrated by an Oxfordshire LEA survey in 1982 — see Table 3.4.

These figures suggest that the variation is not very substantial. Almost all the schools below 280 minute daily class contact were middle

Table 3.4   Variation in length of school days in secondary schools in Oxfordshire LEA, 1982

Number of minutes of lesson time per week	Middle schools	Secondary schools
250	2	
255	–	
260	3	
265	1	1
270	1	–
275	–	1
280	8	18
285		3
290		6
295		3
300		7
305		–
310		1
TOTAL	15	40

Source: Statistics supplied by Oxfordshire LEA.

schools, with half their pupils below the age of 11. Only two secondary schools fell below that figure, and those only slightly. Nearly half the schools provided 280 minutes. However ten were providing 15 or 20 minutes more than 280, equivalent to 75 – 100 extra minutes per week or 47 – 63 more hours per year. It is my impression that these figures are typical of most LEAs, and that extreme variations are created by a few rogue schools. It is also my impression that since 1982 there has been a tendency for these extremes to fall closer to the norm. There is however much more variation between schools if one measures 'total contact time' (i.e. including registration, assemblies and pastoral time), and more still for 'total school time' (including breaks and circulation) and 'school day span' (including lunch-breaks).

The impact of the 1989 DES circular remains to be seen. The draft circular suggests that the typical secondary school should increase lesson time by twenty minutes per day. In practice schools would tend to provide perhaps half of this by absorbing circulation time/short breaks and even part of assembly time into lesson time. This means little real increase in effective teaching time. The remaining ten minutes would probably be sprinkled across the day by expanding two periods by five minutes, again making little real difference to the delivery of the curriculum. The circular illustrates the weakness of making pragmatic adjustments to the school day without an underlying analysis. If an extra hundred minutes a week is to be added effectively, more strategic change is needed.

Number and length of periods

Five main variations are in use:

Variation	Total minutes per day	Total periods per week	Maximum circulation times times per day*
A 8 x 35 minutes	280	40	5
B 7 x 40 minutes	280	35	4
C 6 x 45/50 minutes	270/300	30	3
D 5 x 55/60 minutes	275/300	25	2
E 4 x 70 minutes	280	20	1

* lesson-to-lesson changeovers excluding movement to and from registration/assembly, one break and lunch.

These models do not often exist unadulterated, because of the use of double, treble or even quadruple periods (or split 70 minute periods). This is particularly important for model A which in practice will often be closer to model E since many of the 35 minute periods will form 70 minute doubles.

A number of schools also mix period lengths, e.g. 55 and 60 or 35 and 40 minute periods. But a wider mix is uncommon, e.g. 35 and 50 minutes, presumably because of the arbitrary losses or gains of time this gives to subjects (this is particularly sensitive if they only have one block of time each week).

Five factors seem to account for these variations:

1. *Movement*   Large sprawling schools lose more learning time from each changeover from lesson to lesson, and so prefer to reduce the number of changeovers. Also the more circulation time, the more scope for behaviour problems.

2. *Subject requirements*   Different educational activities have different optimum durations. Oral work is suited to short periods; practical activities involving getting out or putting away equipment, cleaning up, changing clothes or showering, need more time. So foreign languages and to a lesser extent maths will prefer 35 – 40 minute periods, with their greater frequency each week; PE, CDT, art and science (practical) will opt for 55 – 70 minute periods, with a preference for the 70 minute end.

   This conflict has led to experiment with 50 minute periods (model C) as a compromise which with their reduced concentration span and high weekly frequency look attractive. However, they are not really long enough to satisfy the second group of subjects and double periods of 100 minutes are wastefully overlong. Probably this explains why model C has not proved popular (they are, however, common in European countries).

   This conflict between short and long period subjects has led, I think, to the general popularity in England and Wales of an eight period day, since it makes possible a double tier system of single and double periods. However, other attempts have been made to resolve the conflict.

   A few schools have introduced 20 minute units, allowing periods of 40, 60, 80 or 100 minutes. This obviously gives greater flexibility but it is difficult to timetable. Banbury School, Oxfordshire, one of its first exponents, operated the following timetable for a long period, (although it is now discarded):

8.50 – 9.00	Registration
9.00 – 11.00	Units 1 – 6
11.00 – 11.20	Break
11.20 – 12.40	Units 7 – 10
12.40 – 1.50	Lunch
1.50 – 2.10	Assembly/Tutor periods
2.10 – 3.30	Units 11 – 14

   This approach has been adopted by the City Technology Colleges, which are tending to use 25 minute units.

   An alternative approach is the block timetable which takes longer blocks of time, often each timetabled for a year group with a faculty, and then allows them to be broken up by informal arrangement to suit actual activities and staff (this is explored more fully in chapter six). This system particularly suits large, faculty-run schools, though it is not always easy to balance the blocks of teachers and activities.

A variant is the half-day timetable operated for example in the Sutton Centre, Sutton-in-Ashfield, Nottinghamshire. Here the timetable is divided into ten half-days, each taken for one group by one teacher who inserts breaks and changes the activity when appropriate. A small number of other schools use similar half-day blocks. The reasons put forward are that they facilitate less formal learning methods, team teaching and individualised learning, meet many of the needs of prevocational education, encourage integration of subjects and cross-curricular assignments, and assist interaction with the community. Indeed a strong case can be made that for younger secondary students such blocks lead on naturally from the more integrated single-teacher day of the primary school, and for 14 – 18 students are well adapted to many current developments. However, they do create difficulties where there is strong academic expectation, and tend to be resisted by foreign language and maths teachers in particular. Some schools such as Pike Deans Community High School, Livingstone in East Lothian, have given up this system largely for such reasons. However the difficulty, as often, seems to have arisen from trying to insert a sub-system into a system which is unfriendly to it. If timetabling can modify or split some of the blocks to meet special subject needs, this model could become increasingly attractive, given current trends. It has much in common with the time slots devised by Keith Palmer (see chapter seven, on modular time), and the sophisticated timetable refinements which he suggests could make it more acceptable.

A promising variation has developed at Blyth Tynedale Upper High School, Northumberland. Here blocks are staffed by teams, each led by three coordinators and working with a year group of 190. Teams are responsible for courses, teaching arrangements and groupings. Most important, each team is kept free for one block (guaranteed not to be used for absence cover) so that this time can be used for curriculum and materials development, course moderation and INSET.

3. *Frequency of teacher contact*　Most subject teachers prefer to see a class twice rather than once a week, three times more than twice, etc. The increased number of contacts improves the consolidation of learning, assists the setting and prompt return of homework, and reduces the effect of student absence. In the earlier list of period variations, models A and B would increase contact frequency most, except when their use of double periods reduces it. Advocates of model C suggest that in practice it often offers the greatest weekly frequency of contact.

4. *Curriculum requirements*　The fewer periods in the week, the harder it is to fit in the full range of subjects, particularly for students aged 11 – 14, and the sharper the time difference between one subject and another. So many schools using model D and E, or even C, work their timetable over a ten-day cycle. A subject can then for example be allocated an average one and a half periods per week in the form of one period the first week and two periods the next.

5. *Student and teacher needs*   Student concentration spans were largely considered under subject needs above. Probably both students and teachers are fatigued by too many lesson changes in a day, although I am not aware of any research to substantiate this.

The daily period patterns of secondary and 9 – 13 middle schools are set out for Oxfordshire LEA in 1982 in Table 3.5.

The majority of schools worked an 8 x 35 minute day or a close relation to it, and the only other contender was 5 x 55/60 minutes. It is my impression that this situation is still typical of the country as a whole.

Finally, it is worth pointing out that these tensions over period numbers/lengths only exist within the rigid, sealed-system timetable. Outside such a system, before or after school or in a 'flexible day' or a community education context, it is possible to create optimum period lengths whenever a class is not preceded or followed by another commitment for the teacher or students.

Example
A French teacher, allocated Friday periods 7 – 8 of an 8 period day with a class, could (in theory, if not often in practice!) negotiate that class and teacher go home after Friday period 7, but reinsert a single period after school ('period 9') on another day. Quite a fair exchange!

A scattering of such before and after school periods do appear, particularly in urban schools and usually in response to timetable pressures. There are occasional examples of twilight courses,

Table 3.5   Period patterns in 9 – 13 middle and secondary schools in Oxfordshire LEA in 1982

Model*	Periods		No. of schools	% of total schools	Remarks
	8/9 × 30	minutes	3	6	All middle schools
E	4 × 70	minutes	3	6	
A variation	8 × 30/35	minutes	4	7	
A	8 × 35	minutes	22 } 38	41 } 70	All middle schools
(A/B)	8 × 35/40	minutes	8	15	
(A/B)	8 × 40	minutes	1	2	
B	7 × 40	minutes	2	4	
C	6 × 50	minutes	1	2	
D	5 × 55/60	minutes	7	13	
Others	various		3	6	
			54	102	

Note: * refers to text

Source: Statistics supplied from the LEA

sometimes linked with school consortia or technical colleges, or adult education classes treated as an extension of school for some students. There are also the 'eleventh session' arrangements used at the Sutton Centre and Dukeries Complex in Nottinghamshire.

Grouping and distribution of periods

The number of periods in the day partly determines these groupings. For example, when the periods in the day are an even number, i.e. four, six or eight, the day will almost always be divided into sessions of two or four periods. There are a few examples of three period sessions, but these seem to be perverse since they reduce timetabling opportunities for double periods. An odd number of periods in the day require that one block will contain an odd number of periods, usually three. This third period creates timetabling problems since it is more difficult to use it for any subject which must have a double period. The proportion of lessons in the morning session is also influenced by the number of periods:

Model	No. of periods	Reasonable division into two sessions
A	8	4 + 4 periods or 6 + 2
B	7	4 + 3 periods
C	6	4 + 2 periods (or 3 + 3, but 50% less scope for double periods)
D	5	3 + 2 periods
E	4	2 + 2 periods or 3 + 1

Clearly the main choice lies within the eight or four period days, and here most schools current operate 4 + 4 or 2 + 2 periods. However the anecdotal evidence in favour of 6 + 2 or 3 + 1 is very strong. Schools adopting this distribution report a more positive start to the day and a stronger finish. Although the morning is long this is more than offset by a short afternoon without any drag in periods 7 – 8. Afternoon truancy seems to be less. I do not know of any school which has tried this system seriously considering changing back. In fact the evidence is strong enough to suggest that any school currently working a 4 + 4 period day should re-examine the position critically. However with 6 + 2 a start to the day at 8.45 or earlier is necessary to keep lunch before 1 p.m. (see example on page 50).

Some schools distribute periods unequally across days of the week. In the 1982 survey of secondary schools in Oxfordshire mentioned above, four schools had one day shorter than the others. Usually this is to provide games or activities opportunities, or to shorten Friday afternoons. Often the time saved is sprinkled across the rest of the week by lengthening some periods slightly. Two schools gave their first year students (eleven year olds) a little less time each week.

Another factor affecting period distribution and the timing of the day is links with other schools. Consortia arrangements for sixth form or minority subjects, leisure activities or linked courses with technical colleges may all require adjustments of times in the schools involved.

Secondary schools in Scotland

While the English school day scene is relatively static, apart from the small portion of schools described later which are trying out compressed or flexible days, in Scotland a strong new trend is apparent. It is a good example of curricular and organisational needs changing period patterns.

In the very large Strathclyde Region, almost all secondary schools previously had a 40 x 40 minute period week (Roman Catholic schools preferred 45 x 35 minutes), with some double periods in years $1-2$ and the majority doubles in years $5-6$.

In 1981 a regional working group recommended that lessons for students in the first two years should be at least one hour, to reduce fragmentation of the curriculum and enable students to be taught by fewer teachers. This led to discussion of the practicability of 25 x 60/65 minute periods in schools.

Then in 1983 the Scottish Education Department published '16 – 18s in Scotland, An Action Plan' which aimed to develop a wide range of modular courses, create vocational and technical programmes which could be mounted in a range of institutions, rationalise uneconomic provision and extend opportunities to a larger number of students. To implement this Strathclyde set up a structure of consortia of secondary schools and FE colleges. This made a wider range of courses available to students, introduced more of them to further education, and rationalised small classes. It has also led to increasing attendance of adults in school classes.

To facilitate the Action Plan and the consortia, the Region strongly encouraged schools to introduce sixty minute periods since these assisted student travel to other centres and suited adults. By 1988 nearly 90 per cent of Strathclyde schools were operating them. A survey of schools which had adopted this period pattern in 1984 showed that schools would not wish to move back and that parents, pupils and adults preferred the change. To facilitate travel to consortia centres many schools have adopted a 1 + 2 + lunch + 2 pattern with some double hour periods for fifth and sixth year students. Start/lunch/finish times need to be synchronised between schools.

The change has been consolidated by the introduction of Standard Grade instead of 'O' Grade courses, mainly for $16-17$ year old students. These encourage an increased number of options beyond the core subjects and so favour a 25 period week (compared with the previous week largely made up with double periods approaching 20 in number). The introduction of TVEI in Scotland has also fitted well into the new pattern.

This is an interesting and well documented change. Further analysis is useful:

1. The change has been surprisingly rapid and extensive for a decentralised educational system.
2. It represents a planned and rational attempt to solve specific curricular and organisational problems — not always common in school day design.
3. Inevitably it is to some extent a compromise. The two hour blocks of time are too long for some purposes and some teachers, and the single hour blocks are not ideal for oral foreign language teaching.
4. It attempts to resolve many of the conflicts described earlier. The 60/65 minute periods are just long enough for equipment using subjects and PE; the weekly period frequency of 25 periods is higher than a 40 period week where a high proportion are doubles; and the double-periods (two hours) provide many of the advantages advanced by the advocates of morning or afternoon blocks of time.
   BUT – and an important but:
5. Its introduction has been appreciably assisted by the fact that schools in Scotland had longer contact time than those in England (about 320 minutes per week compared to 280). This made 60/65 minutes possible. In England schools operating a similar pattern usually adopt 55 minute periods, or a mix of 55 and 60. The difference between 55/60 and 60/65 is probably sufficient to tip the balance — 55 is rather short for 'long period' subjects.

Secondary schools in Northern Ireland

The main difference from England and Wales is that class contact time is often longer (typically 9 x 35 minute periods, but with some 30 minute periods in some schools). However, as the day often starts slightly earlier and assemblies are short, schools still normally finish by 3.30 or earlier. The central regulations for the school day are similar to those which prevailed in England: instruction is required for four and a half hours (not four hours as in England), still a minimal requirement.

Independent schools in the United Kingdom

It is very difficult to generalise about the independent sector. There are approximately 2,500 independent schools in the UK, and great variations among them. Each school is separately managed and has its own traditions. So it is difficult to choose a representative sample and more difficult to collect data. It is also harder to quantify time in independent schools because they commonly have afternoon games which are not counted as 'lessons' but which in state schools would count as lesson time. Similarly out-of-school activities can be mounted in timetabled sessions during the week, sometimes with an obligation for a student to enrol for a minimum amount, so that they should perhaps be counted as contact time.

The remarks below are drawn from my own impressions and conversations and from detailed responses from over twenty varied schools. Even from such a limited study some tentative conclusions can be drawn:

1. There is probably more variety of school day within the independent sector than in its state counterpart. Overall there is certainly much more variation in day length, class contact and total contact time, and pattern of week.
2. Some of this variety springs from the boarding tradition. In boarding schools since students are on campus all week there is every incentive to use the time available fully. There is also a strong disincentive to leave tracts of time where students have nothing to occupy them! However there is also a strong tradition, dating back to Thring in the 19th century, of the value of activities outside the classroom. Most boarding schools devote some or even all afternoons (sometimes in the summer term the late afternoon) to games, extra-curricular activities or cadet force/pioneering/estate/community work. On some afternoons these are followed or preceded by lessons. School days can also be treated flexibly – lessons or activities can be inserted into afternoons or evenings or switched.

   Most day schools follow a different pattern with lessons finishing by four p.m. or soon after. However the boarding tradition extends into them, with some afternoons kept for games and sometimes other activities like community service. (Many girls' day schools however timetable games periods, as in maintained schools.) Some day schools also retain Saturday morning school although this is tending to fade.
3. There is considerable variation between schools in daily and weekly contact time. In my small sample one school worked only 36 x 40 minute periods, while another had 44 x 40 minutes. A number worked 40 x 40 minutes giving more contact time than in state schools (particularly where additional games sessions are added). However, this is at least partially offset by the shorter school year (see next chapter).
4. The predominant lesson length appears to be 40 minutes, with some examples of 35 and a few of 45. I have not found an example of a school using lessons of 50 or 60 minutes and it is my impression that double periods are fewer than in state schools, although they may be increasing. So independent schools use a system with shorter periods but greater frequency of teacher contact. In some boarding schools circulation time is timetabled,

perhaps reflecting dispersed premises. At Eton this extends to a ten minute break between lessons, similar to the common European pattern.

5. Generally less time seems to be allocated formally to registration and tutorial activity — this may reflect independent schools' smaller average size, better pupil-teacher ratio and perhaps a more limited range of pastoral problems, but also it is offset by a good deal of ad hoc tutorial counselling. However breaks seem to be slightly longer (fewer problems of social control?) and lunch hours considerably longer (usually to create time for activities and to break an intensive day). Starting times mainly range from 8.40 – 9.00, with 8.50 perhaps an average.

6. The use of time by day schools depends a good deal on their catchment area. Some schools draw students from a wide area and so have to finish reasonably early. So they operate a somewhat breathless, very compact day, with activities packed into lunch hours though spilling over after school and on Saturdays.

7. Out of school activities are a much more prominent feature. The take up per hundred pupils is much higher. They are seen as an integral if informal part of the working week, affecting all students (in some schools by regulation).

8. Despite the flexibility and variation within the independent sector, schools do not on the whole appear to analyse their management of time very systematically. Most maintain a traditional inherited system which works acceptably and modify it pragmatically to improve it or accommodate new pressures. (But probably the schools would argue that if the system works, why disturb it?) There is often an ad hoc use of voluntary coaching by staff for gifted or dyslexic students, or minority subjects. Almost always students are taught in their own age cohort, although accelerated courses are often operated in maths, English or foreign languages whereby students take examinations a year or part-year early.

New developments

In the last few years three new approaches to the school day have developed in England — time shifting, time flexing and the extended school day. Time shifting alters the hours of the day to lesser or greater degree, but not the time structures within its boundaries. Time flexing attempts to make more flexible use of school time. The extended school day has been developed by the City Technology colleges both to increase curricular time and incorporate enrichment activities. The three approaches are not in opposition: one tends to lead to the other.

Time shifting

As previously noted there has been a marked trend towards shorter lunch-hours and some tendency to start the school day earlier. There is a clear trend for schools with eight (or four) lessons a day to put six (or three) before lunch.

Much more important has been the establishment of the 'compressed day' or so-called 'continental day' in a number of schools. This had previously been adopted as an expedient, for example in the hot summer of 1976 or at time of union action over lunch-time supervision. It is of course not continental, as the next chapter shows. Few of the European countries operate a long morning-only day, and this has not taken root in England in its pure lunchless form.

The best known example of the compressed day is Tideway School, Newhaven. The headmaster Ken Saxby introduced this in September 1981 because he felt that children worked better in the mornings, the long lunch-hour was unproductive, and a 'free' afternoon would provide time for out of school activities and personal leisure interests. Initially the year's trial was approved by parents two to one, despite some scepticism on the part of the LEA, and its permanent retention was backed by 85 per cent of parents. It now seems a permanent feature of the school.

There have been only minor alterations to the new day since its introduction, principally extension of the lunch break from 30 to 40 minutes. With a start time of 8.10 a.m. and a finish at 2.15 p.m., it is set out in the Appendix, Example 4. This form of day is different in timing but not much in structure from the typical English school day set out in the Appendix, Example 2. It has three features which in combination create its 'compressed' character:

- an early start (rather earlier than the other schools with this type of day)
- a lunch hour 20 minutes or so shorter than most schools
- a 6:2 division of lessons before and after lunch (but similar to many schools with traditional days)

Other schools looking at the Tideway example have found that a whole range of minor changes are possible to starting time, breaks, lunch hour and lesson pattern. A five minute adjustment to these can often alter the feel of the day substantially. For many schools reasonable minimum lengths for lunch break, short breaks/circulation and registration/assemblies would be 40, 20 and 20 minutes respectively, totalling 80 minutes. Combined with four hours 40 minutes lesson time this creates a school day span of six hours. So it is not possible to finish school at 2.30 without either starting at 8.30 or further compressing these breaks, etc.

A number of schools have now adopted a compressed day, mainly in initial response to problems with lunch-time supervision during teachers' industrial action, but retaining it because they preferred it, for example:

- Light Hall School, Solihull (1981) with an 8.45 a.m. start and lunch break of 30 minutes (now amended to 9.05 start; 35 minute lunch and 3 p.m. finish)
- Sydenham School, Bridgwater, Somerset (1982), starting at 8.30, finishing at 2.30, with 35 minutes lunch
- Bentley Wood High School, Harrow (1985) starting 8.40, finishing 3.00, with 30 minutes for lunch.

Some schools have removed the lunch break, although leaving breaks for snacks:

- Kingshurst School, Birmingham (1979, closed 1988), starting 8.50, closing 2.15, with one 20 minute break but with the cafeteria available after 2.15.
- Court Moor School, Fleet, Hampshire, start 8.30, finish 2.20, with two short breaks and meals available after 2.20.

One school, Whitesmore School in Birmingham, adopted a lunchless day, 8.45 – 2.05 in 1980, but reverted to a traditional day in 1982. Another, Tudor Grange School in Solihull, ran an 8.25 – 1.25 day in 1979 but reverted because it seemed tiring.

An unusual form of day operates at Ernesford Grange School and Community College, Coventry. This has a period 0 at 8.30, with the main day from 9.10 to 3.40, but with some year-groups finishing at 3.0/3.15 on some days and with a staggered lunch hour.

Some LEAs have considered the compressed day as an authority-wide strategy. Dorset set up a working party in 1981 to consider a 'restructured day' for all schools, in a context of severe impending cuts where such a day could bring possible savings on meals, supervision and heating. The working party report (September 1981) concluded that 'it would be educationally feasible to restructure the day in most schools'. It suggested that the difficulties, e.g. in break-time supervision, rearranged transport, general school organisation and linked courses with colleges, could either be overcome or would be less of a problem than financial cuts elsewhere. However, the proposal ran out of steam. Officers were uneasy about the countywide proposal and logistic problems surfaced. Political opposition developed and there was an outburst from parents with a large petition. Financial pressures eased and the proposal was dropped – though the county did stop providing meals in primary schools.

Avon LEA undertook widespread consultations in 1987 about proposals for an 'alternative day', arising mainly from the problems of lunch-hour supervision. Two models were suggested, one 8.00 a.m. to 2.00 p.m. with a break for light snacks and lunch available at the end of the day, the other of a compressed day type with examples similar to those above. The proposals were overwhelmingly rejected, but afterwards the LEA did issue helpful guidelines for schools which were considering change.

One LEA, Hampshire, accepted the compressed day on a wide scale. A group of schools approached the LEA in 1984 about the possibilities of a compressed day. One of these, Court Moor School described above, introduced it on a one year basis, gaining 73 per cent parent approval (subsequently 86 per cent). By September 1986 eight schools were operating in this way and the LEA drew up ground rules. The compressed day was defined as a school day finishing before 3 p.m., or with a lunch break of less than half an hour. The earliest acceptable start was seen as 8.20 a.m., and the shortest break to serve food as 20 minutes. Arrangements to develop out of school and supervised homework activities in the afternoon were to be included.

By September 1987 25 schools in Hampshire had adopted this pattern of day, most impelled initially by lunch hour supervision difficulties. Reports from school governors generally suggested that the advantages outweighed the disadvantages.

Supporters of the compressed day list a number of advantages:

1. It is more businesslike. Students seem to work better in the mornings.
2. Lunchtime problems are solved. Behaviour is much better, damage reduced and supervision problems overcome.
3. Out of school activities regrow in the afternoon, which also provides more daylight hours for them in the winter.
4. Community activities can expand in the afternoon — often substantially.
5. Individuals put their time to better use. Students have more time for their own leisure pursuits (and shared family evening activities need not be spoiled by homework). Staff meetings and activities are held without pressure from the end of the day.
6. Homework seems to improve, both in quantity and quality. Students do not feel so much conflict between homework and leisure and can often do it at home in more quiet and with less television distraction than in the evening.
7. Students, parents and teachers on the whole seem to approve.
8. This type of day is easily explained, and the administrative change is very simple.

On the other hand, there are disadvantages:

1. It is a very compressed day (to secure an early closure some of the timetables compress class time below that for 'normal' timetables). So there is little time for informal contact or discussion between teachers and students. There is also less contact between staff, and communication is more difficult. Staff also tend to arrive at school less in advance of the first bell. New staff take some time to adjust to the day.
2. Some teachers clearly prefer a longer lunch period for relaxation or preparation and may suffer increased stress from the lack of it. Preparation for science practical lessons and some other practical lessons is more difficult.

3. Some schools find providing snack-lunches in 40 minutes difficult or uncivilised (but some could use a staggered lunch-hour to reduce this.)
4. Schools heavily dependent on contract transport may find afternoon activities poorly supported unless extra transport is arranged.
5. Sports fixtures with other schools still often involve a long wait until the end of the afternoon.
6. Invigilation of external examinations in the afternoon can create difficulties.
7. Particular problems arise for special schools, boarding schools or day schools with a boarding hostel or houses, and schools whose contract transport is inflexible.

It should be said that none of the heralded problems seem to arise. There is no evidence of a falling off in school work — if anything the reverse; there is no increase in truancy (rather less), and no upsurge in vandalism in the community. And there is no rebellion from working parents.

The compressed day is clearly both workable and acceptable and is now well established in the schools that use it. Broadly it trades a more businesslike morning and a freer afternoon against an early start and a slightly rushed quality. It does have two limitations: it does not significantly affect the curriculum (though there is a tendency for minority subjects and some quasi-curricular activities to reappear in the afternoons); and it lacks any staffing resources to exploit the splendid time resource of the free afternoons. However, it may well marry in time with its time-flexing cousin.

Time flexing

This has developed over a range of schools. It seems to have arisen out of disillusion with the conventional day and the rigidity of the conventional timetable, their unfriendliness to new learning approaches and activities, and the separation of the school day from community time.

DAY 10: STANTONBURY CAMPUS, MILTON KEYNES, BUCKS
The oldest and perhaps best known example of time flexing in the UK is Day 10 of the Stantonbury Campus. This originated in 1974 as a compromise in a debate on cross-curriculum learning approaches. It fitted neatly into an existing ten day timetable and allocated one Friday each fortnight as Day 10. In 1977 timetable pressures made Day 10 monthly, but supplemented it with a 'Week 10' in the summer term.

On Day 10 the normal timetable is stood down and replaced by a menu of 80 day long courses for which students opt. Some courses have restricted enrolment, many are open to all years. Some continue on other Day 10s, although most are freestanding one-day events. They cover a full range of academic, sporting, arts and crafts activities and special events/visits (some of the latter involving costs).

Day 10 requires a strong administrative structure. It has in effect its own self-contained faculty, with a volunteer committee, funds, and monthly administration of computer processed option choice sheets and notification of choices/changes/vacancies through tutors.

Day 10 has a number of virtues: it offers great variety, a high spot each month; it harnesses the enthusiasms of staff and interests of children; it offers a good stretch of time for each activity (plus access to a long weekend, if needed). It is a popular and well-established feature of the school, but it does require considerable commitment and energy from the staff. While Stantonbury Campus has been able to generate this, replication has not occurred elsewhere.

ACTIVITIES WEEKS

A growing number of schools have adopted an easier alternative — 'activities week', usually in the post-examination period of the summer term. Typically the timetable is wound down for a whole week and replaced by a range of week-long activities similar to Day 10, sometimes using an adjoining weekend. There is a similar options booklet and choice procedure.

While activities weeks only provide half the time of ten monthly Day 10s and are not so suited to single day activities, broadly they offer similar advantages and are much easier to administer. There is only one round of activities instead of ten, and the whole year is available for preparation. As the fifth year have left there is a 20 per cent improvement in student-staff ratios (more for schools with sixth forms, and over 35 per cent more for some 13 – 18 upper schools).

DAY 5: BROOK SCHOOL, SHEFFIELD, (NOW PART OF HANDSWORTH GRANGE SCHOOL)

A similar but more limited development is Day 5, introduced for the fifth year in the Brook School from 1982 and copied to some degree by other local schools. The school operated a four period day and previously allocated four periods per week to fifth year PE, careers, social education and religious education. This time was now blocked and recycled on Fridays, with generous staffing (1:15). In the autumn two circuits of taster options were operated, followed the next term by a choice of these options and some visits and special events (sometimes using the adjoining weekend).

The reaction has been very positive. Fifth year students liked the more integrated day, increased contact with the community (both coming in and going out), greater variety of learning situations, more responsibility and better relationships with staff. Teachers have gained by working outside their subject boundaries, in teams, using their strengths. The initiative has continued to develop, with improved team work and greater use of a student portfolio. Sarah Draper, Day 5 Coordinator, has completed a useful evaluation (1986). The main difficulty in replication is I suspect that many schools do not give 20 per cent of their fifth year timetable to those areas. However, the device is a useful one and could be used for other age-groups and for combinations of other subjects. It will probably become increasingly valuable as the need grows for greater emphasis on process and so for cross-curricular and combined academic/pastoral activities.

'ELECTIVES': ARCHWAY SCHOOL, STROUD, GLOUCESTER-SHIRE

Experience of an activity week in 1981 led the staff of Archway School to explore ways of retaining its virtues within the normal school week. 'Electives' were accordingly introduced in 1983. Years 1 – 2 were given two elective sessions of one and three quarter hours each and years 3 – 7 three, the time being found by trimming time off registration and some periods, removing afternoon break and some timetable reallocation. The day is a busy one with nine 30 – 35 minute periods. Two of the three sessions are whole afternoons, with the possibility of early start or late finish.

As with Day 10 and activity weeks, the fifty electives of each session cover a full range of activities, from minority GCSE subjects to fun and leisure. Some last a term, others a year, some are part of a two year course or spread across two sessions. Most span several year groups, and many are open to parents and others. Their expressed aims are to provide greater opportunities for excellence; extend horizons and widen opportunities, academic and other; tap the skills and interest of staff, parents and students more fully; strengthen links with the community; develop more active learning methods and encourage greater cooperation among students and with adults.

The scheme is now well-established with a positive aura. It brings valued variety, flexibility and enthusiasm and is encouraging new learning and working approaches. It is interesting that the school's three best years examination results have come during the scheme. It was evaluated by LEA inspectors in 1986. They concluded:

> ...we share the feelings of the overwhelming majority of staff and students that the programme represents a genuine enrichment of the curriculum for most students, and that it is the source of very considerable enjoyment, and that it should continue to develop with the positive encouragement of staff and student alike.

THE FLEXIBLE DAY: HOLYROOD SCHOOL, CHARD, SOMERSET

In 1981 there were staff discussions about the possibility of a flexible pattern of school day. The rationale was that the existing rigid school day (a typical one with 4 + 4 35 minute periods) made it difficult or impossible to provide many activities, e.g. short courses, all-age courses, activities for special interest or ability groups, different time allocation for different pupils, individualised study and full use of learning resources, etc.

As a result a ten week trial was operated in the summer term 1982. This involved:

1. starting at 8.30 a.m.
2. mounting the existing timetabled periods 1 – 6 before lunch at 12.45
3. providing *four* periods after lunch, in which the two periods remaining from the normal day either
   (a) could be reinstated in their usual form (normally periods 7 – 8, 1.45 – 2.55) or
   (b) the staffing could be recycled in entirely different flexi-classes periods 7 – 8 or 9 – 10 Mondays—Thursdays (3.00 – 4.10). These flexi-classes were similar to the Day 10, activities week, and electives courses described above. Students had to choose a minimum number, but could choose more.

Each faculty offered a programme of flexi-classes, in which it was asked to provide some or all of:

   −   a variety of course lengths (10 weeks, 5 weeks, other)
   −   supplementary courses for the able, talented, enthusiastic, or students with difficulties
   −   keep-up classes for students who were struggling
   −   revision courses for examination students
   −   small groups or individual coaching
   −   leisure activities/visits/field work.

In addition, community education mounted an extensive programme of adult classes which students could join, while adults could join many school classes. Main bus departures were at 3 p.m., with a smaller run at 4.15. (About 30 per cent of the students took the bus.) The afternoons were quite different from normal afternoons. Staff, students and adults from the community came and went throughout − students and staff could on different days be free after lunch, go home at 3 or at 4.10.

Response to the trial was very positive on the whole. The administration went smoothly and the main problems were over mismatches of demand and supply (e.g. two hundred would-be archers for sixteen places!) The adjustment to the new day was very swift. Flexi-courses produced the same interaction of enthusiastic staff and volunteer students as the Archway electives. The interaction with adults was also valuable, with student involvement in adult classes small-scale but promising. Many visitors commented on the positive reactions of students and on the atmosphere of the afternoon — low key, quiet, civilised. Discipline problems were virtually nil, and there were no problems out in the community nor any increase in truancy.

Many parents liked the scheme, particularly if their children enjoyed it, but a number disliked it, usually because of car transport problems and difficulties with the early or irregular return of children. Replies to the question 'Would you like to see a continued trial of a 'flexi-week' in some form?' were (percentages):

	Yes	Not sure/it depends	No
Parents	45	24	31
Students	61	25	13
Teachers	72	20	6

As a result a Mark II pattern of day was introduced in September 1983 which retained flexi-classes although the afternoon structure was less flexible. The morning was similar, with six periods before lunch. In the afternoons normal school periods 7 – 8 were 1.45 – 2.55 p.m. However, the 'day' was shortened by 15 minutes through reduction of tutor-time (offset by the introduction of a tutor period) and this 15 minutes per day was rolled by staff agreement into one double period flexi-class per week for each teacher in flexi-time 3.00 – 4.10 p.m.

In some ways this pattern was more conservative, since it largely excluded community classes which needed to start before 3 p.m. and created less afternoon flexibility. However it was a stable model. Improvements included an extensive supported self study system which was always available for students in flexi-time, and better computer programmes to identify students' disappointed choices and process alternatives. Flexi-time was also used to relieve timetable pressures, for example, for the second foreign language which could spill into it.

This pattern was continued the following year, but modified again in 1985, broadly similar but allowing a little more flexibility in lessons 7 – 8. Self study has increased in importance, and joint sixth form-community classes developed. A modular curriculum for fourth and fifth years has also been assisted. In 1989 flexi-time operates Tuesdays – Thursdays, leaving Mondays after 3 p.m. available for meetings (see Appendix, Example Five). Some scheduling has been introduced to avoid clashing with team fixtures.

Detailed reports on the original trial and the subsequent developments are available from the school. Some valuable lessons emerge:

1. The 'flexible day' becomes very acceptable. Beforehand the idea of flexibility is disturbing to many. Parents are the most dubious, but they do work out solutions to transport and family problems. Teachers and students soon become familiar with it and learn to make use of its possibilities. So the flexible day becomes a normal, everyday feature of school life.

2. In the flexible part of the day, control of the timetable reverts to the individual teacher and the faculty. They decide what activities should be provided for whom, and when. The timetable becomes servant.

3. Timetable flexibility is quite different. The normal school timetable fits x items into x slots; flexi-time puts x items into 2x or even 4x slots. So there is great freedom to switch teachers, classes, rooms or days, often at short notice. To give just one example, a weekly single period can often be converted into a fortnightly double — the intervening week being free for both teacher and taught.

4. The potential for developing individualised study and interaction with community education is tremendous.

5. Flexi-time is *different* — and as such brings welcome variety... and flexibility. The greatest potential advantage is probably the one which has not yet been found. Of course that cuts no ice as an argument, but it is probably true. The possibilities and limitations of the fixed day are well known, but those of the flexible day have hardly been explored.

OTHER FLEXIBLE DAY SCHEMES
Devizes School, Wiltshire
This school introduced a scheme originally based on that at Holyrood School as a seven week trial in 1985, with a full year trial 1986 – 87. The scheme has developed strongly and is now well established and extensive. It provides an 8.50 a.m. – 2.40 p.m. main day (50 minutes lunch), with flexi-courses offered every day 2.45 – 3.45 p.m. These cover a very extensive range of the electives type. All students choose an average of two per week all year, and some more. Fig. 3.2 gives an example of part of the leaflet for parents.

An evaluation in 1987 gave the following results:

Percentages in favour of restructured day and flexi-courses continuing

		Yes	Yes with changes	No
Parents	(55% return)	48	31	21
Students	(90% return)	57	35	7
Staff	(70% return)	76	21	3

Ansford School, Castle Cary, Somerset
The school operated a flexible day of a similar type in the summer of 1985 which was evaluated later in the year. Comments from staff, parents and pupils were generally favourable and similar to that at Chard and Devizes. An interesting feature was that Ansford is a small secondary school, with most students bussed, and undertook this as a possible means of improving its provision. A significant finding was

DEVIZES SCHOOL FLEXI COURSES AUTUMN TERM   SEPTEMBER-DECEMBER 1988

Length (Half terms)	Course	Years & Notes		Code		Room
	THURSDAY					
5/11	GCSE Italian	U6*		6 XIT	W Th	27
6	Typewriting	6		6 XTY	Th	FE
5/11	GCSE Geology	5*	c	5 XGE	Tu Th	61
5/11	GCSE Design & Communication	5*		5 XDC	W Th	44
5/11	GCSE Music	5-6	PA	XMU	Th	48
11	GCSE Geography	4*	P	4 XGY	M Th	40
11	GCSE Religious Studies	4*	P	4 XRS	M Th	59
2	Computing	6		6 PBM	Th	96
2	Wordprocessing (3 45)	4-6	P	WP	Th2	96
2	Roundway Covert Conservation	6		6 SMH	Th	64
2	Ceramics	6	c	6 IRL	Th	22
2	Home Economics	6		6 DCS	Th	46
2	Play Rehearsal	5-6	PA	BGW	Th	85/MH
2	Keyboarding (3 45)	4-5		KB	Th2	FE
5	Discovering Waiblingen (Exchange arrangements and German Conversation)	2-4	PA	DJP	Th	50
2	Careers	3-5		VJW	Th	19
2	Revision and Coursework	All		CJS	Th	12
2	Problem Solving	2-3	A	TGJ	Th	74
6	Design in Wood	4-6	c	RGA	Th	45
6	Design & Make a Remote Controlled Car	3-5	A c	PNJ	Th	31
2	Canvas Work/Needlepoint	2-3	c	SYB	Th	80
2	Tasty Cookery for Slimmers	4-5	c	SJH	Th	47
2	American Football (Boys)	4-6		RCP	Th	
2	Badminton (Mixed)	3		3 MTW	Th	P.Sp
2	Keep Fit (Girls)	2-3	PA	MMW	Th	B.G
4	5 a side Soccer	6		6 PXM	Th	
1	Trampolining (Mixed)	3-6		REH	Th	G.G
1	Badminton (Mixed)	4		4 GMK	Th	Sp.H
2	Hockey (Mixed)	2		2 WER	Th	

Notes

1   The lengths of courses are shown as half-terms. 5/11 means that there are 5 half-terms remaining of a course that lasts for 11 half-terms.

2   Some courses run for one half-term only.

3   Please note that a few courses start at 3 45.

4   Some courses are for pupils from several years, others are more restricted.

5   Years/Notes/Codes:

P - parents are welcome to attend as students if numbers permit.
A - adult helpers would be welcome; qualifications or experience may be necessary.
c - there will definitely be a small charge to pupils, usually for materials or transport.
C - a larger charge to cover fees, equipment or more expensive materials or transport will be necessary.
* - a course running on two or more days per week.
X - a course leading to an examination.
R - restricted numbers, very few places available

Each course has a code indicating the member of staff or subject involved, a day (or days) of the week and sometimes a number. Please use the correct code when you complete the form.

6   Supervised Private Study/Homework is available throughout flexi time. It is also possible for pupils to use the Library. To choose either of these please use the appropriate code: ST - Private Study/Homework
LY - Library

7   Remember that choices are being made for next year's years, eg, present 2nd years choose courses available to 3rd years etc.

CJS
6 6 88

CJS/SGS

PLEASE KEEP THIS SHEET FOR FUTURE REFERENCE

Figure 3.2 – Part of Devizes School Flexi-time leaflet

that although there were increased transport costs, these were less than might be expected.

Greendown Community School, Swindon
This comprehensive school, opened in 1986, operates an unusual and imaginative type of day which includes a flexible element. The day itself is compact, with an 8.45 a.m. start and a short break and lunch period (see Appendix, Example Six). There is an additional enrichment session at 2.10 p.m. on four days of the week. One of the four enrichment sessions is compulsory (physical recreation) and students have to choose at least one of the others (and can choose two or even three).

The activities for enrichment sessions are mounted by three 'curriculum schools' (a descriptor for three large faculties) each providing two options per day making six in all. Enrichment activity modules last for about six weeks. In all 144 modules are provided per year (including sport/recreation) of which students must choose 12 and can choose up to 24. The activities are planned by each curriculum school as part of their total provision, and so extra curricular activities are part of the total curriculum. For the last week of each module period enrichment activities are wound down to provide time for reporting to parents. During (and after) the enrichment session community activities also take place.

The Greendown School day has some other unusual features. The main lesson sessions are unusually long, one hour 20/25 minutes, three per day; each session for a year group is blocked with one of the curriculum schools; and the session on Mondays from 2.10 p.m. is allocated for staff planning and curriculum development.

Marlborough School, Woodstock, Oxfordshire
The school originally ran a very extensive electives programme involving all pupils and staff each day. This proved difficult to sustain with the right quality and so in 1988 was contracted into a whole afternoon (Wednesdays) 1.00 – 3.05 p.m. This is additional to 24 hours per week class contact time provided within an 8.30 a.m. – 3.05 p.m. day (45 minutes lunch).

Electives can be one or two hours in length and last a term, although they can be linked together over a longer period. As at Greendown School they are mounted by faculties and are seen as part of the total curriculum provision. As such, definition of objectives, syllabuses and self-assessment by students are being developed.

A related activity is the '3 – 7 programme' which is operated twice a week 3 – 7 p.m. as part of the community education programme. Senior students may enrol for informal use of the sports hall, library, music block, and for other activities. A similar programme operates on another day '3 – 5' for younger students.

North Area College, Stockport
This a new sixth form college which also has 12 – 16 pupils phasing out from the previous school. For them it provides academic education 9 a.m. – 1 p.m., with complementary studies Monday – Thursday afternoons 1.40 – 2.55 p.m. of which students must choose two, and can choose more. The range is wide, largely but by no means solely leisure and practical activities, and library facilities are also available.

The extended school day in City Technology Colleges
From the outset the proposals for the CTCs included the suggestion of a longer school day. The DES publicity document of 1986 stated, 'The school day and the school term are likely to be longer than the minimum required by law for LEA-maintained schools. All pupils will be expected... to participate in extra curricular activities including residential field trips.' This perhaps unexpected feature seems to have arisen from the need for additional curricular time, given the CTC emphasis on science and technology, and a stress on positive values and the contribution of out-of-school activities. This thinking can perhaps be traced back to the Newsom Report extended day and also to the independent school model.

The idea was developed further in working documents, with suggestions for a school week comprising:

	per day (average)	per week
formal teaching	5 hours	25 hours
enrichment activities	1 hour 20 minutes	6 hours 40 minutes
assemblies, registration, breaks and lunch	1 hour 40 minutes	8 hours 20 minutes
School day span	8 hours	40 hours

Periods of 25 minutes, creating lessons of 50, 75 or 100 minutes were envisaged. Enrichment activities were suggested such as sport, 'clubs', Duke of Edinburgh's Award, performing and expressive arts, community service and outdoor pursuits. The school year was seen as comprising the standard 38 weeks, but with many students and most teachers involved in five – ten days of enrichment activities during the vacations.

Detailed arrangements can be seen in the proposals for Thamesmead CTC set out by its sponsors to Bexley LEA in July 1988. The school day outlined here starts at 8.30 a.m. and ends at 4.50 p.m. (4.05 on two days). During the week 60 25-minute periods would provide 1,500 minutes of class contact, 100 more than in a typical secondary school. Seven enrichment sessions of varying lengths provided another seven hours per week. Example 14 in the Appendix sets out the model. It can be seen that the greatest change from the traditional school day is the greater school day span, the inclusion of enrichment activities within it, and the varying lengths of day.

Central government has recently shown interest in extending the school day in maintained schools, probably because of the difficulties discussed in chapter six of squeezing the national curriculum into the present day. It has been suggested that the current English day is shorter than its European counterparts — not actually true, as the next chapter shows, though it does compare badly with Scotland and Northern Ireland. However it is not clear whether the CTC model will be copied — it does depend on students and teachers who have opted for the regime, and would be more difficult for a governing body to develop even under the provisions of local school management. Also, assuming that teachers can be persuaded or directed to work a longer day, it isn't clear whether the best use of their extra time lies in the extended day model, which is still broadly a traditional type of day, or in a more developed flexible day such as that suggested in chapter twelve.

Initiatives in Local Education Authorities
COVENTRY LEA
In 1981 a full study was made of post-primary education in the LEA, leading to the publication of a report 'Comprehensive Education for Life'. One of the working documents for the report examined the structure of the school day. It criticised traditional 'daily and termly routines... usually imposed on all secondary pupils regardless of their age or education requirements' and illustrated possible changes with a model of a long morning, followed by afternoon and evening for a whole range of activities ('A' level consortia, school clubs, work experience, sport, music tuition, adult education and community activities, etc). The full report floated a different possibility, with mornings used mainly for 11 – 13 programmes, and afternoons and evenings for 14 – 18 and community programmes. In the upshot although the report has been very influential in Coventry and beyond, the school day recommendations have not developed.

THE OXFORDSHIRE DAY
In June 1982 the Oxfordshire LEA circulated a paper to schools 'A change in the Oxfordshire school day?' This questioned aspects of the existing day, and encouraged secondary schools to look at three options:

1. An 8.30 a.m. – 1.30 p.m. long morning, providing at least four hours lessons, with lunch during or after it, and with school transport; followed by a *voluntary* afternoon for club and leisure activities, individual study

and community-linked activities, and possibly links with further education.

2. Similar but with a slightly later start, a short lunch-break, and with compulsory involvement for students in the afternoon activities, with transport at 3.30 p.m. 'The afternoon provides extension and addition with possibilities for mixed age groups, individual study, work alongside adults and off-site projects without disruption to the basic curriculum. All pupils would have access to good private study conditions and have library time for project work regardless of home conditions.'

3. Retaining the traditional day, but developing Day 10s and activities weeks.

For primary schools the paper suggested a more cautious approach 'with the youngest children requiring more supervision and less able to work on their own and with a different rhythm of school day'. However, it saw possible developments in association with parents, particularly the spread of afternoon family/community workshops, and did not discount the possibilities of using options 1 or 2 above, possibly linked with adjoining secondary schools.

The Chief Education Officer, Tim Brighouse, addressed a series of large public meetings — often tumultuous. Apart from the shock of such an assault upon tradition, option 1 created fears because of the voluntary nature of the afternoon, while option 2 could lead to increased hours for teachers. The paper stirred up ideas about school time in the LEA but led to limited result. The main immediate development was that described above at Marlborough School, Woodstock.

The experience of these two LEAs together with Dorset and Avon over the compressed day suggests that innovation in school day structures by LEAs is difficult. It seems to provoke and amplify opposition. LEAs can operate more effectively by loosening the constraints and encouraging schools to experiment — particularly in the new climate now being created by the local management of schools.

* * * * *

The overall school day situation in the UK is very interesting. The great mass of schools still operate school days which are of the traditional form, different only in detail from those of the early part of this century. However never has there been so much trial of alternatives as in the last ten years. Some of these have been in response to pressures — some of the compressed day changes, for example. But many reflect a systematic attempt to rethink and replan a school's management of time — particularly the changes in Scotland, the flexible day developments and the new arrangements of the CTCs.

Many of these schemes were difficult to introduce, meeting scepticism or resistance. The LEA initiatives seemed particularly threatening. And even now, despite wide publicity for these new models, the rate of change is slow. Many schools still retain school day features which are clearly inefficient — the 4 + 4 model, for example.

Yet it is significant that most of the new models have rooted themselves very firmly. It is the implementation of change which is difficult. However there is now sufficient collective experience of such change to ease this implementation and to present change positively. The latest, and uncertain factor, is the spread of local management of schools. Will the new 'market economy' make schools more nervous of a change which might disturb parents? Or will it lead them to think more positively about the cost-effectiveness of their present school day arrangements and to redesign them?

4   The school day world-wide

The present school day in Europe

Table 4.1 sets out the position for the EC. Caution in interpretation is needed, since lesson-times can include breaks or circulation, and games are often not included. At first sight the table suggests an incoherent assortment of historical traditions. But careful study suggests some common features, a range of variations and some trends for change.

Common features

By English standards most European schools start early in the day, mainly between 8.00 and 8.30 a.m. This does not seem related to climate or hours of daylight — Danish, Norwegian and Swedish schools begin at 8.00 or soon after.

Partly as a consequence of the early start most countries' school days are morning heavy, with short or nil afternoons. The exceptions are France, Belgium, Luxembourg, Spain and Ireland, and of course where double shifts operate. Most of the former group have long lunch-hours.

No country provides registration-by-tutor, assemblies and pastoral time comparable to the arrangements in Britain, usually attributed to the 'in loco parentis' tradition of British schools. Many European countries make no such provision, although it can exist concealed in the working of the class as a unit.

In most countries the school day is an on/off operation. Either students are all in school or they are all out. The main exceptions occur in France, where it is accepted that students can leave early or arrive late if they do not have a lesson, and in Hungary where a 'lesson zero' (i.e. a lesson before school) and extension classes after school are sometimes provided, mainly for able students.

Variations

STARTING TIMES
The earliest are 8.00 a.m. in Denmark, Hungary and West Germany, the latest 9.15 a.m. in the Netherlands.

FINISHING TIMES

The earliest are found in Austria, 12.00 for primary schools; Italy, 12.30 for primary and some junior secondary schools; and Denmark 12.00 for younger primary pupils. However for the first two this is offset by Saturday morning school. West German schools finish early, 1.00 p.m, again offset by Saturdays. A late finish occurs in France, Belgium, the Netherlands and Luxembourg, with the latest Spain (5.00 p.m. but after a three hour midday break). This reflects a difference between 'mornings only' countries (e.g. Italy, Austria, Germany, Greece); 'mainly mornings' countries (e.g. Denmark, Norway, Sweden); and 'mornings and afternoons' countries (the remainder). Shift systems are quite commonly operated in Greece, Italy, Portugal and Yugoslavia, usually mornings and afternoons. Occasionally in Portugal a three shift system is used.

LUNCH BREAKS

The 'mornings only' countries by definition have no lunch-break, although snacks are eaten in a reasonable length break. Otherwise, lunch-hours vary between 30 minutes and three hours (Spain). There are also contrasts in lunch arrangements — for example, lunch is provided by schools in Belgium but not in the Netherlands.

SATURDAY SCHOOL

This occurs, mornings only, in Austria, France, Italy, Luxembourg, West Germany (but in some *Länder* only two Saturdays a month, in others none) and a few Irish schools.

MIDWEEK BREAKS

France, Belgium and Netherlands operate a half day, usually on Wednesday, often used for games (two half days in Luxembourg).

LESSON LENGTHS

There is more uniformity here. In most countries lessons are 45 or 50 minutes long. In Sweden lessons are 40 minutes long, in France 55 and in Austria and Italy 60. Some countries such as Finland and Hungary operate a system of nominal 'hours', in which 45 minutes or so is lesson time and the rest recreation (a similar system is used in Japan). Others such as the Federal Republic of Germany commonly timetable circulation time between lessons.

CLASS CONTACT TIME

The greatest variation in Europe occurs in primary education. In the Scandinavian countries the youngest children may attend for as little as 11.25 hours contact time per week, with a graduated rise throughout the primary years. (Children also enter school later, at seven years.) This contrasts sharply with most other European countries which make little or no distinction between younger and older primary children. Most provide about 22 – 23 hours of lesson-time, but this is exceeded in Spain (25), France (27) and Luxembourg (30). France is unusual in that primary school contact time slightly exceeds that of secondary schools.

Variation for secondary children is much less, with most countries providing 22.5 – 25 hours of lessons. This is exceeded by Belgium (26 hours 40 minutes), Ireland (28) and Italy, Luxembourg and Portugal (30). Some countries provide a set amount for all students of the same age, while in others it varies within or between schools, sometimes quite considerably.

Table 4.1 sets out comparative data for EC countries.

Care is needed in such international comparisons, both for Europe and for the other countries described below. Daily times need expressing as a weekly total because of the incidence of Saturday

Table 4.1 School hours and school years in the EC

| | PRIMARY | | LOWER SECONDARY | | | |
	Class hours per week	School days per year	Duration of lessons (in mins)	No. of per week	Class hours per week	School days per year
BELGIUM	23.3	182	50	32	26.7	182
DENMARK	11.25 – 21.75 (c) (d)	200	45	24 – 34 (c) (d)	18 – 25.5	200
FED. REP. GERMANY	12.75 – 21.0	200/226 (a)	45	29 – 33 (c) (d)	21.75 – 24.75	200/226 (a)
GREECE	17.25 – 23	175	40 – 45	23 – 30	17.25 – 23	175
SPAIN	25	185	flexible	flexible	25	185
FRANCE	27	158 (b)	55	24 – 27.5 33 (f)	22 – 25.2	175 (b)
IRELAND	23 (e)	min. 184	40	42	28	min. 180
ITALY	24	min. 200 (a)	60	30	30	min. 200 (a)
LUXEMBOURG	27	216 (a)	50	30	25	216 (a)
NETHERLANDS	22 – 25 (c)	200/240 (a)	50	24 – 32	20 – 26.7	195
PORTUGAL	23.75	175/208 (a)	50	30	25	164
UK	c.23.7 (h)	190	35 – 60	40 – 20	c.23.4 (h) c.26.7 (j)	190

Key: (a) Six day week system
       (b) 'day equivalents'
       (c) graduated by age
       (d) graduated by ability or interest
       (e) plus 2.5 hours religious education
       (f) vocational lycee
       (g) includes rest periods
       (h) plus 1.5 (primary) or 2.5 (secondary) 'other contact time'
       (j) in Scotland

Source: Adapted from EURYDICE 'Tables on the School year in the Member States of European Community 1987', with additional information from EURYDICE 'Regulations Concerning Compulsory Schooling in the Member States of the European Community'.

school. Even weekly totals are misleading, because total contact time is also affected by the extent of the school year and the number of years of schooling (see next chapter).

The overriding impression is of eccentric national variations which defy rational justification. Variations for apparently similar countries seem to be created not so much by local custom or circumstance as by past bureaucratic decision which has created its own momentum and tradition.

An interesting footnote is provided by British schools for armed forces children outside Britain, many of which retain the British school day but some of which adapt to local conditions:

In West Germany, Belgium and the Netherlands	(86 schools)	Typical British school day
Denmark and Norway	(2 schools)	8.45 – 14.20/14.45, with short lunch hour
Naples, Sardinia	(2 schools)	Typical British school day, but mornings only in the summer
Gibraltar	(2 schools)	9.00 – 15.30/16.15, but mornings only in summer
Cyprus	(9 schools)	Early start, 7.30 – 8.00, finishing at 12.00/12.30 (infants) to 13.15/13.30 (secondary)
Brunei	(4 primary)	7.30 – 13.15/13.30
Hong Kong	(8 schools)	8.20/8.45 – 14.45/15.00

It appears that the exported tradition remains strong and relatively unaffected by local native schools. However, it is affected by climatic conditions, although not uniformly. Moreover one can see the beginning of that local self-perpetuating momentum, e.g. in Cyprus, which is such a powerful force in the use of school time.

Trends

Saturday morning school is shrinking. In West Germany it was previously universal, but now several *Länder* have removed it (lesson time is increased on other days). There are experiments in Italy to do without it, and it is more uncommon in Ireland.

There is also a trend for activities to fill empty afternoons. This has been most marked in Germany with the development of *Ganztagsschulen* (all-day schools), particularly in many of the *Gesamtschulen* (comprehensive schools). Here a range of lessons and activities are provided, mainly voluntary, including some lessons not easily fitted into the mornings, extra help for students with difficulties, supervised homework and clubs and activities. Often pupils have to choose one a week but may choose more. This development has also led to the provision of lunches (see Appendix, Example 8).

The school day in North America
The North American school systems have developed their own traditions in time use, very different from their European counterparts.

The typical school day
In the USA the day in primary ('elementary') schools will typically be six hours long. Its general form is not dissimilar to that described for the UK earlier. In secondary (high) schools, the day normally lasts about seven hours.

The traditional US high school day has two characteristics: long lessons, usually of 55 minutes, allowing five minutes circulation within the hour; and a regular daily pattern where the same class occurs in the same period (i.e., at the same time) each day. The day commonly begins with a short 'home room' session for registration. In this traditional pattern there are six such periods in the day, sometimes seven, and sometimes shortened to 45 minutes. Sometimes the last period of the day is an access period where teachers are obliged to be available and students can request additional help.

A new trend provides a more flexible or modular system, often taking advantage of computer timetabling assistance, to offer lessons for longer lengths of time but only two or three times per week, the total weekly duration for each subject being similar to the traditional pattern.

Guidelines for the school day are laid down by states and vary between them. Start and finishing times and length of lessons are established by school boards, but tend to be similar throughout a state. In general US schools tend to start early, often by 8 a.m, and finish by about 3 p.m. Lunch hours are short, commonly 30 minutes or so, usually with staggered sessions.

Canadian high schools, which originally had features of both the English and US school day, have now moved closer to the traditional US pattern in that they commonly use long periods which follow a regular weekly pattern. Provinces and county boards lay down overall regulations and guidelines, but within these schools are free to work out their own timetables and times. There is probably more school by school variation than in the USA. In Ontario, for example, some schools offer 6 x 55 minutes plus lunch, others 4 x 75 minutes plus lunch. (See Appendix, Example 10.) Classes occur regularly each day, but some schools alternate the times, for example

Period	Day 1	Day 2	Day 3
1	Course A	Course B	Course A
2	Course B	Course A	Course B
3	Course C	Course D	Course C
4	Course D	Course C	Course D etc.

The extended day

THE IDEA

In the 1970s concern grew in the USA about the limited duration of the school day. This sprang partly from research interest in the importance of school time as a factor in school achievement, but mainly from an awareness that students in Europe and the Pacific nations achieved better than their US counterparts and spent more time in school. This was highlighted in the influential report of the National Commission on Excellence in Education, 'A Nation at Risk' (1983). It found

> three disturbing facts about the use American schools and students make of time: (1) compared to other nations, American students spend less time on school work; (2) time spent in the classroom and on homework is often used ineffectively; and (3) schools are not doing enough to help students develop either the study skills required to use time well or the willingness to spend more time on school work.

The Commission concluded that students and teachers should spend more time on educational tasks and recommended 'school districts and state legislatures should strongly consider seven hour school days as well as a 200 – 220 day school year'. (It also made a comprehensive range of other recommendations to improve the use of time, including more homework and instruction in effective study methods, better classroom management, provision of time for remedial and gifted students, improved attendance policies, reduced classroom disruption and interruptions, less administrative work for teachers, and placing and promotion of students by achievement and not age.) Other current arguments for extending school time were the problems of increasing curricular demands and the social problems of working mothers.

However, caution has taken hold. First, research evidence of a direct correlation between allocated time and learning achievement is slight. The quality of time is seen as much more important than the quantity (this is discussed more fully in chapter eight). Second, the cost is formidable — calculated by Odden (1983) at over US$20,000,000,000 per annum for the USA to extend the school day to eight hours (or the school year from 180 to 200 days). So it has been seriously questioned whether if such funding was available this would be the best value for this expenditure. So far there has been a slight tendency to lengthen the school day and year, but no marked shift.

THE EXTENDED DAY IN PRACTICE

In some areas modified school days have developed to meet special needs, e.g. of underachieving students, supported by the development of mastery learning strategies.

In 1979 – 80 Shreveport (Louisiana) operated an extended day programme. Three hundred students scoring twenty percentage points below the state mean for study skills participated, from four secondary and five primary schools. They were bussed after the school day to two learning support centres, attending from 3 to 6 p.m. (they could leave earlier if they wished).

Test results suggested that 71 per cent of these students gained four months or more in achievement over a four month period, and teacher assessments suggested that most students improved in homework, classroom performance and behaviour. Improvements in absenteeism, participation in extra curricular activities and attitude to reading were also reported (Gilbert and Price, 1981). The programme was financed by Federal funding and ended when this was withdrawn in 1983. Small scale extension has continued.

A similar but much more extensive programme was provided in Dade County, Florida 1978 – 83 under the same Federal funding. Here 37 schools provided compensatory education for disadvantaged children in the form of 80 minutes additional instruction after school four days per week, either in basic maths and reading, or in one area plus skills application. In 1979 – 80 this programmme involved over 13,000 students in grades 1 – 6. It was withdrawn in 1983 because of declining teacher and student enthusiasm as well as reduction in Federal funding. However a modified version after school and on Saturday mornings still continued.

In New York city a number of school districts operate extended day programmes. In 1985 – 86 the City Board established a project in five of its districts, involving 82 elementary schools and nearly 7,500 students. The programme was focussed on children who had no adult supervision after school. Schools provided free programmes from 3 to 6 p.m. These varied from school to school, but included educational activities such as English, maths and computers; homework; and recreational and arts and crafts activities. The cost in one district was US$3,000,000 plus supplementation. The programme seems to have been popular with students and parents, and there were long waiting lists. Teachers considered the programme improved homework, general achievement and social behaviour. Under a separate programme extended day activities of a 'club' and small group type were provided by some New York City middle schools as part of a scheme to improve attendance and reduce dropouts.

Such extended day programmes clearly have great merit. The problem, as for the Newsom Report discussed in chapter two, is that they are expensive. If they come as a free gift they may be welcomed

—but not necessarily if one asks whether they provide the best return for the money invested. A workable low-cost solution could possibly be developed with the extensive use of volunteer helpers.

The four day week

In 1980 the Colorado State legislature authorised schools to explore alternative school calendars with fewer but longer days. There was already experience of a four day week over several years at Cimarron in New Mexico. The initial motivation was economic — to save heating and transport costs. Perhaps surprisingly, the trials showed no evidence of decline in achievement, while the new arrangement was very popular with students, parents and staff.

The annual minimum instructional hours, 990 for elementary schools and 1,080 for secondary, remained unaltered. Typically school days were extended to seven and a half hours, from about 8 a.m. to just after 4 p.m, for a 144 day year. About half the schools closed on Mondays, the others on Fridays — the former saved more fuel, the latter made Friday available for games and activities and so reduced midweek classroom disruption. There is a tendency now to prefer Fridays for this reason.

Financial savings were appreciable — about 7 – 25 per cent for heating, and about 20 per cent for petrol and vehicle maintenance. There was some increase in custodians' salaries, but sometimes reduction in other ancillary salaries. The substitute teacher bill was reduced by 25 per cent.

An evaluation carried out on behalf of 12 districts in Colorado, (Richburg and Sjogren 1982) showed that 91 per cent of parents, 93 per cent of students and 95 per cent of teachers preferred the four day week. Reasons were mainly personal — more time for family activities, vacations, work in business or the home. Many parents felt their children's attitudes and achievements had improved. On the fifth day children often helped their parents or worked for employers or the family, paid or unpaid. Teachers tended to use the fifth day for preparation and in-service training. They approached teaching in the extended days differently, using a greater variety of methods. Student and teacher absence was less.

Test scores compared the performance of elementary school students in their previous two years on a five day week with their first year on four days. The pattern was inconsistent, with some gains and some losses, but no evidence of overall decline in achievement. There was some suggestion that the new week was less favourable to special needs students and to extra-curricular activities.

This movement spread rapidly. By 1988 20 per cent of the Colorado school districts used the four day week calendar, and another 15 per cent used some form of extended day/shorter year calendar (for example, an extra half an hour on the day which allows 15 – 20 four day weeks in the winter months). One district operated a 7.50 a.m. – 4.30 p.m. schedule but found this too long. The trend has spread to other states such as Minnesota, in all some hundred districts in ten states.

Caution is needed. So far the four day week has only been adopted in rural districts. There it produces strong support and clear social and personal benefits. There is some suggestion that it leads to better prepared and more varied teaching, but no evidence as yet of improvement in student achievement. There is still risk of the Hawthorne effect operating — though the Cimarron operation still works well. The effect on extra-curricular activities and community education needs study.

The school day in other countries

Australia

The main parameters, including hours of instruction, starting times, length of breaks and number of school days are defined by the separate states. There are slight variations between them. However reasonable latitude is often given to principals, teachers and school councils to determine the exact timing and the period patterns of the day. Considering that the Australian states have rethought their school year pattern more thoroughly than any other country (see chapter five), and given the growth of the school self-management movement in several of the states, it is slightly surprising that more change has not developed in school day patterns.

In most states the school day begins quite late, typically 9 a.m. (in New South Wales primary schools as late as 9.30). The Northern Territory is the exception, 8.00 to 8.30 a.m., although schools in some of the hotter areas also begin earlier. Required instructional time is commonly 320 or 330 minutes per day, a slightly high figure compared with most countries, although in practice this can include registration, assemblies and circulation or short breaks. Lunch hours are typically about an hour.

In secondary schools the traditional period length has been 40 or 45 minutes. In New South Wales in particular there is now greater school to school experimentation with new arrangements, including six day cycles. There is not much variation on the standard type of day, although in New South Wales some students start earlier and finish later if taking 'in depth courses'. One new trend is the rapid growth of cooperative programmes between schools and further education colleges in some states, e.g., Queensland, involving both linked courses and integrated programmes. This has led to some synchronisation of timetables and school day arrangements.

New Zealand

There are significant differences to Australia, despite an apparently similar heritage and context. The secondary school day is longer than primary and markedly more varied.

Primary schools are closely regulated by the central Board of Education, but with some local variations. Typically they open at 9 a.m., work to noon with a 15 minute break, take one hour for lunch and close at 3 p.m. This provides approximately 285 minutes of contact-time per day.

Among secondary schools much greater variation occurs, and the principal with the board of governors decide actual timings within national limits. Typically schools begin at 8.30 – 8.45 a.m. and close 3.15 – 3.30 p.m., with 50 – 60 minutes for lunch. They provide 300 – 330 minutes of instructional time, often including an assembly or form period, and sometimes up to 15 minutes per day of movement time. Previously the normal pattern was 8 x 40 minute or 6 x 50 minute periods, but within the last ten years almost all schools have moved to 6 x 55 or 5 x 60, the 'nominal hour'.

In some schools some senior classes operate before school, 7.45 – 8.00 a.m, or after school, to increase the options available.

Japan

Japanese schools usually begin at 8.30 a.m. Lessons are 45 minutes in primary schools, 50 in secondary, each followed by recreational breaks to make up the hour (i.e. 15 and 10 minutes respectively). Wednesday and Saturday school is morning only. Primary schools provide 25 periods a week for the first grade rising to 29 in sixth grade. Junior High Schools provide a minimum of 30 periods per week. A little daily time is devoted to classroom cleaning and meetings. Schools normally end about 3 p.m. — exact times are established by the school principal. (See Appendix, Example 11.) After-school activities are very popular and there is a heavy homework load, especially in high schools. Regular homework is commonly set in primary schools from the first year. A high proportion of primary and particularly junior high school students go to cramming schools two or three times a week.

China

Schools in the Beijing municipal education area begin at 8 a.m. and close at 4 p.m. Primary schools take a two and a half hour lunch-break, 11.30 a.m. – 2 p.m. and secondary schools one and a half hours, 12 noon – 1.30 p.m. Total daily instruction is 200 – 240 and 270 – 315 minutes respectively. In secondary schools 7 x 45 minute periods are usual. There are some before school reading classes and evening self study classes.

Taiwan

Secondary school hours are very long, starting at 8.05 a.m. and finishing at 4.20 p.m. with only two 30 minute breaks, and with compulsory Saturday mornings.

Singapore

Singapore is unusual in that most schools operate a two shift system. In primary schools the first shift session usually starts at 7.30 a.m. and ends at 12.50 p.m. The second session begins at 12.55 and finishes at 6.15 p.m. (See Appendix, Example 12.) Students in the first two years leave 30 minutes earlier. Because of the shift system there is no lunch period and only a 20 minute break. Each session therefore provides 300 minutes of instruction. Each shift is self contained for pupils and teachers but there is a common principal.

Arrangements in secondary schools are similar, with two shifts in most, usually from 7.40 a.m. to 1 p.m. and 1.05 to 6.25 p.m. Normally there are 8 x 37 minute lessons per day, again providing 300 minutes.

Many schools, both primary and secondary, organise supplementary, remedial or enrichment classes before or after the main sessions, on Saturdays and in holidays. There is now a trend towards single session schools, to allow such developments in the afternoons as well as extra curricular activities.

Israel

The system is the compressed, lunchless type. Primary classes begin at 8 a.m. and end between 12 noon and 2 p.m., according to age. There is no lunch session, only a 20 minute break. Some schools may begin at 7 a.m. one or two days a week, and others are funded for additional classes until 3 or 4 p.m.

Secondary schools typically work 8 a.m. – 2 p.m., with a 20 minute break, creating a long day of 340 minutes. There are commonly seven lessons of 45 – 50 minutes.

Pakistan

Seasonal timetables operate. In winter the typical primary day is 9 a.m. – 2 p.m., secondary 9 a.m. – 4 p.m, with one hour lunch. In summer this changes to 7 a.m. – 12 p.m, and 7 a.m. – 1 p.m. respectively, with half an hour lunch. In both cases there is a six-day week. Secondary periods are 40 minutes.

India

Typical school times are 10 a.m. – 4 p.m., but again seasonal timetabling commonly operates.

Shift systems, worldwide

Many countries operate multiple-shift schools, mainly where funds are lacking or demographic pressures strong. Examples occur in S. Europe and even the USA but are most numerous in developing countries.

In a thorough recent survey Bray (1989) describes the main variations in detail. The most common type has two shifts within the school day, end-on, as in example 12 page 217. Some schools operate triple or even quadruple shifts, usually of shorter length. Sometimes shifts overlap.

Bray suggests that the economic advantages can be substantial. Multiple shift schools cut capital and other expenditure and reduce unit costs, and may require fewer teachers (if teachers teach more than one shift), so offsetting teacher shortages or reducing costs. Students can earn while attending school and teachers may be able to augment income.

Educationally, there is little or no evidence of lower achievements. Multi-shift schools can substantially improve access to education. However they often have inferior atmosphere, problems of identity and management, and reduced out-of-school activities. Afternoon shifts in hot countries are less attractive. So shift schools tend to be unpopular, with low status. Bray's analysis however suggests that their positive value is often underrated while good design and management can overcome many of the problems.

What does it all mean?

It could be argued that all this variation in school days is not very important; that it is simply a reflection or expression of national culture, rather like national dress or cuisine, a cherished local idiosyncracy. Certainly differences of school day between countries are very enduring and apparently unaffected by alternatives in neighbouring countries; witness the considerable difference between the Netherlands, Belgium and Luxembourg, and even between England and Scotland.

Yet I would argue that certain types of day, period lengths etc. can be seen to be more effective vehicles for learning than others. Given thoughtful analysis it is possible to design new and better models and to implement them — as the examples from England, Scotland and North America show.

The main problem seems to be that the pattern of the school day is to a greater or lesser extent established by central or regional governments and then strongly entrenched by custom. So it is difficult to change. However if the trend towards local management of schools extends, we can expect to see in more countries a greater local influence over school time structures, both macro and micro. And perhaps even central governments will begin to see that they ought to put as much research and care into the development of school day design as the curriculum. After all, one is the container for the other, and 'you can't cook a good stew in a bad pot'.

5 The school year and the total quantity of schooling

There is no evidence that Neanderthal man operated a three term year, but we are certainly looking at an institution rooted in the distant past.

In most countries the school year is not really designed. It has just evolved, the product of religious festivals, the agrarian calendar, summer heat, factory shut-downs and family vacations. So attempts to reshape it encounter hallowed tradition.

Criteria for school year design

Any attempt to design the school year rationally should try to meet the following criteria — although some of these will conflict:

Term durations should be of the optimum length to:

- prevent student and teacher fatigue
- maximise student and teacher performance
- reduce student and teacher illness and absence/absenteeism

Start-up and wind-down time loss should be minimised. The main loss at the end of each school year should be reduced as much as possible, although some loss is unavoidable. For the other main breaks the end of term will create some loss, the beginning little. The fewer the terms the less the loss. Short holidays of a week or so create little loss.

Term length patterns should assist course planning and organisation. This implies, ideally:

- equal length terms or part-terms
- calendars which are virtually the same each year
- an even rather than odd number of terms
- minimum disruption from examination and testing, special activities or events
- the minimum possible number of single days' holiday.

Holidays should:

- coincide with the best vacation weather and long daylight hours
- provide opportunities for families to take long or short vacations at different times of the year

- provide opportunities for school expeditions and activities
- include the main religious and New Year festivals.

Finance. School year design should:

- maximise economies in heating, lighting, caretaking and cleaning, premises maintenance, transportation of pupils, teaching and non-teaching salaries, and other school expenditures
- achieve the best real return for the capital and revenue resources committed.

Present practice: the European tradition
The three term year with a long summer holiday prevails almost throughout Europe.

The United Kingdom
REGULATIONS
The school year in England and Wales is determined by the Education (Schools and Further Education) Regulations 1981, amended 1986 and 1987. These require that a school shall meet for not less than 380 sessions in each academic year, there being two sessions per day (except schools open on six days in a week may have only one session on two days). In other words, schools are to be open for at least 190 days or the equivalent. The length of year in Scotland and Northern Ireland is the same.

THE PRESENT SCHOOL YEAR
The actual dates of terms and holidays are laid down by LEAs, with some latitude for decisions by schools. However in practice the outline of the year is set by Christmas/New Year and Easter. There are also three public holidays:

- May Day (first Monday in May),
- Spring Bank Holiday (a Monday at end of May, in a week increasingly used for factory closure and holidays),
- Summer Bank Holiday (a Monday at the end of August).

There is a further constraint. The pay year for a teacher nominally runs from September 1st to August 31st. So any LEA starting a term in August rather than September can be liable to additional salary payments for teachers joining the authority.

The autumn term usually runs from the first week of September to a few days before Christmas, a period of 16 weeks or slightly less. This is widely felt to be too long, and is normally broken in state schools by a week's half term holiday.

The spring and summer terms together last normally from early January to about the third week of July, roughly 28 weeks, less about four weeks for Easter and half-term holidays, giving a total of about 24 weeks for the two terms. However the movable date of Easter creates havoc. The spring term can be as short as 11 weeks or as long as 14, and the summer term as short as 12 or as long as 15, excluding half term holidays. The only fixed element is the second part of the summer term, from the spring bank holiday week, usually six to seven weeks. (A few LEAs have variations on this pattern, arising from local holiday traditions.)

The system is manifestly a poor design; in fact it fails to meet most of the criteria.

1. Terms are unduly long. The autumn term is always so, and one of the others can be. There is a general view, although not much detailed research, to suggest that this creates:
   - fatigue and loss of motivation for children
   - fatigue, stress and fading performance from teachers
   - increased illness of teachers and students, particularly in the autumn term (from fatigue and a build-up of infections)
   - increased student absenteeism

2. The spring and summer terms can vary considerably in length. This makes course planning difficult (increasingly important with the spread of modular approaches).

3. The summer term is severely disrupted in secondary schools by public and to a lesser extent internal examinations.

4. The summer holiday period of late July/August has inferior weather and less daylight than June/early July. It also coincides with a congested holiday period in Europe. The Easter holiday can occur in the late winter.

5. The long summer holiday can cause regression in learning. Turner (1970) gave language based tests before and after the summer holidays to 226 primary children, drawn from two estates, one council and one privately owned. He found:
   - of children on the council estate 42 per cent regressed, 17 per cent gained
   - of children on the private estate 25 per cent regressed, 36 per cent gained

The disparity was most marked for children of lower ability.

Unless Easter becomes a fixed date (the first Sunday after the second Saturday of April is often suggested), or Good Friday becomes a free-standing public holiday or no holiday at all (as in the USA, where it is a working day), the weaknesses in the system cannot be completely overcome.

VARIATIONS

There have been some attempts to modify the system. Some LEAs have switched one week from the summer to the Christmas holiday to save fuel. In 1976 Wiltshire LEA estimated their savings as likely to be £15,000 — a very modest economy. This move has proved unpopular and the traditional pattern has tended to be restored.

There have also been attempts by some LEAs to move unilaterally towards a four term year by shortening the summer holiday and moving the start of the autumn term forward until it virtually becomes two terms. However these collapsed because they increased teacher salary bills and were unpopular with families whose parents taught or children went to school in LEAs with different holidays. The attempts to establish a four term year nationwide are described in the last section of this chapter.

The introduction in 1987 of five obligatory professional days for teachers has injected a little more flexibility, in particular allowing schools to close to students for a full week at each of the half-terms. On the other hand they have slightly reduced the school year in some LEAs. LEAs which previously opened schools more than 190 days now find the five professional days press them to reduce their school year to the minimum.

In secondary schools the least productive part of the year is the last two or three weeks of the summer term, after external examination groups have effectively left and often after internal examinations. Hence the growing tendency to fill this with activity weeks or work experience. A very few schools like Sheldon School, Wiltshire have actually introduced their September timetable at the end of the summer term, to induct their new intake and ensure a quick start-up in September.

In many schools leisure schemes are operated in holidays, often by community education providers. There have been few examples of 'catch-up' learning skills schemes on the American summer school pattern.

INDEPENDENT SCHOOLS

Holidays in independent schools are almost always longer than in the state sector. Commonly boarding schools will be closed for 18 – 19 'week- equivalents' (i.e. including aggregated part-weeks), and day schools for 16 – 17, compared with the state equivalent of 14.

However, longer holidays don't necessarily mean fewer hours of education. All boarding schools and some day schools work on Saturday mornings. Some weekday afternoons may be devoted to games or other activities outside the classroom, but these are normally compulsory and so should count as part of 'school learning time'. In any case weekly class contact time is greater in most independent schools, and extra-curricular activities play a much larger part.

It is therefore very difficult to compare the two sectors. On paper independent schools usually teach for fewer full day equivalents (i.e. aggregating two half days as a day). However in practice it seems that many, perhaps most, equal or exceed the total annual class contact time and certainly the total educational time provided by their state counterparts.

Within the independent sector there is considerable variation. For example, in the sample referred to in chapter three, day schools varied from 174 to 187 school days per year. Boarding schools were usually open for just over 200 school days, including Saturdays, equivalent to a range of 178 – 187 full days, with one outlying at 193. There does not seem to be an automatic offsetting of shorter year with longer days — some of the schools with the shorter years showed lower weekly contact time, and vice versa.

There is also variation in the short breaks — one day school for example, taking three days for the October half term and another two weeks. However the major holidays were generally fairly uniform — with probably less variation than would be found between LEAs. The longer Easter holiday in independent schools is less affected by the variable date of Easter, and so the dates of terms are more constant than in the state sector.

Continental Europe

There is a strong European tradition of a long holiday in the summer, beginning with rare exceptions in June. The holiday can be almost three months in the Mediterranean countries, less in Scandinavia. So there is variation in the start of the new school year, ranging from mid August to late September. Compared with the UK there are shorter holidays in Western Europe at the Christian festivals of Christmas and Easter, and often additional weeks in October or in February, sometimes connected with carnivals or winter sports. A summary of the number of school days per year in EC countries occurs in Table 4.1.

Belgium Schools are open for about 182 days each year. Holidays comprise two weeks at Christmas and Easter, eight in the summer (July and August) plus 14 term-time days for national holidays and short breaks. Easter holiday dates are set separately for the French-speaking and Dutch-speaking communities. For the former they occur in the first two full weeks of April, regardless of the date of Easter.

Denmark Schools must be open for 200 days (the highest number in Europe for five-day week schools). The Ministry of Education lays down the number of days and the beginning dates of the summer holidays, but the local authorities fix all other dates. The school year usually begins in the second week of August.

France Primary schools are open for 316 half days, equivalent to

158 days, the shortest school year in Europe. Secondary schools are open for 351 half days (175 day equivalents), but with some variation for individual students. Holidays comprise about one week at the beginning of November, while two weeks at Christmas are common to all schools. Others are staggered across three regional zones: ten days winter holiday in late January or February, two and a half weeks at Easter and ten weeks in the summer.

Finland The school year begins in August and ends by June 6th at the latest. The Christmas holiday has a minimum of ten days, the Easter holiday four, and the winter sports holiday six.

West Germany Schools are open for about 226 days (about 207 or 187 if alternate or no Saturdays are worked). The administrative year begins on August 1st. Both dates and durations of holidays are staggered across the 11 *Länder*. They comprise a week in October or early November, over two weeks at Christmas, one and a half weeks at Easter, a few days at Whitsun and six and a half weeks in the summer.

Greece There are 175 days in the school year. Holidays comprise two weeks for Christmas and Easter, about 11 weeks in the summer for primary schools and nine for secondary schools, plus ten national or religious holidays.

Italy Schools are open for at least 200 days each year. Two weeks holiday are provided at Christmas, one week at Easter, and over two and a half months in the summer.

Luxembourg Schools are open for 217 days (in weeks of six days of which three are shortened), making 181 full day equivalents. Holidays comprise one week in October, two at Christmas, and three more one- or two-week breaks before eight weeks in the summer, plus five extra days.

Netherlands Primary schools are open for 200 days, secondary for 195. Holidays comprise a week in October, two weeks at Christmas, a few days in February or March, a week and a half at Easter and six weeks in the summer. The start and finish of the last is staggered over four weeks.

Portugal Primary schools are open 175 days, secondary 164. The school year begins about September 21st.

Spain Primary schools are open 185 days, secondary 170. The school year begins on September 15th.

Sweden The school year comprises 40 weeks, divided into two terms. The autumn term lasts from about August 20th to Christmas, the Spring term from about January 10th to June 10th (including winter sports and Easter holidays).

Switzerland In the Zürich canton the school year begins in late April. There are five holiday periods: five weeks in July/August; two in October; one or two over Christmas and the New Year; one or two winter sports holidays; and two or three in April.

USSR The school year begins on September 1st and ends on May 30th.

Present practice: the North American tradition

North America too has developed a long summer vacation feature, no doubt originally in response to the same agrarian needs and summer heat as Europe. However, the USA has also adopted a semester (a term lasting half a year) and not a three term system. The length of the school year is regulated by each state legislature and comprises around 180 days, made up of two 90 day semesters. There has been variation of year lengths between states. In 1985, 55 per cent required 180 days, 28 per cent 175. The lowest requirement was North Dakota with 173, and the highest the District of Columbia with 184.

Actual dates of terms and holidays are fixed by local school boards. Typically semesters run late August to mid January, and mid January to the beginning of June, each subdivided into two nine-week periods. Christmas and spring vacations are short, typically one and a half weeks and one week respectively, the latter often not coinciding with Easter. A common feature in the USA is summer schools, principally to enable students to improve their school performance but also for acceleration by more able students.

The school year in the 1980s has come under new pressures. First, there has been the concern about the efficiency of education in the USA compared with other industrialised countries, highlighted in the 'A Nation at Risk' report. The actual argument here is interesting: 'In England and other industrialised countries it is not unusual for academic high school students to spend eight hours a day at school, 220 days per year'. Actually, English students typically spend four and two thirds hours in class, and six and a half in school (including the lunch break) for 190 days. Even in a six day week country like Germany, a student may spend 220 days in school, but only have a maximum of four and a half hours lessons (and five hours school time) on each day. But myth was always stronger than truth!

'A Nation at Risk' specifically urged states and school boards to consider a 200 – 220 day year, but the response has been minimal. North Carolina enacted a pilot programme the same year with two districts operating a 200 day year with seven hour days. In one there was great community dissatisfaction and the decision was reversed. In the other, both teachers and parents were almost equally divided. There was no strong support for the change and it was terminated. Nationwide this fear of community opposition linked with concern at the cost and findings from research that merely increasing the quantity of education had little effect on achievement. So there has been little change. There has been a slight trend to bring school years up to an 180 day norm, and also to close loopholes where school days could be taken up by teachers' inservice training or bad weather closures. Indiana has introduced a 20-day extension to the school year for students failing to achieve required grades.

Pressure has also come from a different quarter. The tourism industry has mounted extensive lobbying to prevent the school year starting before September 1st, to increase tourism in August. It has been resisted as unwarranted interference by school boards, but so far nine states have adopted the policy. This is a new factor affecting school year design — the modern equivalent of the old farming lobby.

Economic pressures have affected the school year in the USA in two other ways. First, a drive to save energy costs created the four day week movement described in the previous chapter, which reduced the school year in the districts concerned to 144 days but kept the quantity of schooling constant. Second, the pressure to maximise use of premises and to reduce the need for new buildings have led to the Year Round Schools movement discussed later in this chapter.

In Canada a somewhat similar system prevails. The number of instruction days per year is set by the provinces, with calendar arrangements by district boards. In Ontario for example there are currently a minimum of 194 instructional days in high school, less 5 – 15 examination days. The school year begins in early September and continues until mid/late June. Breaks during the year are very short as in the USA, one and a half weeks at Christmas and one week in March. Some schools have adopted a semester pattern within this framework.

Present practice worldwide

The Unesco International Bureau of Education Yearbook (1986) surveyed the school year worldwide in primary schools. Of 70 countries, 41 provided 180 – 200 days. Of the 19 with more than 200 days, 15 operated a six day week (mostly in Europe and Asia/ Oceania). Ten provided less than 180, the lowest being 150 in the Central African Republic and 155 in the rural areas of Turkey.

The most widespread model worldwide is the European one, with a long summer vacation and the school year beginning immediately afterwards, although the actual dates depend mainly on the climatic calendar. In Africa one group of countries (mainly in West Africa) operates a long holiday in the July-September period, often beginning the year in October; another group, mainly in East and Southern Africa, begins the year in January or February and spreads vacations more evenly. Kenya, for example, allows one month in April, August and December.

In Latin America there are again two groups. One (Argentina, Brazil, Chile, Paraguay, Peru, Panama) closes in November-December, and reopens mainly in March; the other (Mexico, Venezuela and various Caribbean states) have their main vacation in July and August and reopen in September. Colombia operates both systems in different areas.

In Asia and Oceania, school calendars begin early in the year: January in Malaysia, February in New Zealand, March in the Republic of Korea and Pakistan; April in Japan. Exceptions are China, September, and Indonesia, July. In Japan the main long holiday in July-August breaks the school year instead of concluding it. In Arab states the school year typically ends in June, begins in September.

Clearly climate is the dominant factor in the placing of the long vacation. However, there are a number of exceptions which do not conform. There are also variations both in the timing and length of the main holiday which do not seem to be climate related.

New developments in school year design
The four term year
IN ENGLAND AND WALES

The traditional year has few friends — but its enemies seldom manage to agree. The main arguments have been those outlined at the beginning of this chapter, with added concern from the disruption of the summer term by examinations and congestion in the summer holidays. In the 1970s three of the main teacher unions produced reports recommending the four term year. But none took root.

The issue emerged again in the 1980s, this time pressed by Local Authorities. The Association of County Councils (1986) produced a well-argued report and concluded 'educational benefits are likely to flow from a reordering of the school year'. It summarised these as follows:

(a)   Depending on existing LEA policies it would be easier for summer-born children to gain early admission to the infant school. There would be four rather than three opportunities each year for children to be admitted, and it would be possible to consider changes in transfer dates between nursery, primary, middle and secondary schools.

(b)   Shorter, more even terms should lead to more effective pupil performance and fewer absences of teachers resulting from stress-related illnesses.

(c)   The 'dead' post-examination period for secondary schools at the end of the summer term would be avoided.

(d)   The effect of (b) and (c) together would lead to a more even distribution of work and more effective use of teaching time over the whole year and facilitate curriculum planning.

(e) The avoidance of over-long breaks away from school and of half term breaks which disrupt without providing a proper rest would assist continuity of learning, especially for younger children.

The report suggested five possible arrangements, but later consultation showed the preferred version to be four ten week terms with two week holidays at Christmas/New Year, late March and early October and six weeks in June and July.

Response to the report from a wide range of audiences was favourable. Unfortunately it was rapidly eclipsed by the proposals for the Education Reform Bill, and the Secretary of State clearly did not feel the time was right for a change of this kind. Undoubtedly it might have provoked more debate and uproar than all the other reforms together! However, in 1988 eleven Midland LEAs are exploring the possibility of a regional change (Times Educational Supplement, December 9th 1988). Meanwhile...

In Australia the four term year has been adopted

The traditional pattern followed the English three term year, beginning in February, with two short vacations and with the long holiday in December – February. Total school days for students were 196 – 199. Criticisms similar to those raised in England were made of the three term pattern.

Queensland introduced a two semester year in 1981 and the Northern Territory in 1982, both in effect four term years with one or two-week breaks in mid semester and longer breaks between semesters. New South Wales followed in 1985, with Western Australia and Victoria following. The advantages and disadvantages for Victoria were systematically reviewed by a working party (1984).

Generally the four term year seems to have taken root quickly, but not without problems. The summer holiday has to commence before Christmas and now often ends earlier than previously so that school begins in the hottest season. This can only be adjusted by shortening other holidays or reducing the number of school days. Initial reluctance to set the first term holiday independent of Easter created unequal length terms. Considerable difficulties arose over the staging of the tertiary entrance examinations.

Most states have now fine tuned their schemes. They seem to be working better and are probably permanently established.

Year-round schools

This is the most radical development. There is a good summary in Ballinger, Kirschenbaum and Poimbeauf (1987) and a good account of one development in Parker (1986).

In one sense it is not new. In the 19th century many US urban schools operated for 48 weeks or more. However, by the early 20th century this had contracted to the pattern of the rural areas, with a 190 – 195 day year and three month summer vacation. By the 1950s the year had shrunk further to 180 days.

In the 1950s the student population grew rapidly, with costly building implications. School districts began to experiment with year-round schooling schedules, primarily to reduce overcrowding, maximise use of buildings and reduce capital and revenue costs. Later, stress was laid upon the educational benefits.

A number of different systems have developed. Most can be either single-track or multi-track. In single track schemes all students follow the same calendar, being in school and on vacation at the same times. This realises the educational advantages but not the economic ones. In multi-track schemes students on the different tracks have the same type of year but different, staggered calendars. This realises both sets of advantages but also creates more problems. Examples of the main schemes are:

THE '45 – 15' YEAR
This was first introduced in the Valley View district, Illinois. In the multi-track version, students are divided into four groups, each attending 45 days and off 15 in a staggered rotation through four 60 day sessions (with four additional weeks available for holidays common to all groups). Students attend 180 days of the 240 days the school is open. This system allows enrolment of 33 per cent more students within existing buildings and creates a series of nine week terms and short vacations. However, it creates organisational and curricular problems for secondary schools. The single track version is much simpler, in effect a four term year.

THE FOUR QUARTERS YEAR
This was first introduced in Atlanta for high schools. Here students worked three of four 60 day quarters, again with a 33 per cent increase in premises use. This fitted the curriculum better and allowed some students to accelerate by working all four terms. But it fits family vacations less well.

CONCEPT SIX
Developed in fast growing Jefferson County, near Denver, Colorado, in the early 1970s, this divided the year into six 42 day terms. Students work two terms school, one term vacation, two terms school, etc, and are in three rotating groups so that two are in school and one off. This is a more cost efficient form of year in that school buildings are in use for 252 days and can house an additional 50 per cent more students. It provides only about 170 days schooling, though this can be offset if days are lengthened slightly, or by other devices. Students are able to take an additional (fifth) term of schooling if they wish.

The system became well rooted in Jefferson County. It was clearly preferable to the previous overcrowding and so well accepted by communities and parents. Students' achievement did not suffer and there was some reduction in per pupil school costs. Recently, however, as demographic pressures have eased a modified system has been introduced with a uniform but reduced summer vacation.

FLEXIBLE ALL-ROUND YEAR

Here school is open for fifty weeks. Students can start at any point, and plan their own programme subject to a minimum attendance. In some cases the year is broken into sixteen three week units, with students choosing twelve (or more). This is the ultimate in calendar flexibility, but depends on an individualised learning system.

OTHER FORMS OF YEAR

These include the 'Quinmester', where students attend four of five nine-week 'quins'; the $60-20$, $60-15$ and 'trimester' (all of which provide longer terms and vacations but do not fit the semester system); the $90-30$, two semesters with more evenly spread vacations; and five track, five term (multi-track only, students taking 45 day terms, leaving one free and with a short three week summer break common to all). These are less popular, being less flexible or worse suited to family vacations.

The financial savings are long-term. Initially there is a need for increased clerical staff, extra school cleaning, greater heat and light and transportation costs. There is more wear and tear of buildings. However long-term the new schemes utilise buildings more fully and cut capital expenditure. There is additional opportunity for teacher earnings and student employment.

The main academic advantages claimed are that learning is evenly spread and not interrupted by long breaks (particularly important where English is not a student's first language), and the 'intercessions' (vacations) offer better opportunities for instant remediation or enrichment. There is some improvement in student and teacher attendance. Students' achievement does not seem to decline and there is some evidence of improvement.

Socially all year schooling has been well accepted by parents and communities. It has allowed staggered entry of children into the school system and exit from it. Families have been able to choose a school calendar to suit their needs, and vacation activity has been spread more widely.

There are a number of fairly obvious organisational difficulties, and initially at least there is obviously resistance. Each scheme has some disadvantages, and none suits both primary and secondary schools perfectly.

So far schemes are operating in 15 states and affecting some 350,000 students, including a quarter of those enrolled in the Los Angeles school district. They have been commonest in suburban areas. It is not yet clear whether all year schooling is a permanent trend. It has been driven mainly by demographic pressures, and when these ease the multi-track versions may fade, leaving a change which is mainly driven by educational and social factors, not unlike the four term year movement. However these US developments are more varied than their Australian counterparts and have designed the use of the whole year, holidays and all. The concept does seem likely to suit the next century better than the unbalanced North American school year or the traditional three terms of Europe.

The total quantity of education

Common sense suggests that the quantity of schooling will affect, up to a limit, the quantity of learning. However, it is a hypothesis which is difficult to prove.

Definition of the quantity of schooling for international comparisons isn't easy. It ought to be the product of its three components:

No. of school days × number of instructional × number of years
per year   hours per day   of education

However, there are problems with each. Information from countries on the number of school days isn't always clear, particularly regarding inclusion or exclusion of single day holidays. The situation is worse for instructional hours, since 'lesson time' often masks recreational time, pastoral time, registration and assemblies, class movement, etc. The number of years of education is complicated by the extent and nature of pre-school education. In countries such as France and Belgium this is almost universal, and in the Netherlands is now unified with primary education. It is also affected by the duration of compulsory education, the degree of staying on or dropping out, and to a lesser extent by grade repetition.

The IEA (International Association for the Evaluation of Educational Achievement) conducted exhaustive surveys of data collected in 1970 from twenty-one countries. In an overview (1976a: 260 – 269) it found considerable cross-national variation in the number of instructional hours per year at both primary and secondary levels, and also in the total hours of instruction provided for compulsory education. Here totals ranged from 10,520 (Scotland) to 4,800 (Chile) with a median of 8,160. The three countries at the lower end (Thailand, India and Chile) averaged 44 per cent fewer hours than the three at the upper end (Scotland, Australia and New Zealand).

Similar variations in the total hours of instruction per student (compulsory plus post compulsory education) were also striking and perhaps more surprising. Three countries at the lower end (France, Japan and Chile) averaged 10,279 hours, 25 per cent less than the three at the upper end (Scotland, Australia and Italy) averaging 13,554.

The survey then tested the hypothesis that hours of instruction are positively related to mean country achievement levels. It found that 'the country rank order correlation coefficients between hours of instruction and the test scores of the relevant population do not support the expectation that the two variables are positively related. The coefficients are in general low, and indeed have negative rather than positive signs'. Some countries, for example Japan and Hungary, ranked high on school achievement but provided relatively few hours of instruction. It seems clear that there are far too many variables, cultural as well as educational, to allow the hypothesis to be tested on an international scale.

An associated IEA study (1976b) examined the variable of quantity of instruction against achievement in six study areas. While there was only a little relation to scores in reading comprehension, literature or science among fourteen year olds, there was strong correlation for science in the pre-university population and for English and French as foreign languages. For the last two the number of years of study was the most important predictor of achievement. (Time spent on homework showed a similar association for these three subjects.)

Holsinger (1982) reviewed this IEA evidence for the US National Committee on Excellence in Education. He concluded:

> Achievement is dependent upon the emphasis given in school through the curriculum, which in turn is contingent on the time available or allocated to a subject area. The student's own motivation and willingness to work in and out of school is also part of the total picture. The greatest advances will be obtained by addressing fundamental social and economic disparities.

So in general the riddle remains. Does the quantity of schooling a nation provides affect achievement? I suppose most readers will say 'yes', partly on common sense grounds that more time means a larger curriculum (a typical argument for raising the school leaving age) and that 'missing school' is seen as a handicap; and partly from sensing a logical problem — if we don't think the quantity of schooling affects achievement, logically we should *reduce* it until the point where there is evidence that it does.

But if it does affect achievement, why is it that we cannot prove the connection? Even within a country the riddle persists. Frederick & Walberg (1980) concluded from an extensive review of research studies that, other things being equal, the amount learned is generally proportional to the time spent in learning, but that 'time devoted to school learning appears to be a modest predictor of school achievement'. The noise from the other variables is too loud. It is only when we concentrate on the active element of time allocated, time-on-task, that a strong link with achievement emerges (see chapter eight).

Perhaps the riddle needs a Delphic answer: 'other things being equal, the quantity of schooling increases achievement...up to the point where it does not.' For there is a saturation point; there are opportunity costs to students of the additional time they spend in school; and the quality of school time is much more important than the quantity.

6 Time for the curriculum, and beyond

The problem

The problem about time for the curriculum is simply that there is not enough of it. Curriculum documents refer to 'pressures', 'overcrowding' and 'new demands'; popular articles see the problem as squeezing a quart into the pint pot. Yet this time pressure is relatively new. It is doubtful if schools felt it last century.

Pressure has been created by the information explosion and by the increasing demands which societies make on their schools. The former is well charted — the massive growth of printed material, the opening of whole new areas of knowledge, the acceleration of global communications. The latter is more complex. As a society — almost any society — is affected by the technological, economic and social changes of the late 20th century, so the changes in society and the strains which they create generate new activities for schools. Hence, current demands for expansion of information technology; design and technology; careers, prevocational and technical education; drugs and AIDS education; personal, social and moral development...and doubtless in the future for 'global systems studies' and the study of information itself.

It is not surprising that this trend, coupled with the pressures from the information explosion (for example, DNA from Nobel Prize research to main school syllabus within ten years), has created time management problems for the curriculum.

Current solutions

Time allocation

The answer, worldwide, is time allocation. Time for the curriculum is carved up like a cake. Schools, local boards or authorities, state or national governments allocate it either in hours per week or as a percentage of the available week (in effect the same thing) to subject or activity areas. A typical example of prescriptive time allocation by a central government can be found in the German Democratic Republic. (see Table 6.1.)

A similar example comes from Japan (see Table 6.2). However in the near future the proportion of elective subjects for junior secondary schools will be increased.

Table 6.1 Curriculum time allocation of the General Polytechnical School of the German Democratic Republic (hours per week)

Subject	Grade 1	2	3	4	5	6	7	8	9	10
German	10*	12	14	14	7	6	5	5	4	3
Russian	–	–	–	–	6	5	3	3	3	3
Mathematics	5	6	6	6	6	6	6	4	5	4
Physics	–	–	–	–	–	3	2	2	3	3
Astronomy	–	–	–	–	–	–	–	–	–	1
Chemistry	–	–	–	–	–	–	2	4	2	2
Biology	–	–	–	–	2	2	1	2	2	2
Geography	–	–	–	–	2	2	2	2	1	2
Industrial art	1	1	1	2	2	2	–	–	–	–
Gardening	1**	1	1	1	–	–	–	–	–	–
Polytechnic instruction***	–	–	–	–	–	–	4	4	5	5
History	–	–	–	–	1	2	2	2	2	2
Civics	–	–	–	–	–	–	1	1	1	2
Drawing	1	1	1	2	1	1	1	1	1	–
Music	1	1	2	1	1	1	1	1	1	1
Sport	2	2	2	3	3	3	2	2	2	2
TOTAL	21	24	27	29	31	33	32	33	32	32

Note: *   11 lessons during the first six months

      **   Starts at the beginning of the second six months

      ***   Is subdivided into the subjects Introduction into Socialist Production, Technical drawing and Productive Work

Optional subjects: Needlework in grades 4 and 5 (1 lesson each). Second foreign language (in grades 7 to 9 three lessons each week and in grade 10 two lessons)

Source: 'Education in the GDR', published Panorama DDR (First hand information), Berlin 1987, page 62.

Some government or state departments recommend rather than prescribe. For example, the Northern Territory Department of Education, Australia (1986) states:

> At secondary level in years 8 – 10, the suggested proportions of time which the average student should spend on the core and recommended components of the curriculum in the seven original key subject areas are:

	%
English	14
Mathematics	14
Science	14
Social and Cultural Education	14
The Visual and Performing Arts	8
Health and Physical Education	8
Life and work Skills	8
TOTAL PERCENTAGE	80

The proportions shown are not intended to be prescriptive and should not be interpreted as placing restrictions on school timetabling or setting finite limits on the time to be spent on a particular subject, nor do the suggested time allocations imply that all students should spend those proportions of their time on the designated subject areas through the years 8 – 10. Thus, if a student has satisfied core requirements in a particular subject, it should be possible — given adequate counselling of the student and his/her parents — for the student to pursue other studies suited to his/her needs, interests and abilities.

Approximately 20 per cent of the total curriculum time over years 8 – 10 remains beyond that suggested for the core and recommended components of the curriculum. The remaining time can be allocated at the school's discretion. It could include, for example, the offering to students of extended experiences in the key areas beyond the percentage of the time suggested and the provision of studies in other areas, especially foreign languages.

A global view of time allocation in practice is provided by the UNESCO International Yearbook of Education (1986). It sets out a comparison of the percentage of time devoted to subject areas in primary schools by world region (see Table 6.3). This shows close convergence in the time devoted to the native language and mathematics, but wide variations in other areas. (Caution is needed

Table 6.2 Curriculum time allocation in Japan

Weekly number of lessons

		Primary					Lower Secondary		
Year	1	2	3	4	5	6	1	2	3
Japanese	8	8	8	8	6	6	5	4	4
Social Studies	2	2	3	3	3	3	4	4	3
Arithmetic/Maths	4	5	5	5	5	5	3	4	4
Science	2	2	3	3	3	3	3	3	4
Music	2	2	2	2	2	2	2	2	1
Arts/crafts	2	2	2	2	2	2	2	2	1
Industrial arts and/or home making	–	–	–	–	2	2	2	2	3
Physical education/ health	3	3	3	3	3	3	3	3	3
Moral education	1	1	1	1	1	1	1	1	1
Special activities	1	1	1	2	2	2	2	2	2
Elective subjects	–	–	–	–	–	–	3	3	4
TOTAL	25	26	28	29	29	29	30	30	30

Note: Primary lessons of 45 minutes, secondary lessons of 50 minutes.

Source: Adapted from Ministry of Education, Science and Culture, Japan: 'Education in Japan: A Brief Outline', 1986, page 7.

however, because this percentage method does not reflect total time allocated by day, year or over a period of years.) The Yearbook also provides similar tables for each region, in which country-by-country variations are at least as great.

Of course this cake-carving isn't new. It has respectable antecedents in the 19th century elementary schools. But as the screw tightens on the curriculum, so those responsible for curriculum management increasingly resort to it. In England, for example, wide curricular freedom is now being replaced by the National Curriculum, which has been introduced in part to guarantee adequate time allocation in key subjects. But it is becoming increasingly obvious that cake carving isn't enough. Pressure requires either that the size of the time cake is increased, or some of the ingredients are reduced or blended, or the cake is cooked more quickly. All of these trends can again be seen worldwide.

Increasing the time available

Increasing time occurs in several forms. There is a general tendency in developing countries for the years of compulsory school to be increased. There is also a trend in developing countries to convert the tops of primary schools into junior secondaries. This does not expand the years of school but does increase the proportion of specialised subject based education. In countries where the duration of compulsory education has stabilised, mainly at the age of 15 or 16, extension continues with the expanded take-up of post-compulsory education. There is also a trend to develop pre-school provision, and

Table 6.3 Percentage of time allocated to subject areas, primary schools world-wide

Region	Own language	Foreign language	Maths	Science	Social studies	Religious or moral	Art	Physical ed.	Political	Practical	Other
Africa	25.5	12.5	18.0	8.5	9.0	4.5	6.0	7.0	2.0	6.0	1.0
Latin America	24.0	0.2	19.5	13.0	13.0	2.5	8.0	8.0	0.2	9.5	2.0
Asia and Oceania	27.5	6.5	18.5	12.0	5.5	7.0	8.5	8.5	–	4.5	1.5
Arab States	31.0	6.0	17.0	8.5	5.5	12.5	8.0	7.0	0.3	3.0	1.5
Western Europe	26.5	6.0	18.5	8.0	8.0	6.5	12.0	8.5	–	4.5	1.5
Eastern Europe	33.0	7.0	21.0	7.5	5.0	–	10.0	9.0	0.3	6.0	1.0
Average	28.0	6.5	19.0	9.5	7.5	5.5	8.5	8.0	0.5	5.5	1.5

Source: From Unesco International Yearbook of Education (1986: 155)

to coordinate this or even merge it with primary education. Unfortunately this ad hoc extension of the duration of main schooling doesn't always lead to a full rethink of the use of the time available over the extended span. For example in England curriculum pressure for the 11 – 16 age-group could be reduced if areas of the curriculum could be transferred to 16 – 18 and the years 11 – 18 treated as a continuum. So, time for say social studies or the arts could be reduced for years 14 – 16 if they were compensated in years 16 – 18.

There is also a growing tendency to regard education as lifelong — 'l'education permanente'. To some extent this justifies a view that items can more easily be omitted from the main curriculum because they can be retrieved later. This has also been a small factor in the growth of modular approaches to the curriculum examined in the next chapter.

Reducing the curriculum

Attempts are also made to release pressure by pruning the curriculum or compressing it. Pruning is difficult. It is always much harder to leave out a familiar topic or subject than to put another one in. Science subjects seem to find this particularly difficult. The current emphasis on process rather than content ought, at least in theory, to make pruning easier — parodied, it's not what you study but how you study it. However this is deceptive. Core knowledge is still important, and the core continues to grow. For example, it is difficult to have much understanding of environmental issues unless one knows about food chains. Moreover, process-orientated education is often more time consuming by its very nature. So unless the curriculum is fundamentally rethought to identify core knowlege and key concepts so that these can be retained as growth points for further learning and much other knowledge removed, the actual release of time pressure is not very great.

Another set of strategies attempts to reduce pressure by combining elements of the curriculum more compactly, or even by dispersing them in a cross-curricular form. For the former we can mention combined subjects such as humanities or social studies, combined or integrated sciences, creative arts or combined craft and technology. Sometimes such compression uses devices such as timetable carousels, options within a subject area or modular schemes.

For the dispersal approach we can see subjects taught 'across the curriculum' — not just skills such as maths and English, but areas like health or careers education. This can be seen as an attempt to provide two curricular areas for the time cost of one which at its best can be educationally very productive. Commonly it just conceals the fact that squeezing say health education into biology and social studies may relieve pressure on the curriculum as a whole but increase it within particular areas. Of course these approaches to combine subject areas or promote cross-curricular activities often arise for educational reasons, but in most there is an element, and sometimes a predominant element, of time saving. They can lead to eccentricities — like the DES official who recently proclaimed that he was confident 120 per cent of the curriculum could now be accommodated within the week!

Of course, the curriculum is also reduced by omission. Often areas are omitted by default and so curriculum managers may not realise that they have avoided time pressure problems. A good example lay in the grammar and secondary modern schools in England in the period 1950 – 1980. Both established their own restricted curriculum by omitting or scaling down important areas — the arts, craft and technology for the grammar schools, science and foreign languages for the secondary moderns. But when the two combined in comprehensive schools, acute problems arose. Algebraically, $C > G + SM$.

Curriculum omission can also arise from the shortage of specialist teachers or skills. For example the limited role of science in the curriculum of many English primary schools has sprung partly from a lack of appropriate foundation knowledge and confidence in the teaching force.

The newly minted National Curriculum for England and Wales set up in the 1988 Education Reform Act shows several of these factors at work. The original consultative document of July 1987 (later amended in detail) proposed that all secondary pupils should continue with maths, English and science for 30 – 40 per cent of the time. It then illustrated how the whole curriculum might be organised in years 4 and 5:

Foundation subjects	%
English	10
Maths	10
Combined Sciences	10 – 20
Technology	10
Modern foreign language	10
History/Geography, History or Geography	10
Art/Music/Drama/Design	10
Physical Education	5
	75 – 85
Additional subjects	10
Additional time (this would include religious education)	5 – 15%

This crude time allocation already showed signs of internal strain:

1.   There was suggestion of combined subjects — 'combined sciences', 'history/geography', and 'a combined course covering art, music, drama and design'.

2.   There was a suggestion of timesaving by teaching some subjects or themes through the medium of other subjects.

     'For example, biology can contribute to learning about health education, and the health theme will give an added dimension to teaching about biology. It is proposed that such subjects or themes should be taught through the foundation subjects, so that they can be accommodated within the curriculum but without crowding out the essential subjects.'

3.   Welsh would be added as an eleventh foundation subject for Welsh schools (and a core subject for Welsh medium schools) — and this implied scaling down of time for the others.
     Indeed logically it implies either that students in such schools will have to omit one of the 'additional subjects', or will reach lower standards in foundation subjects because they have less time for them. If the latter is denied, then logically students in other schools could also include an additional subject without any lowering of standards elsewhere. We are then back to the 'Does the quantity of education affect effectiveness?' riddle.

Other stresses were soon apparent:

4.   Some subjects previously catered for in many schools seemed to be under threat — particularly a second foreign language, home economics, economics and business studies.

5.   There was no mention of time for personal, social and moral education or careers education.

6.   There was only passing reference to the special needs of pre-vocational and technical education.

7.   The working party for the science curriculum soon came to assume 20 per cent as its share of the curriculum rather than 10 – 20 per cent, and this increased pressure on the other subjects. The DES then attempted to damp down this proposal, partly to safeguard other subjects and partly because of concern over the shortage of science teachers.

Speeding up curriculum delivery

The national curriculum working party on mathematics ('Education', August 5th 1988) strongly supported use of electronic calculators in mathematics classes as time-saving devices, freeing pupils to spend more time on more important aspects of mathematics. 'There is no moral gain derived from tackling a thousand long divisions when calculators exist.'

This is a sign of new technology being recognised as an aid to *quicker* learning, freeing students from other activities. We can expect this use of the new technology to become more prominent, particularly in mechanical learning areas such as rote learning in foreign languages, spelling and punctuation, and mathematics calculations.

The limitations of time allocation practices

The prospect for curriculum time allocation is not encouraging. Extending or reorganising the years of schooling, or compressing or dispersing the curriculum may gain a little time. But if we assume that the present pressures on society will at least continue, while the pressure from the information explosion increases exponentially, the respite can only be temporary. Inexorably pressure will rebuild.

The cake-carving approach to curriculum time is a poor one, only made respectable by its ubiquity. It appears to be a common-sense response to a practical problem; it is actually a rather primitive process, crude, illogical, and inefficient.

Crudity

Implicit in this cake-carving is a notion of marginal educational utility. Why does country X allocate 15 per cent of time to activity A and only 10 per cent to activity B? Because it is assumed that the extra five per cent for activity A will have more marginal utility and create more value added than if five per cent or even two and a half per cent or one per cent is transferred to B. Now obviously this is a very crude assumption. There is seldom any firm evidence or even serious study to suggest that this is so. We are really talking about inspired — or uninspired — hunchwork. On occasions curriculum managers will sense a need to increase one area — say a country threatened with economic competition may wish to expand teaching of science or technology. But this can only be done by contracting something else. It's a very crude trade-off calculation, often with only tenuous hope that in the long term measurable or even observable benefit will accrue.

Illogicality

Cake carving isn't just crude. It's also illogical. For it treats all areas of the curriculum alike, as if they all deserve slices of the same cake, albeit of varying size. But different areas of the curriculum have quite different needs for time. For example, some areas have 'low specification outcomes' — that is, we cannot specify their objectives with precision and cannot expect many, or mainly, measurable outcomes. These will be areas dealing with complex verbal or intellectual skills, social skills, beliefs and values, emotional development and personal character traits — largely the areas of personal, social and moral education. These will also occur in specific subject areas, although they may predominate in literature, the creative arts and the humanities. For these 'low specification outcome' activities allocation of curriculum time is really an expression of hope. If we allocate a percentage of the time available to say personal and social education, or the arts, we are saying that we intend these to produce various outcomes and hope that they will do so. But we have no guarantee that this will happen or measure that it has happened. Indeed often we just assume that a student who experiences a particular activity — say reading or acting in an emotionally charged play, or taking part in residential experience — is likely to be affected by it. But there is no guarantee. Allocating time to such activities is a kind of logical gamble.

At the other extreme allocating time to areas of the curriculum which have high specification outcomes is not logical at all. Here we have basic skills and foundation knowledge which are much more amenable to assessment. In effect we are saying 'school, take this amount of time, and teach the learner what skills and knowledge you can in it'. In doing this we are foregoing an opportunity of exploiting the marginal utility or relative efficiency of learning for one student against another, or one activity against another. Why give the same percentage of curriculum time over 'y' years as an equal ration to all learners? Why are we so sure this is the most efficient use of time? Is it not possible that allocating more time to one group of learners and less to another may be more efficient? (To some extent we acknowledge this when we devote more teacher-hours per student to students with learning difficulties.) And why for 'y' years, and not y + 1 or y — 1 for different students? In England, for example, students normally learn English, maths, science to the age of 16, but not normally terminating earlier or continuing later. What is so sacred about the cut-off at 16?

Superficially the present system of time allocation may be defined on grounds of equity, since it appears to give each student equal time. However the system wasn't set up for that reason; it arose in the 19th century out of the practical requirements of a class centred model of education, with all members of a class allocated the same time for each curriculum area. In practice the system is very inequitable, since equal time for a whole class benefits those of higher ability and handicaps those of lower ability, in the way John Carroll has exposed so clearly. We already acknowledge this wherever students are allowed to spend extra time on a subject, perhaps by spending less on another, or taking summer school or receiving coaching, or repeating a grade. Time allocation is only equitable if it meets the individual needs of each student.

Inefficiency

Such monolithic allocation of time is not only crude and illogical, it is patently inefficient. Underlying it is a concept of equity, that all students should have the same share of time. But this is only input equity. It certainly doesn't extend to equity of outcomes (indeed programmes concerned with this often resort to positive discrimination in time allocation). So it doesn't address the question of how much time is needed for each student and how outcomes can be maximised. Let us suppose — wildly — that a new wonder-drug, 'Brainstorm', allows students to learn twice as fast. What would we do about the time allocation for English if all students achieved in three years what previously they gained in six? Do we still allow six years, so that all reach twice the standard? Or do we settle for the same standard with which we were previously quite happy, and divert the time saved from the last three years to other areas of the curriculum? Or do we allow some students to divert time, and others to continue and so raise their standard in a key subject?

This science fiction illustrates the fundamental weakness of current time allocation arrangements. They assume an input model of the curriculum, and in so doing ignore the possibilities of improved productivity. If the educational process is regarded as inputs combined and changed by process into outputs, curricular time is clearly being allocated to inputs and to an extent to process (insofar as one form of process may require more time than another):

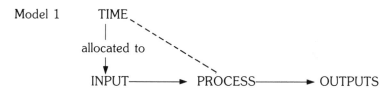

Time allocation linked to outcomes

If however we consider allocating time for outputs, our view of curriculum time immediately alters:

Here for 'high specification outcome areas' time is allocated for the outcomes themselves. So for example, curricular time would not be allocated for 'learning reading' but for 'identified achievement level in reading.' If the level is achieved, there is no justification for further time; if there is no achievement, we need to look at how the time is being used. So teachers, students, and schools would be encouraged to use time more productively.

The output model also has a salutary influence on 'low specification outcomes' activities. For if we allocate time for outcomes we are more likely to think seriously about the best use of time to realise them. David Hargreaves (1983: 140) remarks how his research revealed that many people first developed an interest in the arts from a particular event or experience. He notes that this experience was almost traumatic — a deep, almost wounding experience, often with features such as a shattering of preconceptions, a concentration of attention, sense of revelation, inarticulateness and arousal of interest and enthusiasm. Such experiences often occur *outside* the classroom, and Hargreaves calls this a 'traumatic theory of aesthetic learning'. Many people will recognise themselves in it — the impact of a childhood visit to a play, concert or exhibition, for example. It seems likely that the traumatic theory of learning can be extended to other affective areas of the curriculum. It seems close to real religious experience and related to Benjamin Bloom's idea of 'peak learning experiences'. Similarly, first hand experience of the handicapped or under-privileged, or of an outstanding expert or enthusiast, or of a situation of danger (a typical situation of 'Outward Bound' courses) or even of the realm of nature in certain conditions — all can have a traumatic effect on the person engaged.

> One impulse from a vernal wood
> May teach you more of man,
> Of moral evil and of good,
> Than all the sages can.

If we take curriculum outcomes seriously, how shall we allocate time to maximise this kind of learning? Not by five per cent or two hours per week! At the least we could define it in hours per year — that would suggest more flexibility for residential experience, visits and irregular events, as well as other intense learning experiences such as immersion learning in foreign languages. Perhaps better, we could define it as so many encounters or involvements of specified types per year.

New time allocation arrangements

Table 6.4 suggests how this outcome oriented approach to the allocation of curriculum time could look in practice. Here time has been allocated to subject areas on a different basis. Some has been allocated for specified achievement in high outcome areas — this

Table 6.4   An example of outcome orientated time allocation for the curriculum

| | High specification outcome activities (hours per year for specified achievement) | Low specification outcome activities | | Total time (hours per year) |
		In the classroom (hours per year)	Outside the classroom (hours per year)	
English	85	30	10	125
Mathematics	125	–	–	125
Science	100	15	10	125
Social & Cultural Education	60	60	15	125
Visual & Performing Arts	–	40	30	70
Health & Physical Education	–	50	20	70
Life and work skills	–	30	30	70
Other activities	– – – – – 175 hours in total – – – – –			175
TOTAL				885

implies that the allocation may differ between students, depending on their ability and standard. Other time is allocated for low specification areas, some of this for out of class activities. This too could vary between students, depending on their needs. All the time allocations are shown per year, to encourage special events and compressed learning experiences.

This outcome orientated allocation does not fit current practice. Although it looks like a usual class time allocation but of a different type, in fact it needs to be fitted for each individual. So it certainly does not suit the sort of schools we have at present. It is not easy to see exactly how it would operate in detail. Clearly the staff responsible for the total annual time allocation for a curriculum area would need to plan its use, and perhaps to present a programme to the school's management team. But the mechanism by which time allocations could be adjusted for individual students is much more complicated. This is explored further in chapter nine, page 156. Yet the logic that this represents more effective allocation of time seems strong enough to suggest that it should be taken seriously. And when schools are able to go beyond batch processing and educate individuals as individuals it will become essential.

Outcome orientated allocation of time is desirable for another reason. Most time allocation strategies do not take account of the possibility that the ultimate curriculum is internal to each learner. They allocate time for the external curriculum — the prescribed curriculum

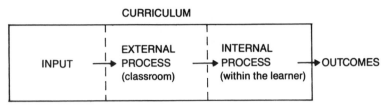

Figure 6.1 – The curriculum internal to the learner

and its implementation in the classroom process — which appears to be common to each classroom of learners. But every learner brings prior knowledge, skills and attitudes, so that what appears to be a common curriculum for all is actually a different curriculum for each. And each learner then internalises it. The process of internal learning and delearning goes on long after the external process has stopped. So each learner makes his or her own curriculum. Each learner decides, consciously or otherwise, which elements of the external curriculum he or she will adopt, to grow and develop into part of his or her thinking, believing or doing, and which will be rejected or die back. Figure 6.1 sets out this view that the ultimate curriculum is the curriculum each learner makes.

If you accept this view, the time implications for the curriculum are substantial. Currently we only allocate time on any scale for the input and external process stages. Should we not also allocate time for both learners and teachers-as-counsellors to develop this internal process? Time for the learner to reflect on the learning process and on his or her internal curriculum? Time for the teacher to counsel, advise, provoke? Time to enlist parents to help this internal process? The logic of this view of the internal curriculum must be time for 'curriculum consultations'. Currently few schools provide this, although to some extent it is emerging for older students with records of achievement, and more rarely for negotiation of the curriculum, for example with the CPVE.

Timetables

New timetabling approaches will be important if curriculum time allocation is to be improved. There are two main types of timetable, closed and open. The closed type, common to most secondary schools, inserts a set number of lessons (each having its own teacher, class and space) in the same number of standard size slots. An open timetable inserts a number of lessons into a *larger* number of slots, and does not necessarily define the size of the slot.

> Example: A closed timetable with twenty classes and four afternoon lessons would have eighty lessons, and eighty slots for them, each

afternoon. If the timetable were 'open', there would still be eighty lessons to insert. But if these could be mounted at any time between say 2 p.m. and 9 p.m. there would be ten lesson slots available for each class, 200 in all. Moreover some classes could probably lengthen or shorten lessons or vary times without disturbing others, as evening classes sometimes do now.

This type is common in technical colleges and adult education centres, and exists around the fringe of some school timetables (e.g. in some independent schools and in the flexible day arrangements described in chapter three). Timetables in primary schools could be said to be 'loosely closed'. They are closed in that classes start, finish and adjourn for breaks at the same time. However because each class spends most of its time with the same teacher, timetabling is much freer.

Timetabling of closed systems is too complicated and specialised to consider here. It has been well analysed in a number of books, e.g. Johnson (1980). Some timetables are moving closer to the open system by the adoption of 'blocking'. Here blocks of time are allocated to clusters of subjects or to a faculty. Blocks tend to be longer in duration, double periods or even half days. They retain the characteristic closed system rigidity of fixed start and finish times, but allow more flexibility within the blocks. If used extensively they can replace the complex whole school timetable with a timetable framework, within the blocks of which faculties or departments can make their own provision. A good example is the timetable of Greendown School, Swindon, where the main part of the day is broken into three core sessions, each provided for a year group by one of three 'curriculum schools'. This can provide a framework as follows: (A,B,C = curriculum school):

(Monday)	Year 1	Year 2	Year 3
Core Session 1	C	B	A
Core Session 2	A	C	B
Core Session 3	B	A	C

Blocking looks simple. One advocate used to boast of doing his school timetable on the back of an envelope in an afternoon! But it is more complex than it appears. Fluctuations in size of year groups, staff limitations, part-time staff, limitations of rooms or special needs of subjects like foreign languages can create serious problems. Also, the longer the block or the larger or more mixed the group of staff responsible for a block for a year group, the greater the risks. Blocking gives more responsibility to middle management — probably a benefit. But it extends scope for mismanagement which because it occurs at a lower level will be less public. It's a little like open plan classrooms. At their best they offer splendid flexibility; at their worst the lack of structure can create problems which aren't immediately obvious.

The idea of blocking has been explored in depth by Keith Palmer in Palmer & Carter (1984) and Palmer (1987). Here he developed the idea of 'time slots'. A time slot is a very simple concept which is difficult to explain. It can be defined as a part of the week where all staff and students are either timetabled or free, and during which the timetable does not change. So Monday period 1 in any school will be a time slot, with a particular combination of teachers, classes and rooms which do not change within the slot. Since that combination clearly can be timetabled, conceptually the time slot could extend all Monday morning. In practice protests would arise because some subjects are not suited to whole mornings — so the time slot could then be split into say Monday periods 1 – 2 and Thursday 5 – 6. But the two sessions are still one time slot, still with the identical teacher-class-room combinations in each.

Time slots have two great advantages. First by keeping the same teams of teachers and groups of classes constant throughout the slot they make ad hoc rearrangement possible, and allow teachers much more control over the time allocated. Second, any activity in the slot can in theory at least be made available to any student. For example, a gifted mathematician in the first year could exchange his or her normal activity Monday 1 – 2 to take fifth year maths, and be sure he or she could make the same exchange in the other half of the slot Thursday 5 – 6. This is particularly important for modular curriculum approaches because it enables students to take a module not originally intended for their year group. In practice time slotting is difficult because of some of the problems mentioned for blocking above. However, Palmer does examine these and suggest technical solutions.

Blocking and time slotting are much harder to operate successfully in practice than at first appears and can brush over real problems. The difficulty mainly arises from operating them within a closed system. If some of the week can be allocated to an open system, extra flexibility is created to solve many of these problems. This possibility is examined in chapter twelve.

Osborne (1986) has taken these ideas further by suggesting blocking the total manpower resources of a faculty, both contact and non-contact time. This allows greater flexibility and can also provide time for covering absences, training and curriculum development. In fact the Blyth Tynedale Upper School blocking described in chapter three is an example of it. The development of a more open type of timetable system either from these ideas or from the two part day model suggested in chapter twelve will make outcome related allocation of curriculum time much more feasible. That would be a great step forward. The South Australia Education Department has produced a useful guide for teachers 'Time Allocation and the Curriculum' (1984) which explores some of these issues in a practical way.

Beyond the curriculum

Extra-curricular activities

In terms of quantity these are marginal to the main curriculum. Even in schools with a large amount of extra-curricular activities, only ten per cent or less of the average student's 'total educational time' would be provided in this way. In most schools five per cent or less would be more realistic. However these are average figures — for individual students the figure could be 20 per cent or more.

In quality, however, extra-curricular activities score highly. Volunteer teachers and students, special interests and small groups all create an ideal learning situation with much spin-off in terms of inter-personal skills and personal qualities.

Most schools just let such activities happen on an ad hoc basis. Some however organise them into a properly publicized and coordinated programme, supported by encouragement and guidance from personal tutors. This is especially true of the independent schools.

A particularly good example occurs at Clifton College, Bristol (a coeducational public school with 670 students, 415 being boarders) which is worth quoting in detail. Here there is a teacher in charge of societies who produces a booklet for the start of the year called 'Not the Timetable'. This lists, with pen sketch details, a whole range of voluntary activities — music (13 groups), art, pottery, crafts, technical activities, computing, printing, drama, publications, sports (including fencing, boxing, weight-training, aerobics and individual sports), libraries, and about 20 societies (including an Amnesty group, bridge, chess, Christian Union, cookery, debating, Esperanto, film, jazz, kites, photography, railways, as well as several subject-centred clubs). Many of the societies are run by senior students. Further details are provided in a weekly 'What's on' sheet.

This booklet also has a section on 'Nearly the Timetable' — a range of activities from which students have to choose one on Monday afternoons. These include an introduction to outdoor pursuits (including climbing, orienteering and shooting), combined cadet force, social service in the local community, Duke of Edinburgh's award, community service (conservation and making toys), instructor corps (learning to lead activities), school service (including work in departments, audio-visual aids, running the theatre, gardening, poster production, school maintenance) and also taster courses in a range of other activities.

Of course a school of this type, with its boarding character and its clientele, has advantages. However, the key principles in this programme could be adopted by any school:

- a teacher in charge
- a booklet listing all activities plus a weekly bulletin sheet
- a 'requirement' for students to choose from some activities

- heavy involvement of senior students
- strong overall support from the school staff and encouragement to students to join.

The flexible day programme described in chapter three includes some of these features. Schools operating a compressed day also have an ideal environment for developing such a programme.

Community activities

Community schools are well placed to organise extra-curricular activities through their community education department. The '3 – 7' activities at Marlborough School in chapter three are a typical example. There is also considerable scope for all schools to enrol responsible members of the community or parents to run school or school-and-community activities. However this will not develop fully unless someone is responsible for organising it — as discussed in chapter ten.

The programme of classes and activities for older members of the community itself offers an opportunity for students. There is no reason why 11 or 12-year-olds — or younger — should not be encouraged to join adult classes for activities such as arts and crafts, household skills and sports. Younger students learn a great deal in adult groups — not least that some people come to school voluntarily and want to use every minute! If there is no charge, a requirement or at least recommendation for students to enrol in such an activity could be made.

Activities away from the campus also contribute to students' total education. Some schools do build close links with local clubs, publicise their activities and encourage students to join them. Undoubtedly this can be expanded if someone has responsibility for it.

There are also important learning resources within the community — work experience in various forms, training centres, libraries, museums and record offices. These could be used much more extensively, particularly if school time arrangements encouraged this and if credit for off-campus learning was given. In Ontario, high school students can take 'cooperative education courses', with both an in-school and an out-of-school (usually work-based) component, both of which can provide credit towards the Secondary School Diploma. It is also possible to gain credits for this Diploma by independent study in school or out of it, correspondence and continuing education courses, and summer schools.

Vacations

Apart from organised expeditions, many schools in England regard this as dead time. However increasingly holiday schemes are being organised, and there is no reason why these should not be extended to enrichment and remediation programmes on the US model. There are however funding implications.

One-to-one coaching

Voluntary coaching of individual students has always been provided outside the main school day by teachers, parents, siblings or friends. However the amount of private and paid coaching has increased in recent years, particularly but not solely for students facing examinations. Most schools ignore coaching and almost seem to disapprove of it. However the quality of coaching time is, at least in theory, good: one-to-one teaching, directed at a specific need, with voluntary enrolment (at least by parents if not by children).

It is possible for schools to offer informal coaching. The common North American arrangement where staff remain in their classrooms at the end of the day and are available to give help to individual students is a good example. But provision of structured, regular one-to-one coaching is much more difficult because of the resource implications.

If staffing resources are not available, there is no reason why schools should not mount, promote and sell coaching programmes in the same way as they mount community education programmes. There will be reservations of course — mainly that some students are excluded by financial circumstances, and perhaps a concern that such a programme admits deficiencies in the school's main provision. The former is a perfectly reasonable objection on grounds of equity, and there is no reason why it cannot be met, just as it is in community education. Reduced or nil charges can be made to needy students, offset by higher charges generally and/or by a subsidy from the Education Authority (ideally a matching grant to encourage development). The second objection has to be rejected. It is more honest to admit that some students need or would benefit from extra coaching than to pretend the problem does not exist. Some independent schools have been able to offer additional paid-for coaching without undermining their own reputation.

A properly planned and promoted coaching programme, however resourced, would have much to commend it. It would be related to the known needs of the student as seen in the school; there would be integration with the main programme through staff and common materials, and it would enable the school to exploit the favourable time conditions that coaching offers. It could lead to a significant increase in total educational time.

* * * * *

In this chapter I have really tried to suggest two things. First, that the current 'time input allocation' approach to the curriculum, although universally used, does not stand up well to close examination. It is crude, illogical and inefficient. A 'time outcome model' will be harder to operate, but much more likely to meet the needs of individual students now and in the future. Such a model will depend on the use, at least in part, of open timetable systems.

Second, I have suggested that we should acknowledge much more strongly the value of extra-curricular time such as out of school activities, community and off-campus activities, and individual coaching. Just nodding the head in assent is not enough. We need to manage this time as positively as we do time for the conventional curriculum and to create the proper school day environment where it can flourish.

7 Modular time

Modules have their own inherent logic which determines how time is used.

What is a module?
Definition
A useful definition is: a module is a unit of learning with its own integral coherence which can be related to or exchanged with other modules.

This definition is similar to that used by Watkins (1987: 18) in his comprehensive survey of modular approaches to the secondary curriculum. It is strengthened slightly by including interchangeability (in everyday life a module is increasingly seen as something which is pulled out and replaced).

Context
Within this definition modules have been widely used in education, although the great majority of courses worldwide still do not have a modular form. The USA and provinces of Canada have long used a course credit system which is modular in nature, although the traditional semester courses are larger in terms of time than modules elsewhere.

In higher education modules are increasingly used. Many degree courses have options which are treated as modules. Some degree courses go a great deal further, notably in the USA. In the UK a leading example is the totally modular degree course offered among others by Oxford Polytechnic. The Council for National Academic Awards (CNAA) has a credit accumulation and transfer scheme for higher education awards, and the Open University operates entirely on a modular system. Modules are also commonly used in training for the armed forces, industry and commerce and the public services.

In the UK modules have only recently appeared in schools. They have been common in further education, particularly in courses certificated by CGLI and later by BTEC. In the 1970s these bodies began to develop prevocational courses for schools, some of which had a modular form. The new prevocational course set up in 1984 for 16 + school students, the CPVE, uses a modular system.

The main impetus in the 1980s has come from two quarters. In

Scotland the Scottish Action Plan (1983) proposed a very extensive range of forty hour modules for 16 – 18 students in both schools and colleges which has now been implemented by the Scottish Vocational Education Council (SCOTVEC). Some of these modules are suitable for pre-16 students. In England modular schemes developed almost spontaneously in a number of areas, driven by discontent with the weaknesses of traditional long courses and often introduced as a feature of TVEI. All of these developments are described fully by Watkins (1987).

Purpose

Modules can mean all things to all teachers. However they seem to have two inherent purposes. First they are seen to provide more effective learning and be more attractive to students. Their more immediate and often more tightly defined objectives, often related to outcomes or criteria, coupled to more immediate feedback and assessment bring improved student response. They also tend to require increased counselling and curriculum negotiation and allow easier retrieval and credit accumulation. Evaluation of modular courses so far suggests that all of these factors increase student motivation and success.

Second, modules increase curriculum flexibility. They make it easier to combine subjects, introduce at least elements of new subjects, sustain minority subjects and mount cross-curricular or integrated courses. They encourage students to opt for a module (as opposed to a full course) which is stereotyped for the opposite sex and facilitate joint provision by different institutions, centres or consortia. They also are more suitable for supported self study and distance learning, because of their compactness and shorter duration. Modules make it easier to achieve breadth and balance in the curriculum, and often do not need to be age-related. They also facilitate curricular change because the scale of change is smaller.

There is a third purpose, relating to altered teaching methods, which is not inherent in modules but which is often attached to them. Teachers often suggest that modules are better suited to emphasising curricular process and aspects such as problem solving and experiential learning, and that they encourage more open learning situations and increased student responsibility for learning. Some teachers have also found that modular provision has encouraged longer blocks of time, sometimes whole afternoons, which has made possible new learning approaches. Watkins (1987) examines many of these aspects.

Despite differences in the nature and purposes of modules used in different contexts, there is a logic about modularity which produces particular patterns of time use.

The effect of module certification

A module will normally be assessed and often will gain credit or certification in some form. This certification operates rather like a currency, ranging from soft to hard, and the variation directly affects the use of time.

The softest form of certification is assessment by an individual teacher with no relation to assessment of any other teacher or body. An example is a teacher breaking up a long course into a sequence of units. Almost as soft is certification by departments or even by individual schools. Under these conditions modules can be of almost any time allocation and duration. Teacher controlled modules can operate quite independently of other teachers' courses, except that they need to observe normal timetable constraints. Departmental modules may need to adopt a broad uniformity of time use within the department, but not beyond it. Similarly, a school with a totally modular curriculum with internal assessment may need to set up its own internal time framework, but this can operate quite independently of other schools. An excellent example is the modular scheme for years 1 – 3 operating at Greendown Community School, Swindon. Here the whole curriculum is delivered in the form of half term length modules. So there have to be uniform changeover and assessment dates within the school, but these are not related to other schools.

When however certification is used with a harder currency, increasing constraints are imposed. The broader the area of the certification (i.e. regional rather than local, national rather than regional) and the greater its status or value, the stricter the requirements become. Certificating bodies will tend to homogenise the modules, making them broadly equivalent in their time requirements. This time allocation may be indicative — CGLI, for example, often indicates broadly the time requirements for a course — or specific, as the 40 hours for SCOTVEC modules. Significantly in Scotland this firm time commitment led to many schools revising their timetable arrangements, as discussed in chapter three.

Time use can be affected in another way. The higher the status of certification, the greater the likelihood of strict conditions being imposed on the content of modules and their inter-relationship: rules for combination, aggregation and also retrieval. This can have considerable effect on time use, discussed in the next section. Such regulations may include provision for combining modules as a subject or integrated award. The Oxford Polytechnic modular course established in 1973 has its own vocabulary: basic and advanced, single and double modules; acceptable, recommended, prerequisite, compulsory and unattached modules. It is interesting to see the same concepts emerging in GCSE modular subjects — an indication that the modular approach has its own logic to unwind.

The number of modules involved in a combination has time effects. If an odd number of modules is involved over a span of more than one year, certain consequences flow. Either there is a greater number of modules in one year than another, creating greater time pressures in one and probably underusing time in the other, or one module has to cross over from one year to another. Some of these problems have sharpened where English examination boards have accepted five module combinations. Also there will be a tendency for examination boards to adopt fewer, larger modules to reduce the time spent on assessment and administration.

'Hard' certification has created modular time sub-structures in schools, with uniform times for assessment, changeover and negotiation, often conflicting with the times traditionally used for this in continuous courses. If modular courses became widespread they would create pressures for two semester or four term years and for terms of even length.

The effects of module links

Modules will commonly be linked together in subjects, courses or some overarching award. If the certification is 'hard' the linkage will be determined by the certificating body, but links may also be required by others such as employers. In addition the school or even the teacher may establish their own links, for philosophical or practical reasons.

What matters for time use is not the linkages themselves but their rigidity. If modules are chained in a firm succession which is not normally altered or broken, then in effect a linear course is recreated which can operate under the normal time arrangements for linear courses. The modules it contains may be useful for short term objectives or immediate feedback but they will not require different time use.

At the other extreme are linkages which allow great flexibility. This may be initial flexibility, over students' choice and combination of modules; en route flexibility, where alternative or branching possibilities open; or ongoing flexibility, where at each change-over point students may rechoose quite freely. The US semester unit credit system is of this kind. In the UK a good example is the nine week (quarter year) modules of about 40 hours provided for fourth and fifth year students at Ysgol Emrys ap Iwan, Abergele, Clwyd. At the end of each module period students choose again and change extensively.

This flexibility requires different time treatment. First, it requires time built in for student negotiation of module change. Second, it requires exact and specified changeover points. Third, it may have fundamental timetabling needs if the full implications are accepted. These may be set out logically:

	Modules without a requirement for sequencing can be taken in any order
Therefore:	such modules do not need to be age related
Therefore:	For a module to be available to more than one year group, it must be in the same time-slot for each year-group.

Example:

```
    :           Time slot A              :
    :                                    :
    :      5th Year History module       :
    :                                    :
    :     4th Year Geography module      :
```

Here a fourth year student could take a fifth year history module.

Therefore: A time slot type timetable is necessary for non age-related use of unsequenced modules

This is not just a debating point. Combined year-group classes can be valuable in supporting minority or under-subscribed subjects and extending the provision of small or falling roll schools. US high schools have a time-slotted timetable and commonly have courses which are not age-related.

The effect of closed timetables

Most modules operate within closed timetables of the kind described in the last chapter. Several issues arise.

Time allocation for modules

There is considerable divergence of view on ideal module length. It must be long enough to provide coherence and reduce administrative problems, but short enough to retain short term objectives and flexibility. Examples are:

U.S. semester credits	approximately	80 hours
SCOTVEC modules	"	40 hours
Four module GCSE schemes	"	37 hours
Five module GCSE schemes	"	30 hours
Ontario Secondary Education Review Project	"	30 hours
Northern Examining Association Modular GCSE schemes	"	12 − 20 hours

ILEA ISS programme learning units approximately		15 hours
Northern Partnership for Records of Achievement	"	variable (can be less than 10)

Hard certification modules in the UK have mainly stabilised at 30 – 40 hours.

Lesson lengths

In some schools, particularly those with TVEI courses, there has been pressure for longer lesson lengths to accommodate modules with prevocational activities. Normally this has been offset by the longer lessons being less numerous. An example is: two hours 15 minute lessons, twice a week for nine weeks, as at Abergele, compared with one hour 10 minute lessons, twice per week for 18 weeks (a typical four module GCSE course)

Timetable blocking and time slots

For similar reasons modules have created pressure for blocking of timetables to allow teams of teachers or groups of classes or activities to operate. Where these blocks extend across more than one year group they can be termed time-slots. Here modules seem to be reinforcing an existing trend.

Limitations of closed timetables

Modules mainly exist in closed timetables for one simple reason: most schools operate closed timetables. However closed timetables create an unfriendly environment for modules:

- they damp down the flexibility for both students and teachers which is such an attractive feature and which can best be exploited in an 'open' timetable (see the next section)
- they restrict credit accumulation, because the fixed timetable only allows a set amount of modules to be gained at one time
- closed timetables conflict with the tendency for modules to be outcome oriented and criterion referenced. This tendency arises partly from the sharper definition of more immediate objectives, and partly because modules tend to be more process orientated. But allocation of a fixed duration — 40 hours for example — conflicts with the principle of criterion referencing and excludes any possibility of increased productivity. The CPVE avoided time allocation for its modules for this reason. It is worth noting however that modules also have tended to introduce more course work assessment and this could have the effect in practice of requiring extended time allocation. This can create problems for students who wish to take courses in less time — adult or one year 6th students for example.

Modules can therefore operate in a closed system and will continue to do so. But an open timetable system is much more favourable. Once again this is an example of a new subsystem (modules) being introduced into an existing time system without the implications for adjustment being thought through.

The effect of open timetables

Opportunities for exploiting the possibilities of modules are much greater in an open system of the flexible day/extended day/use of twilight or evening/college day type which is explored more fully in chapter twelve.

Problems over lesson length are reduced. Lesson lengths can be adjusted to meet the needs of the module, and can even be varied from week to week for special activities. There is even the possibility of taking a module in very compressed time — say one week's full time field study plus preparation and follow up. This is equivalent to at least forty hours study, and may well be more educationally effective because of its intensity.

The range of choice open to students increases, since modules can be selected from an extended timetable. It is easier for students to choose modules offered at other centres or by consortia since travelling and personal timetabling fits in more easily. Also modules offered in adult and community education classes are available and it is much easier to mount modules which are accessible to students of all years.

Open timetables also make it easier for students to take additional modules by supported self study, use of computerised and electronic technology and distance learning. Opportunities for access to learning resources and equipment are improved. It is easier for students to increase their total take-up of modules and speed up their learning. The choice of modules can be both extended and fitted more exactly to the learner's own needs. But the implications are that a more developed student counselling, negotiation and monitoring system is necessary.

Modules have not appeared as such in primary schools, although they have always existed loosely in the form of curriculum units and projects. Possibly the compact, programmed nature of modules has less appeal in the more spontaneous and interactive primary context. However, they could be very useful for delivering effectively curriculum areas such as science or technology. If so, the flexible timetabling context in primary schools will ease their introduction.

*　*　*　*　*

The general conclusions are clear. Modular approaches make the use of time more flexible, more directed, and probably more effective.

But they may also create needs which conflict with the existing time systems. They will tend to create pressures to change these, to change the pattern of the school year, lengthen lessons and increase block timetabling. Although most modules will continue to operate within a closed timetable, logically they demand the extension of open timetable areas.

8 Time in the classroom

Classroom time is the one area where research, particularly in the USA, has built up a theoretical framework. It gained great impetus from John Carroll.

Carroll's 'Model of School Learning'

John Carroll's original article (1963) has been very influential. As an educational psychologist he had been puzzling about the process of learning, particularly foreign languages. Clearly students enter the classroom with differing knowledge, skills or abilities, and under *fixed time* conditions these differences are translated into differences in student achievement. What would happen to such differences under non-fixed time conditions? Individual student differences would be translated into individual differences in the amount of learning time needed.

The heart of the model is the statement that 'the learner will succeed in learning a given task to the extent that he spends the amount of time that he *needs* to learn the task.' Carroll identified five factors which determine how much time is needed or spent (see Fig. 8.1).

1. Factors affecting the time needed:

    (a) *aptitude* — defined as the time required for the student to learn a defined task. This time will be determined by prior learning and the student's personal characteristics
    (b) *ability to understand instruction*
    (c) *quality of instruction* — the organisation and presentation of the learning task by the teacher and the learning resources, and its appropriateness for the learner

Factors (b) and (c) clearly interact, and (a) can affect (b) and (c)

2. Factors affecting time spent in learning:

    (d) *opportunity to learn* — defined as the time allotted for learning by the teacher or school
    (e) *perseverance in learning* — defined as the time the student is willing to spend on learning — itself determined by motivation, persistence, morale, self-image, etc.

Factor (e) will be affected by (c) and possibly (b) and (a).

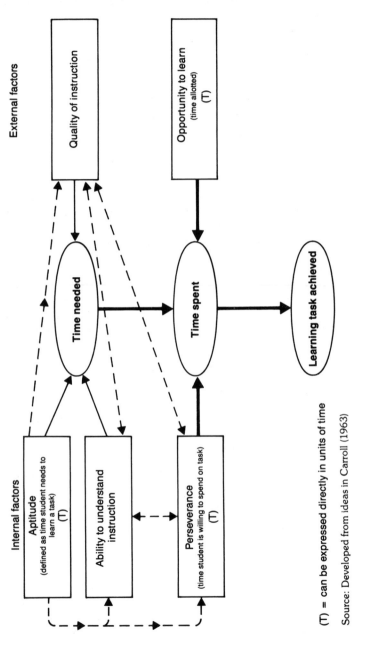

(T) = can be expressed directly in units of time

Source: Developed from ideas in Carroll (1963)

Figure 8.1 – Carroll's 'Model of School Learning'

Learning is thus seen as a function of the extent to which a student *spends* the time he or she *needs*. So:

$$\text{degree of learning} = f\ \frac{[\text{time actually spent}]}{[\text{time needed}]}$$

The more the student spends the time he or she needs, the more is learnt. Time actually spent will be the *smallest* of:

1. Time needed i.e. (a) related to (b) and (c).
2. Time allotted i.e. (d).
3. The time the learner is willing to spend i.e. (e).

These are represented by the bold arrows in Figure 8.1.

Carroll suggested that most school learning could be expressed in the forms of learning tasks, clearly described and with a means for judging whether they have been achieved. He admitted that in practice learning is not necessarily broken into tasks, but conceptually it could be. The model was not intended to apply to goals relating to attitudes, values and personal qualities.

The model of school learning has been developed and refined and used in a wide range of different contexts (see Carroll, 1989). It has been criticised for being too wedded to the identification of learning tasks and inappropriate to affective and higher order educational processes. But it has a number of strengths:

- It is boldly optimistic. Its redefinition of aptitude as time required to learn suggests that human potential can be developed much more fully once we break out of the time-ration situation.
- It is simple.
- It produces a formula to explain learning and highlight the variables which affect learning outcomes and their interaction.
- It provides for measurement of variables in a common unit — time — thus allowing comparisons. Three of the factors can be measured in time, and the other two can be related to other time-measured variables.

For a few years the 'Model of School Learning' made little impact. Then it was taken up and extended by Benjamin Bloom.

Mastery learning

Bloom (1968) criticized the wasteful and destructive nature of fixed-time instruction, with its expectation of failure and practice of grading along a normal curve of distribution. He took Carroll's view that aptitude is the amount of time a learner requires to master a learning task, and suggested that implicit within it was 'the assumption that, given enough time, all students can gain mastery of a learning task'. In theory anyone can learn anything but the time required may be infinite (Carroll, incidentally, gently dissociated from this view). Bloom supported this standpoint with the evidence of grade norms for standardised tests, where the scores for high grades in one year-group are achieved by many more students in older year-groups.

Bloom conceded that a small percentage of students have special abilities or disabilities for learning a task, but suggested that for 90 per cent of individuals, aptitudes are predictive of the rate of learning possible. 'Given sufficient time (and appropriate types of help), 95 per cent of students (the top 5 per cent + the next 90 per cent) can learn a subject up to a high level of mastery'. However he did see that one problem could be to find ways of reducing the time needed for slower students to the point where learning a task was not prohibitively long.

Bloom then suggested a range of approaches which could improve the quality of instruction for individual learners and so help them understand instruction better and improve perseverance. All should help individuals make more effective use of their learning time, and so either decrease the time they needed or increase the time they spent.

These suggestions were developed into a complete strategy, involving:

1. Defining mastery, with identified outcomes and criteria of mastery.
2. Division of material into units, each backed by formative, diagnostic tests.
3. Planning with appropriate activities and materials — particularly support activities and materials for failing students.
4. Teaching geared to expectation of success and aiming at criteria for mastery, with appropriate feedback and correction.
5. Grading for competence and not competition.

The mastery learning approach has spread extensively in the USA and beyond, mainly for grades 1 – 8 (ages 6 – 13). Research suggests it can be more effective than traditional approaches in grades 5 – 8 and with less able students. There is also the interesting suggestion that students on mastery learning programmes tend to require progressively less time to achieve the same performance in successive units. But it does need thorough organisation in both the classroom and the school as a whole. There can be problems. Insistence on full mastery can hold students back and slow learners may need an unacceptable amount of extra time. It has been criticised as being too mechanistic and narrow, less appropriate for more open subjects and demotivating for the most able.

A good overall survey of the practice of mastery learning, with a full set of references, can be found in Burns and Kojimoto (1988).

Time as a classroom resource

This new attention to time highlighted its importance for the individual learner. It brought out the obvious truth that teaching does not in itself cause learning; teaching causes learning only in so far as it affects students' behaviour so that learning results. So the new phase of research concentrated on student behaviour and the effect of different uses of time upon it. In particular it concentrated on the way time, both teacher time and student time, was allocated within the classroom.

One approach conceived of time as being allocated by teacher and student decisions, and so susceptible to the same economic analysis as any other scarce resource allocated in a production process. Brown and Saks (1980) saw the classroom as a workshop (but not a production line) where varying kinds and quantities of inputs are transformed into different outputs. They saw the teacher seeking to achieve 'maximum utility' in the allocation of time resources by deciding to switch from one activity or student to another in order to produce the maximum overall learning. They produced economists' equations and graphs to illustrate time allocation in the classroom. They also suggested (1975) that teachers might have different strategies to seek maximum utility, and distinguished between 'levellers' who spread their time evenly among students to increase the average gain and 'elitists' who concentrate it on the most able students to increase best performance.

This economic analysis of the classroom has been well described by Simkins (1987). He however points out that there has been surprisingly little analysis of the production function of schools, partly because values, preferences and learning outcomes at the whole school level are more ambiguous and less easy to handle than those of individual teachers and pupils in the classroom. For example school level outcomes are much more complex than the selected outcomes measured by the research on the allocation of classroom time, which are typically limited to standardised test scores.

Time as a measure

Time has proved a very useful unit of measurement of classroom activity. It is relatively easy to use, with a wide range of units from macro (years) to micro (seconds). It is expressed in equal, universally understood units and has an absolute zero. Most teacher or student activities can be expressed ultimately in terms of time, and so comparisons are facilitated. So it is not surprising that classroom research increasingly resorts to measurement in time.

However, such measurement does encourage concentration on aspects which can be easily measured and so emphasise the quantitative at the expense of the qualitative. It could possibly lead again to a cult of efficiency similar to that prevailing in the era of 'scientific management' in the 1920s.

Allocation of classroom time
Levels of allocation
The umbrella term 'time' shelters many different meanings. So the total time provided for schooling will only be a nominal quantity. By no means all of it will be used by the student for learning. At each level as it trickles down time is deducted for non-learning activities.

We can set out these levels of time allocation (and time deduction) for each student as follows (see Fig. 8.2).

TOTAL SCHOOLING
The number of hours in the school day, multiplied by the days in the school year and the number of years of schooling.

TOTAL TIMETABLED CLASSROOM TIME
Total schooling less breaks and *timetabled* activities such as inter-class movement, registration, pastoral time and assemblies. In effect this is the time when the student's individual timetable shows him or her in a class.

TOTAL CLASSROOM TIME USABLE FOR LEARNING
Total timetabled classroom time less:

- student absence from school
- teacher absence (this does not prevent learning since teacher cover is normally provided but makes it less effective)
- student or teacher lateness (including inter-classroom movement which is not timetabled)
- school closures (bad weather, emergencies, industrial action, etc)
- scheduled school events which set aside class time (e.g. sports days, concerts, speakers, examinations and large-scale general tests and other special events)
- withdrawal of students from class (e.g. for counselling and guidance, discipline interviews, interviews with other staff or office queries, medical inspections), and similar pull-out events. Withdrawal of students for remedial teaching may also be included, since it may reduce study of part of the curriculum (even though it creates learning elsewhere).

In effect this is all the classroom time when a student is present and in a position to learn — what Carroll called 'opportunity to learn'.

ALLOCATED TIME
Time allocated from usable classroom time to a particular curriculum area or activity.

This allocation of time is particularly important in primary schools, since there it is principally the classroom teacher who makes the

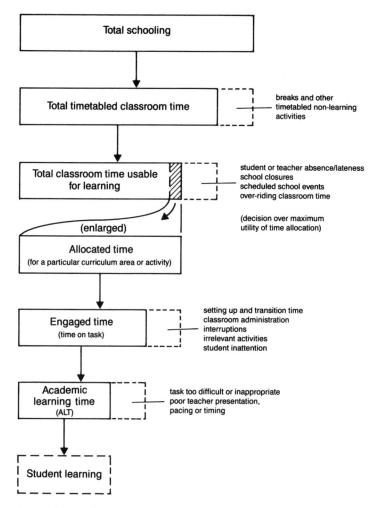

Source: Adapted from Husen and Postlethwaite (1985: 5266)

Figure 8.2 – Allocation of time for learning

allocation. In secondary schools the allocation is largely made through the timetable and the formal syllabus. However, the increasing emphasis on curriculum process rather than content and the growth of cross-curricular themes and activities is beginning to make time allocation within the classroom by secondary teachers a more important issue.

Whether curriculum time allocation occurs from pressure from national or state governments, local administrators, heads or principals, curricula and syllabuses, examinations and tests, or from the local decision of the teacher, the same issue discussed earlier of achieving maximum utility arise. Any decision on time allocation inevitably incurs opportunity costs — the cost of the next best curriculum opportunity which has been foregone.

Note: some of the time originally allocated will not be usable because of the time lost by absences, closures and school events, described above. Such losses may bear more heavily on one curriculum area than another — particularly if with a fixed timetable it occurs at a set time only once or twice a week. For example activities timetabled on a Friday are more likely to lose time from absence.

ENGAGED TIME (sometimes called 'active learning time' or 'time-on-task')
This is that proportion of allocated time which the student actually spends on a learning activity, i.e. allocated time less:

- setting up and winding down time
- transition from one activity to another
- classroom administration (including non-timetabled registration)
- interruptions
- activities not relevant to the allocated curriculum time e.g. diversion of the teacher to another topic (the 'red herring syndrome')
- student inattention or distraction.

In most classrooms 60 to 90 per cent of time is engaged on task, and the percentage of allocated time can be termed the 'engagement rate'. However, the fact that a student spends time on task does not guarantee that learning occurs.

ACADEMIC LEARNING TIME (ALT)
This term was coined by the Beginning Teacher Evaluation Study (BTES), a very extensive research project in California. The project concluded that for learning to occur from engaged time, the task needed to be sufficiently easy and appropriate for a high rate of success to be attainable. ALT is made up from (a) allocated time, (b) engagement rate, and (c) success rate (the percentage of engaged time that the student experiences high, medium or low success). Time spent where the task is too difficult (or easy) or inappropriate to the learner, where teacher instructions or presentation are unclear, or the pacing and timing is poor, can be deducted; it does not provide ALT.

The project's research found a high correlation between ALT and achievement scores. The conclusion was that not only is ALT the crucial residual time element necessary for learning, but that also it can be treated as a proxy for learning, removing the need for much testing. If ALT occurs learning is likely to occur. Moreover, ALT unlike other classroom variables such as resources is very much under the control of the classroom teacher.

Classroom time of students and teachers

Galton and Simon (1980) studied by classroom observation students and teachers in 58 classes in 19 primary schools. Their breakdown of the time spent by the typical student was as follows:

Fully involved and cooperating on learning task		58%	
− working on own	40%		
− listening to or interacting with teacher	12%		
− interacting with another pupil in relation to work	5%		74%
	57		
Fully involved and cooperating in supporting routine activity		12%	
Waiting to see or speak to teacher		4%	
Distracted, not working		16%	25%
Other activities		9%	
Note:			
active disruption	0.1%		
horseplay	0.2%		

The time of a typical teacher was spent as follows:			
Actively interacting with students:			
− with individual students		56%	
− with whole class		15%	c.80%
− with groups		7.5%	
Housekeeping, talking to another teacher, resting, or out of classroom			c.20%

However, the teacher's time from the student's viewpoint was very different:			
Portion of the lesson when the student was not interacting with the teacher			84%
Portion of the lesson when student interacted with the teacher:			
− mostly with teacher		12%	
− as an individual		2.3%	16%
− as member of a group		1.5%	

The authors concluded: 'The asymmetry of teacher-pupil interaction, therefore, lies precisely in this, that while the teacher spends most of her time interacting with individual pupils, each specific individual child only receives individual attention from the teacher for a very small proportion of lesson time'.

Walberg (1988) has emphasised the importance of 'productive time' in the classroom. He surveyed recent work on the psychology of learning which shows how time is needed both to transfer items of knowledge to long term memory and to build up and process memory blocks. These findings reinforce existing views about time as a vital ingredient for learning. However Walberg is concerned that 'students who are behind at the beginning of schooling or slow to start often learn at a slower rate; those who begin well gain at a faster rate; this results in what has been called the 'Matthew effect' of the academically rich getting richer.'

Walberg therefore argues that to overcome the Matthew effect and offset differences in students' prior knowledge and learning rates, we need to increase precious 'productive time' when each student is actually learning effectively. This is difficult in a class situation unless instruction is modified to suit individual differences and to enhance learning skills.

Differences in allocation

Research into the use of classroom time has exposed disturbing inequalities in its allocation. A telling example was set out by Berliner (1979) for maths in four second grade classes and reading in four fifth grade classes, using data from 50 classes in the BTES (see Table 8.1).

The table repays study. The percentage engagement rate of allocated time gives engaged time (e.g. for class 5, 71 per cent of 27 minutes gives 19 minutes), and the success rate of engaged time gives ALT (e.g. for class 5, 67 per cent of 19 minutes is 13 minutes). Even a cursory examination shows several features:

1. Allocated time varies greatly between classes. Classes 5 and 21 for example allocate only about 60 per cent of the time to maths compared with classes 8 and 31. The variations for reading are wider still. Other data in the study showed, perhaps predictably, that lower time allocations were related to higher than average time spent on transitions between activities and management of behaviour.

2. Engaged time ('time-on-task') shows similar variations with some classes receiving 100 per cent more than others for the same curriculum area. There is also variation in engagement rates, but these are deceptively high because in this table 'allocated time' excludes transition time (setting up and winding down, etc). If it had been included total nominal allocated time would have been greater but engagement rates would have been markedly lower,

with much sharper variation between classes. Actual engagement time would be the same. (For the 50 classes of the sample, the range of engagement rates was much larger).

3. ALT again varies widely between classes, with some providing virtually 100 per cent more for maths, and others more still for reading. However, as the BTES concluded that this was the most important indicator of learning, perhaps more important is the very limited amounts of ALT actually provided, particularly in maths.

4. The reduction in time from one level to another is very apparent. Thus 32 minutes of allocated maths time per day for class 21 (more if transition time had been included) reduces to 20 minutes of engagement time and only 12 minutes of ALT. This illustrates the tapering effect already described in Fig. 8.2. Berliner remarks that states and school districts often insist on a certain minimum of time per day on certain subject areas. If they allocate say 40 minutes per day to maths, although this probably appears on the timetable the real provision of effective learning time in the classroom can be very different!

5. Year-long cumulative effects accentuate the above variations. The percentage variations between classes remain the same, but the difference in gross provision in hours is much more stark. For

Table 8.1 Allocated, engaged and academic learning time in maths in four 2nd grade classes and reading/language time in four 5th grade classes, California, 1970s

Class Code	2nd grade Maths				5th grade Reading			
	5	21	8	13	1	3	11	25
Allocated time average minutes per day	27	32	50	53	59	66	142	135
Percentage of time students engaged (engagement rate)	71	62	61	78	82	77	84	75
Engaged time, minutes per day	19	20	31	41	48	51	119	101
Percentage of time students are on material of easy difficulty level (success rate)	67	59	65	55	51	61	47	58
Academic learning time (ALT), minutes per day	13	12	20	23	24	31	56	59
Engaged hours per 150 days* in school year	48	50	78	103	120	128	298	253
ALT hours per 150 day* school year	33	30	50	58	60	78	140	148

Note: * Only 150 days because of assumed teacher and pupil absence, bus or weather problems, wind-down of terms, testing, strikes etc.

Source: After Berliner (1979: 127 – 128).

example students in class 21 are only on task in mathematics for 50 hours per year and only receive ALT for 30 hours.

Berliner concludes from the study as a whole that 'many second grade classes have cumulative engaged time, in *both* reading and mathematics, of under 100 hours per year'. (In fifth grade classes engaged time was considerably higher.) Other research elsewhere into engaged time and ALT has shown similar and sometimes greater variations between classes and similar low levels of ALT. An important finding by Brown & Saks (1986), again from BTES data, is that there is significant interaction between allocated time and a student's initial ability. A given increase in time adds more to the score of a lower- than a higher-ability student.

6. Time allocation within curriculum areas shows even greater variation in coverage of content. In the same study Berliner provided details for specific content areas in reading/language in the four fifth grade classes (see Table 8.2).

    Here students in class 11 spent much more time on comprehension than the others; in class 25, in silent reading and spelling; while in class 3 they did little oral reading.

Research also reveals dramatic variations in allocated, engaged and academic learning time between individual students in the same class.

Allocation of time will be affected by the teacher as he or she directs students to particular tasks. The variation will be extreme where students in the same class are working on different curriculum areas, and will be compounded where children have a high degree of choice over their learning activities. This can be particularly marked in integrated day situations, but will exist to some degree wherever students are undertaking different activities. The variation will range not just over content but also over process.

Engaged time will vary between students because of variations in attention, susceptibility to distraction, motivation, etc. The range of variation will be greater where the classroom engagement rate is low, i.e. where the teacher does not succeed in reducing time loss for transitions, misbehaviour and distraction.

ALT will be affected for individual students by both the above factors but also by the level of difficulty of the learning material and its appropriateness for the individual student.

Quality of classroom time and teacher effectiveness

Growing scrutiny of classroom time has led to growing awareness of the importance of teacher choices and strategies. If the quality of the teacher determines the way classroom time is used, then identifying

Table 8.2   Time spent on content areas in reading/language in four 5th grade classes, California, 1970s

| | Time in minutes per 90 school days | | | |
	Class 1	Class 3	Class 11	Class 25
Content areas of the curriculum				
Word structure				
Root words and affixes	232	105	130	125
Syllables	62	56	105	258
Word meaning				
Synonyms	88	143	10	145
Pronoun reference	0	0	9	68
Other word meaning	518	889	1,077	747
Comprehension				
Verbatim (no rephrasing)	191	308	194	395
Translation (paraphrase)	113	142	1,705	465
Inference-synthesis	218	236	1,481	372
Identifying main items	142	228	975	396
Evaluation of fact and opinion	5	0	68	68
Other comprehension	182	304	1,415	291
Reading practice				
Oral reading	560	59	915	371
Silent reading	1,005	679	989	4,426
Reading in content areas	469	240	414	345
Related reading				
Spelling	643	794	687	1,720
Grammar	225	172	888	502
Creative writing	52	322	101	697
Study skills	438	627	279	208
Other	192	644	1,361	518
Total time in minutes	5,334	5,948	12,804	12,117

Source: Adapted from Berliner (1979: 128).

the qualities of the effective teacher should assist teachers to manage classroom time better.

Much recent research in the USA and in the UK has therefore moved towards teacher effectiveness. One important area is seen as learning settings, particularly group sizes and the degree of teacher supervision and interaction with students. It's a matter of trade-offs. If a teacher spends time with one student, he or she cannot interact with others and is less able to supervise them. So a high degree of teacher – single student activity within a classroom tends to lead to less effective management of classroom time as a whole. Conversely, a reasonable amount of teacher – whole class or teacher – whole group interaction maximises the use of the teacher as a learning resource. Glass (1982) found that reducing class size reduces the size of settings and increases teacher supervision, so leading to increases in ALT. This seems to support the traditional parent's view that smaller classes are better for children.

Related is the growing interest in the structure of classroom activities. Well – structured activities lead to better use of classroom time. Mortimore et al. (1988) found that classrooms where activities were loosely structured, or where several different types of activity coexisted, tended to correlate with lower achievement. He suggested that one reason for this may be that it is more difficult for the teacher to use time effectively if he or she needs to keep switching between different types of student activity.

Another important area is the whole set of teacher skills involved in creating positive working conditions — clear goal setting and directions, classroom management, effective planning, monitoring and feedback. These link with teacher attitudes, for example emphasis on academic goals and creation of high expectations. All lead to more effective use of time.

Finally, growing importance is being laid on effective pacing of lessons and matching of content to the level of the learner. The former opens possibilities of reducing the time needed, as opposed to increasing time spent. Indeed one can think in terms of slow teachers, just like slow learners. One of the problems with logging classroom time is that it does not indicate how *effectively* the teacher's time has been used.

What does it all mean?

In one sense, not very much. For emphasis on classroom time has slipped into a circular argument: effective learning is related to effective use of classroom time which is caused by effective teaching. QED, effective teaching causes effective learning.

There are some specific criticisms which can be made:

1. The research tends to concentrate on what is measurable, and by concentration on narrow and restricted learning outcomes has encouraged a more mechanistic approach. Some critics have argued it encourages lower order, even trivial, activities at the expense of others. Also, much of the research is based on primary classrooms, although not exclusively so.
2. Quality of classroom time is undervalued. A student's learning is not just affected by time and success rate. Students certainly believe they learn better with teachers they like, and although this may represent preference for effective teachers, it also reflects affective factors. Certainly students are affected by their own feelings — personal unhappiness can be a poor environment for learning (even if a fertile one for the imagination).

Also, although some researchers have referred to 'extensity' and 'intensity' in use of time, there is seldom much attention to the importance of moments of insight, break-through points and effective learning experiences. Nor is there much attention to the value of experiential learning: 'I hear and I forget; I see and I remember; I do and I understand.' ALT does not discriminate between hearing, seeing and doing.

3. Finally, research on classroom time unduly emphasises learning in the classroom to the neglect of the rich possibilities beyond it. Fig. 8.3 represents these possibilities. It also suggests that the quality of both in- and out-of-class time creates an additional dimension.

Beyond the classroom time can include:

(a) *Extra tuition*
    In Japan cramming schools create a major additional learning input. Some students attend them for three or four evening a week, two to three hours each. In other countries private coaching is often more common than is generally accepted.

(b) *Homework and distance learning*
    Not only does homework extend learning time; by definition, all the time spent on it is engaged (if not ALT).

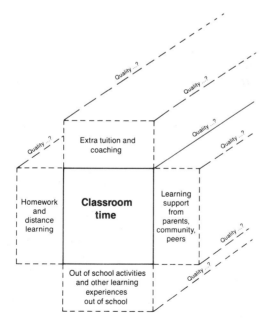

Figure 8.3 – Extending learning time beyond the classroom

(c) *Other learning experiences* such as out of school activities; leisure activities such as TV, reading, home computing, conversation, sports and hobbies; vacations; membership of organisations or of community classes; work experience.

(d) Learning support from other than teachers: parents and friends, peer groups both informal and for organised tutoring, members of the community.

All these beyond-the-classroom activities share several features:

– they are low cost, at least for the school's budget
– they build on the learners' interests and ambitions
– they support and extend classroom learning
– there is no predetermined limit to their growth, and they are often capable of expansion.

So there is a strong argument that time and resources put into expanding out-of-classroom learning could bring at least as good a return as changes in the classroom itself. Some of these possibilities are explored in the next two chapters.

* * * * *

Yet, the interest in classroom time has still brought great benefits.

First, just emphasising to teachers the importance of classroom time is useful. Greater awareness of the effect of the choices they make in time allocation is helpful.

Second, realisation of how good learning time is stripped away by the deductions at each level is helpful. Even sharpening sensitivity to matters like classroom interruption or transition time between activities is useful.

Third, the concept of ALT is important, even though the simple ingredient of 'success with relatively easy material' may be too simple. It suggests that appropriate learning activity does lead to learning — a very obvious point but important because it is largely under the teacher's control. So school — and teaching — matters.

Fourth, many of the characteristics of the more effective teacher which are now being identified can be acquired. They do not demand a personality change.

Fifth, classroom time studies remind us yet again of the importance of time fitting the needs of the individual student (they also question whether slow learners should not be given more time — although in many schools and countries they commonly receive less).

Finally, John Carroll leaves a message of hope. Learning depends on time spent compared with time needed. If we can increase the one and decrease the other, learning can be transformed. We should not under-estimate the possibilities for improvement. Locking the learner in a fixed-time classroom is such a primitive way of freeing the vast potential that lies in every human being.

A practical approach to more efficient use of school time

The US Mid-continent Regional Educational Laboratory (McREL) has used the research and concepts discussed above to develop 'Achieving Excellence' (1988), a tool for schools to improve their efficiency in the use of time. This provides proformas which enable a school to calculate, on a daily basis:

1. Non-instructional *school* activities (e.g. lunch-break, breaks, timetabled registration, intercom announcements, assemblies, as well as an average for early dismissals, fire drills, standardised testing, special events and whole school interruptions).
2. Non-instructional *class* activities (non-timetabled registration, transition activities, lending out materials, interruptions and other time not itself producing learning). These are assessed by 'dip-stick' observation of classes.
3. Student inattentiveness (non-engaged time). Three alternative instruments are provided, one for observation of whole classes, another for selected students, and another for students' anonymous assessments of their own engagement.

A master worksheet leads to the development of percentage rates for these three categories, as well as for student absence. These can then be set out in an 'Academic Efficiency Grid' (see Fig.8.4), on which the remaining engaged time is shown as 'academic efficiency', i.e. that part of the day in which learning should take place.

Figure 8.4. also provides norms for these categories, based upon research in the schools of the McREL region. Clearly the assessment contains some subjective judgements, so it cannot be used to compare teachers or schools. But it does enable a school to analyse more critically its own use of time, and to match this against norms. The programme can also be operated on a computer.

Figure 8.4. also suggests that school, classroom or student management policies can improve the 'academic efficiency index' (AEI). A range of practical improvement tactics are suggested for each (for example, for school management these include ideas for reducing student dropout and absenteeism, whole school interruptions and inefficient scheduling.)

McREL believes 'that a 20 per cent improvement in the AEI is needed to produce a significant difference on standardised tests'. However, this is not as large as it seems:

'If the school day is 400 minutes long and the current AEI is 40 per cent, only 160 minutes a day are spent with students engaged in academic work. A 20 per cent improvement would represent only 32 minutes more student engagement. These minutes can be gained by a slight rise in attendance (say one or two per cent), eliminating five or ten minutes from the non-instructional school time and a comparable amount from non-instructional class activities and decreasing student inattentiveness.'

'Achieving Excellence' contains similar sections relating to effectiveness and excellence, although these touch more obliquely on the use of time. The package has been thoroughly tested in the region and has been well received.

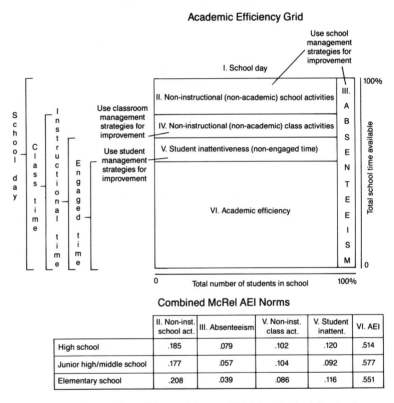

Source: The Mid-continent Regional Educational Laboratory (1988), Policy 1 Figs. 1 and 2 (combined)

Figure 8.4 — Tool to analyse efficiency of school time use

Going further

This chapter can only skim across an extensive literature. Readers will find a good short survey in Husen & Postlethwaite (1988: 5265 ff.) There is also a useful account with practical suggestions in a booklet published by the American Association of School Administrators (1982), 'Time on Task'.

A much fuller survey is Fisher & Berliner (1985). This contains the original papers of Carroll & Bloom and some important recent contributions, including some criticism of school time studies. For British readers more accessible books may be Anderson (1983), similar but less extensive and also with the Carroll & Bloom papers, and Simkins (1987) which gives an account of the economists' approach to the classroom, with a full range of references.

9 Time for individual study

Schools deal with individuals in groups. Yet individuals learn as individuals. So the use of time for individual study is an important aspect of school time management. It will become more important with the spread of new technology and distance learning.

This chapter does not detail strategies for individual study but focuses on the use of time for it. It begins by analysing both the possibilities and problems implicit in individual study. It then examines various approaches within the school day, and a range of possibilities outside it. It concludes by looking at time for support of individual students.

Analysis

Possibilities

Individual study can take various forms:

- general reading, radio listening or TV viewing (serious enough to count as conscious learning, but not structured enough to be always seen as 'study')
- undirected individual study (e.g. a student studying a topic out of personal interest, without help from anyone else)
- directed small-scale independent study, unsupported (examples would be homework, individual study in class without the normal teacher present, or independent fieldwork, and could include programmed learning)
- directed small-scale study, supported (examples would be study of a topic in class, with the teacher providing roving support; project work in a class context; or fieldwork with the teacher providing on the spot advice)
- directed large scale study, usually supported (examples would be a student studying an unusual topic or subject on his or her own or in a small group, possibly within a supported self study framework)
- distance learning of a structured kind (i.e. physical separation of teacher and student, as in correspondence courses, individual learning from radio or television)
- learning from new technology (e.g. computer programmes, interactive video, teletext, audio-tapes).

These categories are not rigidly exclusive. They do however show that there are a number of variables for individual study:

- scale from short topic to whole course
- social context from individual to group
- location from school and classroom to home or other centre, or whole school or community
- support from nil to organised and regular support
- structure of study topic from open-ended or unstructured to closed and heavily prescriptive
- technology from paper and print to electronic.

The variables interact. On the whole more support and structure is needed where the scale is large, the groups small or individuals, or the technology complex.

There are also complications with terminology. All the above can be counted as *individual* study, but *individualised* study should be confined to examples where the tasks are designed for work on an individual basis. *Independent* learning implies that the learner takes some responsibility for the learning, while *open* learning implies open access to learning and direction over it.

Characteristics

Because individual study is tailored to each individual, it has a number of features which affect its use of time.

FLEXIBILITY WITHIN THE DAY

It can occur at any point within the limits of the student's available time. So it is not limited to the slots of the school day. It can be stopped, started, extended or shortened almost instantly. It can be adjusted to fit the unfolding needs of the student. It may however have some fixed times relating to the programming of tutorials, broadcasts, access to resources etc.

FLEXIBILITY IN DURATION

Individual study time can be shortened or lengthened to fit the needs of a student. Well-managed individual study can lead to students spending less time — no longer any need to travel at the pace of the slowest — or more time where it is needed: in effect spending time more effectively. On the other hand it can lead to ill-used time. For some students and some topics efficient and well tried class teaching may be more effective than each student finding his or her own way through the material.

FLEXIBILITY IN SPACE

Individual study on the whole is not tied to group activities at set locations. It is only tied to a location if it needs special learning resources or if a tutor or other learners are involved. So it can occur off the school campus in any suitable location.

ENGAGED TIME
By definition individual study should be engaged time and so is likely
to lead to a higher proportion of ALT. However, individuals don't
always use unsupervised time productively. Much time can be wasted.
So again, good management is essential with effective support and
record-keeping if individual study is to be effective.

LOW COST
Individual study ought to be, and often is, cheap. It may require no
teacher. It may require no premises, other than the home. It could
lead to reduced transport or catering costs. The central expenditure
is on learning resources. A substantial shift to individual study could
have an appreciable effect on educational cost factors and create a
knock-on effect on the cost of school time. However, in practice
support needs for individual study can be substantial, and unless well
managed could even exceed the costs of class teaching.

Also costs cannot be divorced from benefits. Correspondence
courses for example have low costs but high drop-out and sometimes
poor results. When individual study is low cost and effective it is good
value.

ADDITIONAL BENEFITS
Individual study brings its own process, so that students improve study
skills and gain greater independence as learners. These are important
additional benefits to set against the time spent.

Individual study within the school day

The problem!
Time structures required for individual study conflict with those for
class-based instruction. The former needs flexibility — for students
particularly, but also for tutors — together with free access to learning
resources. The latter needs firm timetabling — a merry-go-round of
lessons, turning hour by hour and repeating week by week. It also
creates a compressed day, limiting access to resources.

So individual study cuts across the grain of the conventional school
day. That is why it is often necessary to resort to expedients to provide
it — and more important, why the more systematic approaches
towards individualised supported self study make slow progress.

This is a fundamental conflict.

Expedients
WITHIN THE CLASS
Individual study, i.e. where students are working at their own pace
on different material, has always occurred within the class, for example

for assignments, research and projects. There are some advantages. Supervision and teacher support is built in, and the activity relates to other class work. Students can be freed to work elsewhere in the school. In primary schools this system is used extensively and often very effectively, since the class-teacher has so much daily contact with the class and can exploit this flexibility. However a high pupil-teacher ratio is a limiting factor. In secondary schools the disadvantages are substantial. The pupil-teacher ratio in most classes allows the teacher to answer queries and give help but does not encourage the proper tutoring that is needed by older students. In theory the time is available for the teacher to tutor groups in turn; in practice the presence of the other students, the pressures of their demands and supervision makes it difficult for most teachers to provide this. Also the lesson framework may provide too much or too little time for the needs of the learner at any given moment.

WITHDRAWAL
Students can be withdrawn for study from their normal classes. This provides more flexibility over location and access to learning resources. However it can create supervision problems of students away from their class, and it does not free the class teacher to tutor them. So it is mainly suitable for short-term, directed but unsupported activities. It also implies foregoing the original activity, even though this has been 'paid for'.

STUDY PERIODS
US senior high schools have commonly provided study periods for students who were not occupied in class for a particular hour. However this created a large student mass in a study hall, and despite supervision did not provide an ideal environment. Also of course there was virtually no support. These arrangements have tended to disapppear in recent years.

The John Bentley School in Calne, Wiltshire, introduced similar arrangements in 1981 in two study halls for third to fifth year pupils. This was partly to allow curriculum flexibility, with some students spending more time on fewer subjects; and partly to provide time for homework and private study.

The arrangements worked satisfactorily and were well accepted. Pupils were well trained and so study hall conditions were good. Some pupils gained from the flexibility to restrict their class-time and increase informal study time. However there were limitations — no learning resources at hand, no tutorial support. Partly because of the spread of a core curriculum for all pupils the scheme was abolished in 1989.

Sixth form students in England however have always traditionally had private study periods. These really arise for timetable reasons, but are seen as beneficial providing they do not take too high a proportion of the week. They encourage independent learning and self pacing, and provide flexibility. They may partly explain why some of the leading supported self study developments have developed for this age-group.

AD HOC ARRANGEMENTS
These are sometimes used to squeeze individual study into empty corners of the day — lunch-hours, extra classes before or after school, or free time of students who have dropped a course or option for some reason. This gives flexibility of location and some time flexibility, but it does not in itself provide any time for tutoring. That has to come either from teachers' goodwill or from additional staffing.

Systematic approaches
ALTERNATIVE SCHOOLS
Many of the alternative schools have adopted a child-centred, individualised, student paced approach, often with modular or rhythmic scheduling, e.g. the Montessori, Peterson (Jenoplan) and Freinet schools. These seem to have succeeded because the ethos behind the school as a whole has determined the individual study arrangements. So the learning systems have sprung naturally from this philosophy.

THE DALTON PLAN: AN INDIVIDUAL EXAMPLE
Grafting an individual study system onto a more conventional school is more difficult, but still possible. An excellent example is the way the Dalton plan, introduced to Bryanston the Dorset public school in the 1930s, still flourishes. The system has altered over the years and in response to recent pressures now contains much more class teaching. However the curriculum is still centred on short assignments, typically of one or two weeks duration. Students attend conventional classes for approximately 60 – 80 per cent of the timetable, and work as they choose on their assignments for the remainder, either in supervised 'subject rooms' or in laboratories. In either case teachers are available to help (typically their teaching class contact time is about 50 – 60 per cent).

Students keep a detailed record of how their time is spent, including 'prep' (homework) and hobby sessions, and class teachers enter assignment grades. Each student has a tutor who discusses the record weekly and monitors overall progress.

Although the actual educational content is not heavily individualised, the system certainly is. It allows flexibility for class teachers to cancel classes if they wish, free students to work individually, tailor assignments to some extent to students' individual needs, help students individually in assignment time; it allows the student to pace herself or himself and to choose priorities; it creates slack for activities such as music lessons without disturbing formal classes; and it builds in a system for quality control. It seems to have led to students becoming well organised in their approach to learning. But it is demanding in space because of the extensive study rooms required, and would be more difficult to operate with a higher pupil-teacher ratio.

SUPPORTED SELF STUDY (SSS)

This has developed considerably in the UK since the formation of the NCET's supported self study project in the mid 1980s. Over 40 LEAs now have SSS developments, and a number have appointed full time organisers. In addition there is a large number of schools and colleges operating free-standing SSS schemes, assisted by a loose information network provided by NCET. National organisations like the correspondence colleges and National Extension College are now adapting their learning materials for self study use in schools. A range of publications about these developments are available from NCET, 3 Devonshire Street, London WIN 2BA.

Actual SSS schemes vary greatly in scale and type as well as in detail. Many begin small, but all share some common elements — particularly the stress on support and planned management, and the use of existing materials where they are suitable in preference to generation of new material. Support can range from direction and encouragement to full tutorial support. Management of resources, buildings, finance, non-teaching support, timetable and tutorial time is increasingly seen as a key element.

The motivation for introduction of SSS arises from two main sources. The first is logistics. The circumstances of small schools, minority subjects, retake of examination subjects and minority groups of pupils (the gifted, the retarded, pupils who enter the school late or are ill) have encouraged the adoption of SSS. The second is for educational reasons. SSS is increasingly seen as a valuable educational process, regardless of content or level, developing skills and attitudes which do not spring easily from classwork. Development has been encouraged by the growth of modular curricula, into which SSS fits easily; the new styles of learning and new learning objectives encouraged by the GCSE and TVEI; and the growth of new 'A' level provision, particularly the scheme being developed by Northumberland which is providing 'A' level courses in self study mode, and the Wessex modular 'A' levels where the modular elements (40 per cent) are delivered by SSS.

This growth of SSS has run up against the timetabling problems described earlier. Some schemes have resorted to the expedients described above. Others have built SSS into the school timetable by in effect offering 'SSS subjects' as well as 'classroom subjects', making SSS a required course ingredient, or encouraging SSS as a classroom activity. Indeed the main trend in the UK is to make SSS a mainstream school activity. However, this doesn't really solve the mismatch of SSS time needs with the conventional timetable. So even in schools where SSS operates it usually remains a fringe activity which affects deeply only a small minority of students. It may affect larger numbers but for only a small part of their total school year.

Managing time for individual study

Because of the difficulties described earlier of creating an extensive individual study scheme within a conventional school day, such schemes often 'begin small'. There is much to commend this as it allows natural evolution. However it may conceal the fact that while individual study on a small scale can be administered in an ad hoc way, an extensive scheme requires a systematic allocation of management time (just as a class based system requires time allocation beyond classroom teaching for both annual and day-to-day timetabling, student counselling, reporting to parents, teacher inservice training, etc).

SSS is at its most effective when there are regular tutorials where the tutor and a small group of students discuss the work in hand. The total teacher time required for weekly 20 to 25 minute tutorials for say 30 students in groups of five is broadly similar to that for teaching that number in a class (see Fig 9.1).

If SSS is provided in a class context, tutorials could be more frequent but shorter, possibly in larger groups to assist class management. The aggregate of time required would be similar. For tutoring outside a class situation, savings of staff time per pupil are only possible if group sizes increase or the frequency or length of tutorial falls. In both cases the quality of study is likely to be affected. It is not clear whether SSS requires more or less preparation and marking than class teaching. It is possible that after the initial preparation less preparation time is needed, but this may be offset by time spent looking after or working on materials. So SSS tutoring does increase a teacher's discretionary time, so that he or she can switch tutoring arrangements to free himself or herself for INSET, a meeting or other activity.

So time for tutoring has to be allocated on a broadly similar basis of teaching hours to class-teaching, but outside the class situation it does not necessarily need to be timetabled. Tutor and student can make their own arrangements. (However, this does face the school senior management team with the practical problem of ensuring that the time allocated is actually used for this purpose.)

TIME FOR STUDENTS

This is quite different. Only a small amount of time has to be allocated as tutorial time. For SSS outside the classroom the remainder can be left unspecified, to be determined by the needs of actual assignments.

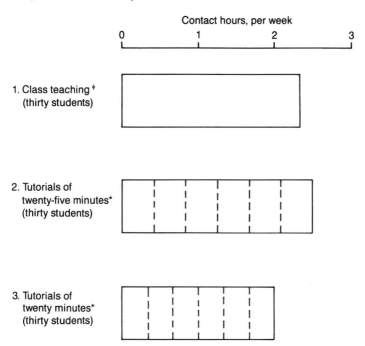

Figure 9.1 – Comparison of teacher contact time for class teaching and tutoring supported self study (out of class)

However there are two provisos. First, younger or less motivated students may not benefit from such an open arrangement. They may need indication of the duration or even the specific time and place of study within the school day. Second, there may be a need for time to be allocated so that there is access to learning resources and technology.

Overall however the change in provision of time for the student is striking. Figure 9.2 shows the possible reduction of timetabled time and expansion in flexible time. It is only for tutorial time that students need to function as groups.

TIME FOR RESOURCES MANAGEMENT

Individual study on any scale implies extended learning resources — reference books and materials, audio-visual material, computer programmes and databases, as well as access to computers and new educational technology. So there is likely to be a need for increased

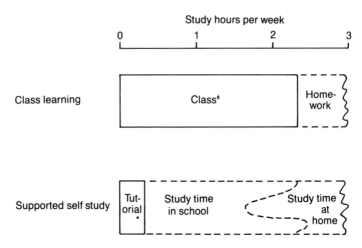

** Typical class allocation in England and Wales
(ten per cent of school week)

* One twenty minute tutorial per week

*Figure 9.2 – Comparison of student time allocation for class learning and supported
self study*

librarian, clerical or technician assistance. Moreover flexibility for
students may imply extended access, in lunch-hours or after school.

TIME FOR STUDENT GUIDANCE

Class based learning is controlled from the nerve centre of the
timetable. An extended scheme of individual study needs an equivalent
— a student guidance system — if resources are to be used effectively
and student underachievement avoided. There are several functions:

1. Counselling and curriculum negotiation to identify the student's needs,
   the learning possibilities and the best match between them.
2. Programming, to establish the necessary arrangements: courses of study,
   learning materials, access to further learning resources, tutorial and
   assessment arrangements.
3. Monitoring, to ensure that the students' progress is satisfactory and that
   arrangements are working properly.
4. Assessment, at intervals and/or on completion, to assess the standard
   achieved.
5. Overall management of the system.

All of these require time, often varying in quantity and sometimes
unpredictable. Some of this time is needed for tutors, in relation to
courses or subjects; some is needed for guidance of students in relation
to learning as a whole — a pastoral tutor (as in the earlier Bryanston

example, or possibly a counsellor as in North American high schools);
and some for the person responsible for general management. This
can be envisaged as follows:

	Subject Tutor	Pastoral Tutor	Overall Organiser
Counselling		*	
Programming	*	?	*
Monitoring	*	*	
Assessment	*		
Management			*

The quantities of time required for each activity for each pupil per
week are very small — often five minutes or less — but in an extensive
scheme the total implications are considerable.

One example of such a guidance system can be found in the Saturn
School of Tomorrow project, St. Paul, Minneapolis which opens with
grades 4 – 6 in 1989. This has made a central feature of a Personal
Growth Plan. It will use IT with purpose-designed software to produce
a plan unique to the learning needs of each student.

Individual study outside the school day
Homework
Homework provides invaluable time for schools, both in quantity and
quality. In quantity it can increase a student's total learning time by
50 per cent or more. In quality it has some of the merits of supported
self study — it is flexible, self-paced and encourages valued personal
qualities — although it lacks the best tutorial support that SSS can
supply. Its home setting has other qualities: it often involves parental
support and increases parental involvement in the child's education,
and it provides underrated opportunities for assignments to be related
to the home, family and neighbourhood. In the future homework can
include increasing opportunities for distance learning.

Homework also has its problems. It presents schools with difficulties
of support and monitoring. Because of its home setting it is affected
by socio-economic and family factors. Some homes have more books
and human expertise and better learning conditions than others.
Homework also has its opportunity costs — the best alternative use
of student's time. So it can squeeze out valuable social or leisure
activities.

In most countries homework is more a feature of secondary schools.
Often homework does not feature in the early primary years. Yet
primary school children often do a great deal of informal homework,
particularly reading, and much of their leisure involves learning

activities. So homework in the broadest sense can be equally valuable for primary schools, although it may not be seen as such.

Considering its value, homework in many schools is under-managed. It operates almost as an appendage to the main school day. Most secondary schools will have notional time allocations per subject per week, and often homework timetables to spread the load. But it is seldom analysed as critically as the curriculum or the timetable. Subject schemes of work generally do little more than assume its existence. There is seldom any attempt to identify the particular qualities of homework time or its value for individual subjects.

Yet homework offers opportunities to subjects like maths and foreign languages for practice; English and humanities, extended research or writing; science and CDT, consolidation of theory, writing up of activities and further research, so leaving more class time for practical activities. To almost all subjects it offers the opportunity to set assignments which involve students in relating their studies to their home and neighbourhood environment, often with parental involvement. Most school homework policies, where they exist in written form, are concerned more with frequency and quantity than with quality and type of activity.

Homework in primary schools tends to be more related to individual needs, but to some extent the same comments about lack of analysis are valid. Moreover much primary 'homework' comprises informal reading and learning activities, often involving parental support, and here some schools could give much more specific and direct guidance to parents.

Unfortunately homework is also under-researched, so there is not too much guidance on the most productive strategies. In a very useful article, Coulter (1979) surveyed the research and summarised some main findings. Homework seems to enhance school achievement particularly when:

1. It involves the cooperation and feedback of parents.
2. It is organised in a 'spiral' form, so that for example in maths it related not just to recent lessons but at times to previously learned material.
3. It is spread over a longer period of time than the period of the topic to which it is related.
4. It involves exploratory home exercises before a topic is introduced.

Findings 2 and 3 seem to be particularly important for average and below average students.

Coulter reports a Belgian study of over 2,000 secondary students where the maximum time spent was over twice the minimum. I suspect that in the UK average times for individual schools could vary by at least that degree, while variation between students could be much greater. Benjamin Bloom pointed out that the study of mathematics homework in the International Study of Educational Achievement

(Husen, 1967) showed that some students spent six times as much time on homework as others.

Rutter et al. (1979) showed that 'schools which set homework frequently and where there was some kind of check on whether staff did in fact set it, tended to have better outcomes than schools which make little use of homework'. The ILEA report 'Improving Secondary Schools' (Hargreaves 1984: 49) saw effective insistence on homework as important in setting standards, involving parents... and providing more time. 'If pupils receive appropriate homework and do it on a regular basis over a five year period, they will in effect be receiving the equivalent to at least one additional year of full-time education.'

Coulter suggests that most teachers do not take sufficient account of individual student differences in setting homework. It is normally set as a blanket assignment, even though it will be undertaken on an individual basis. He points to various possible areas for research, including the structuring of homework assignments, explanation to students of objectives, the follow-up and linking to classwork, and the support given to parents and family.

Coulter argues that homework time deserves the same detailed observation and analysis that has recently been devoted to the classroom. He divides teacher behaviour related to homework into four aspects:

In the initial classroom phase:

- motivating
- facilitating (including guidance over approaches and resources)
- structuring (including links with classwork, and provision for individuals or groups)

In the follow-up classroom phase:

- reacting (including feedback, praise, correction, reinforcement, follow-up)

Coulter also suggests the importance of individual student responses to both sets of teacher behaviour as a key factor in effective use of homework time, as well as more obvious factors such as student ability and home environment. His model is shown in Figure 9.3.

Summing up, homework is a very valuable element of school time which is not fully utilised in many schools in terms of quantity and particularly quality. Almost certainly a small amount of time spent in analysing its potential value and drawing up policies to exploit this would bring a quick return.

Supported self study at home

SSS only needs to occur at school when tutorials or specialised learning resources are required. So logically SSS schemes should push the remaining study needed towards the home, since this reduces the

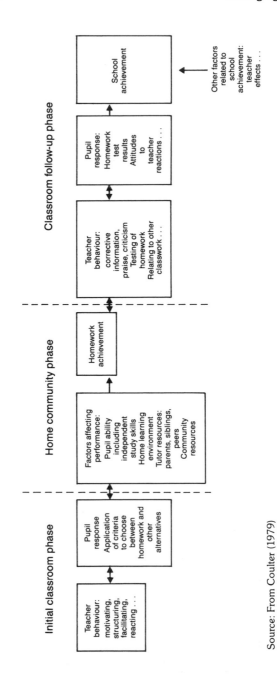

Source: From Coulter (1979)

Figure 9.3 – A model for homework research

pressure on the schools' space and supervision. However self study at home opens the motivation and application problems traditionally associated with homework, and removes opportunity for informal dialogue with other students or staff. So the choice is an open one, possibly to be tipped in favour of home study as distance learning and telecommunication links improve.

Distance learning

At present no one takes seriously the need to consider time for distance learning, simply because few schools or students use it to any extent (leaving aside remote rural areas in Australia and elsewhere). And so far the new technology has not changed the position — it remains peripheral to traditional schooling and has not yet created the powerful interactive and networked distance learning which in theory it could provide.

However sometime in the next generation the situation will change. The development of cheap but much more powerful portable computers, linked by telecommunication to data-bases worldwide, networked to the school and other learning centres and interacting with expert and other learning systems, together with narrowcasting by cable or satellite, must eventually make distance learning a very powerful alternative to traditional schooling.

The time implications will be twofold. First, the learner must have time available at home for distance learning similar to that needed for homework, but competing with it and with self study, leisure and personal needs. So some system for establishing priorities and planning home activity will be necessary. But more important, distance learning will threaten traditional school time structures.

Example

A parent buys an effective distance learning package which can teach French to a reasonable standard to a normal student who is beginning secondary school say in 150 hours, perhaps over the summer vacation. So the son or daughter already has competent French on starting school. What does he or she do? Study French which he or she has already attained for two or more hours each week for five years? Or drop out and find an alternative activity? And how can the hard acquired French be updated and used in an individual capacity?

The time management problems even for one student are considerable. And if others followed? (Primary schools could cope quite easily with this situation; many secondaries would find it much more difficult.)

So distance learning will, perhaps before long, need careful time-provision.

One-to-one coaching

The value of one-to-one coaching was discussed earlier in chapter six, page 119. It has considerable implications for individual study for those students who receive it: it tends to increase motivation and confidence, and improve study skills. At its best it often contains an important if not explicit counselling element.

Informal learning

Children probably learn as much out of school as inside it, from television, reading, hobbies and social or community interaction. Obviously this informal learning time cannot be managed by schools or governments, but it can be influenced. For example governments can influence the quality of children's television and can encourage the educational element in adult television. Schools with parents' support can influence students to modify viewing or reading habits, or to develop hobbies and social activities.

Given the importance of this informal learning area for students' total learning achievement, there is a case for schools and state or national governments to study it more seriously and develop strategies to maximise its benefits. The situation is similar to the under-exploited potential of homework discussed earlier.

Support for the individual learner

Learning as an individual is a lonely business. Learners often need to be helped, reassured and encouraged. So logically schools ought to provide some time for this purpose, particularly where individual as opposed to class study is extensive.

Overview guidance

Apart from help from individual teachers, students benefit considerably if they have one teacher who can take an overview of their learning and has continuity of contact with them. Potentially the pastoral tutor system common in many English and Welsh schools can be used for this, although in practice it is difficult to timetable extended one-to-one interviews on a regular pattern twice or more times a year for each student. Such contact can make use of records of achievement and student profiles, relating for example to skills attained or personal qualities, which can help to motivate students.

However the time implications of such one-to-one pastoral guidance are substantial. If one allows say 45 minutes per student, including subsequent documentation — probably a bare minimum — then a tutor seeing 25 students twice a year requires 38 hours tutorial time, equivalent to say eight school days or five full working days. Apart from the total time commitment, timetabling such review sessions without disrupting class time is difficult. (Southway Comprehensive School, Plymouth, has produced a useful mechanism. One day each week ends with a tutorial period, 2.05 – 3.00 p.m., but with tutors entitled to dismiss the main group at 2.30 and retain individuals for interviews or counselling.)

If individual study in the form of SSS, distance learning and personal coaching develops as an extensive element for many students, in addition to their homework commitments and informal learning activities, then development of an overview guidance system will be essential. For the present it may appear a luxury.

Peer tutoring

Tutoring of students by students increasingly appears to be a very cost-effective strategy for learning. However the time management issues are important.

Levin et al. (1984) assessed the cost effectiveness of four educational interventions in maths and reading in US primary schools: reducing class size, increasing the length of the school day, computer assisted instruction (CAI) and tutoring of students by peers and adult paraprofessionals. He found that both forms of tutoring, and particularly that by peers, was more effective (in student gains) than the other three interventions.

Levin then assessed cost effectiveness in terms of student gains per $100 spent per pupil. For mathematics, peer tutoring was almost four times better than CAI or reducing class size; for reading, marginally better than CAI but considerably superior to the others. (Peer tutoring was more cost effective than adult tutoring because its costs were much lower and its effects greater.) Levin comments 'the same cost outlay would provide almost four times as large an effect on reading and maths achievement through peer tutoring as through reducing class size or increasing instructional time'.

MIXED AGE TUTORING

The most common form of peer tutoring is mixed age, i.e. older students tutoring younger. Previously this has operated for specific reasons: in small primary schools (with antecedents in the monitorial system); as a form of service for sixth formers; and as an alternative activity for disaffected or less able senior students. However it is now arousing interest as an effective learning strategy with general application. Fitz-Gibbon (1988) surveys recent research and describes the main areas where mixed age tutoring has proved useful. He stresses that apart from the benefit to tutees of one-to-one support from their tutors, the tutors themselves register similar learning gains. He also points out that tutoring is a valuable process in its own right, developing general social and specific explaining and coaching skills, and bringing hidden curriculum benefits.

SAME AGE TUTORING

This occurs much less frequently, except for informal tutoring by classmates. In an organised form it seems to be less effective than mixed age tutoring.

TIME IMPLICATIONS OF PEER TUTORING

This is clearly the greatest problem. First, scheduling: if the tutoring is scheduled by withdrawing tutor or tutee from normal classes, they are losing provision which has been paid for. The alternative of pairing whole classes for tutoring is limited. The ideal is to arrange tutoring outside the main school day — and this really needs a new model of day such as that described in chapter twelve. Second, time is needed for training. For tutoring on a large scale a video could be used, but otherwise a teacher's time is needed. Third, time is needed to monitor the tutoring, service it with materials, and sort out problems.

* * * * *

The central argument of this chapter has been that because schools are organised around classes, they will find it difficult to accommodate extensive learning provision for individuals without adaptation of the school day. The provision for individual study that does occur, particularly in homework, is under-managed, and the possibilities for future developments in supported self study, distance learning, individual coaching and peer tutoring are underestimated. Schools will need to reconsider their use of time for these purposes.

10 Time for parents and the community

The time available

The parent body of any school and the community (however defined) which the school serves hold a large pool of time which can be tapped to serve the school and its students. The pool is vast in quantity. If we assume that for each teacher there are say thirty parents, and each parent could devote half an hour a day to involvement with the school or his or her children's education, then potentially we could think of 15 hours of donated time daily to supplement the work of each teacher. The pool in the broader community may be say seven times greater, potentially 100 donated hours daily per teacher. The pool is also rich in quality. The range of expertise, contacts and experience will be much broader than that within the staff of even a large school.

The human and time resources available to schools in this way can be clarified by examining more closely the parent and community groups. The parent body, although at first sight homogeneous, may in effect extend to other members of the family, former parents and even prospective parents. In fact it is a heterogeneous collection of individuals, often almost a representative sample of the broader community for that age-group. So the parent body has the same rich mix described for the community below. What unifies it is its concern for the children and their progress at school; its age range, commonly 25 – 50, and the energy linked to it; and the social contacts which bind it, centred upon the school itself. Primary schools are particularly good at uniting parents in this way.

The 'community' is much harder to identify. Some schools will serve clearly defined communities — villages, suburbs, estates — or a collection of smaller communities. Some will see themselves drawing from ethnic communities, others may draw pupils across a wider area (the new arrangements for open enrolment for schools in England and Wales will encourage this). But all schools unless sited in the remote countryside must be associated with a geographical location and so have potential links with the people that live there. So while what schools see as their community or communities will vary in cohesion and identity, in most cases the key relationship between school and community outlined below will exist.

This key relationship is in principle very simple:

1. The school will often be the largest 'thing' within its community.
2. The community, in its range of human, physical and financial resources, will be vastly greater than the school.
3. The school and its community exist in a symbiotic relationship, each with needs which the other can satisfy and with resources which the other needs.

These three elements can be detailed further:

1. Most schools, primary or secondary, will be the largest 'thing' in their geographical area or their community, however defined — the largest conglomeration of buildings, grounds, and people (both staff and students, and extending out into the parent body). They will often be the most powerful single agent in the community for educational, recreational, cultural, social (and sometimes economic) development. The main exceptions will be schools which have a college, large community centre or very large factory in their area.
2. The community will comprise many more people than the school, in a number of sets and subsets, overlapping, interacting and constantly changing — age groups, occupational groups, social and business groups or organisations, groups with special needs or problems. So the total resources of the community will be vast in comparison with the school: human skills, knowledge and experience; buildings, facilities and services; finance, of organisations and individuals; and the intangibles of interactions, contacts, communications, 'community spirit'. Also, with demographic change in Western Europe and North America, the proportion of the community within 'the grey brigade' — over fifty, active, affluent and better educated — will increase, an important potential source of support for schools.
3. The symbiotic relationship. The school needs time from the community to help its students and activities (as well as additional finance and improved physical resources); the community will have within it a vast range of needs, articulated or unstated, for know-how, assistance, activities, facilities, pump-priming....Each can give invaluable help to the other.

The parent body then, and the community, have vast pools of available time which could benefit the school. The problem of course is how to tap them. Some of the time will trickle in — parents will help their own children without invitation, parents or community members will help the school through casual contacts or requests. But if schools really wish to tap this great reservoir of time they need to manage the situation in a positive way. They need to allocate time for the enlisting of parent and community support and the management of volunteers. The more time they give, the more they are likely to receive.

Help to children at home

Almost all parents assist their children's education at home, whether consciously by listening to them read or helping with homework, or unconsciously by influencing their reading, television viewing, hobbies and activities, or through holidays and excursions. The research evidence both for the scale of this involvement and its importance is strong. Reports such as Plowden (1967) and Bullock (1975) stressed the importance of increasing it through improved parent-teacher cooperation. The NUT has produced a useful pamphlet about it (NUT, 1987).

Recently more specific arrangements have been tested. The use of diaries passing between parents and teachers to chart children's progress, with comments, has proved valuable. Tizard, T. (1982) reported on research in a London borough where children of two randomly chosen classes were regularly heard to read about three times per week on books sent by the class teacher by their parents, who also completed a record card. Virtually all parents took part. They were supported by briefing meetings and home visiting to hear the reading in progress two or three times per term. For one of the classes parents were coached in attitudes and methods. The children receiving this parental help made highly significant gains in reading attainment at all ability levels compared with those in two control classes or in two other classes which received additional reading practice in groups with an experienced teacher.

Subsidiary findings were that most parents were very pleased to be involved in this way. Children reading to parents who were non-literate or not fluent in English still benefited, and such parents were still willing to colloborate. Teachers found the scheme valuable and reported improved keenness and behaviour from the children involved.

Tizard concluded 'The findings of the present study suggest that staffing resources at present allocated by LEAs for remedial work in primary schools might be better employed, at least in part, in organising contact and colloboration between class teachers and parents...on specific practical teaching matters, and that this might prevent many children from falling behind with their reading in the first place.' So the question must be asked — what should schools be willing to give to develop the full potential help of parents in the home? The answer must surely be — rather more than many schools give now. It is a question of cost effectiveness. A little time for a home visitor aide could bring more benefit to children than the same finance invested in teacher classroom time.

Time for help at school
There are innumerable ways in which parents and members of the community can and do help in schools:

- as aides, hearing children read, helping in the classroom or in support of staff, or in the office

- doing things: making equipment, preparing materials, decorating rooms, improving premises
- accompanying school trips
- in the community curriculum, sharing experience or skills with classes, providing placements for community service or work experience.

Many schools are already very active in soliciting parental and to some extent community help. However on the whole the potential supply greatly exceeds the actual supply and even the demand.

If schools are serious in wishing to increase the help from parents and the community, they need first to identify and enrol the helpers, and then organise the management of this voluntary help.

Enlisting volunteers

Schools obviously find it easier to enlist parents as volunteers since they have direct access to them. Moreover parents see that it is to their children's interest for them to help the school. The smaller the school and the younger its pupils, the easier is this enlisting. It is much harder to reach the amorphous community. Yet the volunteers that are needed, however specialist the skills required, often *will* exist, somewhere — and be willing to help — if they can be found and asked. The problem seems to be that most volunteers respond to personal contact and invitation rather than general public invitations. So although appeals in newsletters or newspapers do have their value, the best contact is person-to-person.

So schools need social networks, starting with their own staff, parents, students and existing community people who use or visit the school, which can seek out potential volunteers. Such networks can grow naturally but they will be much stronger if time is found to cultivate them. They will also be fertilised by good public relations and by encouraging members of the community to use the school. But both of these too imply allocation of school management time.

Management of volunteers

The term 'management' may read oddly. However while a small number of volunteers can be looked after quite informally in say a small primary school, large numbers — and in a large school one ought to be thinking of over a hundred — pose different problems. Volunteers need briefing, introducing, settling in and monitoring to ensure they are treated well and are used effectively, and to reduce 'dropping off'; thanking for their services, and offering further involvement or association. So management isn't a bad term for the process. It needs the designation of a person whose job this is and who has time for it — a teacher, or a parent or community person (volunteer or part-time paid). Again, if schools are serious about mobilising parent and community time, then they have to take the management of it seriously.

Help in other ways

Parents and community members can and do devote time to schools in many other ways. Some of this may be programmed, such as belonging to a governing body or a PTA, or attending meetings for parents. Some may arise as a response, for example reading and discussing a newsletter or a student's report. Some of the time will be spent spontaneously — talking positively about the school, resisting or dealing with criticisms, talking to and influencing school students. Even time spent on campus may have positive value in giving the school a stronger adult image and deterring vandals.

Encouragement to people to spend time in these ways can only be indirect, through effective public relations and, equally important, the reality behind them. So schools which positively encourage full use of school premises and facilities (including items such as photocopiers), allocate redundant rooms for parents', community or playgroup use, organise community service for their students and respond positively to expressed needs will receive more community support. But again, all these actions by the school take time and will be more effective if part of a planned programme.

An interesting experiment in this area has been the COMPASS scheme operated by the Thomas Estley Community College, Leicestershire. Funding by the Community Education Development Centre (CEDC) in 1982 – 83 provided a part-time (eight, later 12 hours) organiser to mobilise community support. Various approaches were used:

- Letters to four hundred families   (four replies)
- Adverts in three local newspapers   (two replies)
- Posters in shops and libraries   (one reply)
- Door to door survey   (sixty volunteers)

A register was compiled of volunteers and their skills, which was then used by teachers to enrich the curriculum. Although the initial funding lapsed, once started the register was continued as the responsibility of a community tutor. In 1988 it held over a hundred names, some coming in regularly, others visiting the school on request once or twice a year.

The main lessons of the project seem to be that the door-to-door approach, although time consuming, is crucial for mobilising volunteers; their induction and training is important and under-rated; and it takes time for teachers to appreciate the full potential of volunteers and to think imaginatively of how they can be used. Once the tradition is established, door-to-door visiting is no longer necessary and the scheme has continued strongly with some staff input but little other cost. Further information can be obtained from the school, or from CEDC, Briton Road, Coventry. A useful booklet on volunteer helpers in schools has been produced by the Home and School Council (Bond, 1974).

* * * * *

The central argument of this chapter then is that parents and communities have much more time to offer than schools currently realise or even dream of. But if this disposable time is to be fully tapped, a school first needs to be willing to spend time in enlisting and managing help. But if the school is too calculating, only spending time where it can see a return, in the long run it will gain less than if it spends time altruistically. Communities are quick to sense when they are exploited and only valued for what they can provide.

So the irony is that good community education and parent/community relations are an excellent investment in terms of the time that can accrue to the school; but only the best investment if they are not treated as such.

11 Personal time management

The same problems in the use of time that face a school also confront its managers and teachers. Time is a scarce, limited resource, seldom sufficient for the tasks to be done. Its use is seldom planned. Usually personal time management just evolves, a response to custom, regulations and pressures. Time use for the individual, as for the school, needs analysis and planning.

Problems of personal time management

In general

Almost all managers and professional workers complain of the shortage of time. Early in the evolution of management studies, time management was seen as important. It strikes right to the heart of the management role. What should the manager be doing? What are the objectives and priorities? How can they best be achieved? It needs key managerial skills — planning, delegating, organising, evaluating. And it links uncomfortably to the manager's own style and personality.

In recent years time management has become even more important. The growing complexity of organisations, the acceleration of activity and the growth of stress have all contributed. So business schools now run short courses on time management, and there are a number of specialist books and training materials. Much of this can be applied to schools. John Adair's recent book (1987) is particularly helpful. Although not written for teachers, much of his practical advice is applicable. There are however some specific school problems which can be identified.

In schools

The school workplace is unusual in that virtually all the professionals work on the shop floor. The pressure and priority of the teaching commitment makes effective use of management time difficult. It is as if in a factory the managers, often even the managing director, spent most or some of their time actually working at their lathes. This classroom commitment not only takes up time but also fragments the time remaining.

Schools have their own rhythms which can be unhelpful. The normal day is fractured into relatively short sessions, often one and a quarter to one and a half hours long, divided by breaks, which make sustained management activity difficult. The day itself is short compared with the world of commerce, and during most of it staff are tied to their classrooms, so that the time available for discussion and meetings is limited. In England an opening assembly often ties managers at an important time of the day. The annual rhythm of terms and holidays also has an effect. Manager activity is less effective in the first and last few days or so of each term. On the other hand school holidays although poor for some management activities are excellent for others, for which they can provide flexibility of time and freedom from distractions.

Schools are people-centred organisations. A relatively small staff is involved mainly with personal interactions, staff-pupils-parents-others. This inevitable priority for people matters, mainly of a day to day nature, tends to squeeze out longer term planning.

Finally, schools are experiencing increasing time pressures like their business counterparts but often without their ability to hire extra staff to deal with it. Some of the pressure is self induced. A good head or school will try a new activity, and if it is successful probably retain it. This works like a ratchet, increasing the management work load by one notch. Seldom do managers look at the whole to see if pressure can be released elsewhere. A good example of this 'ratchet law' has been the growth of meetings with parents — rare in the 1950s, universal and frequent today.

Much of the current pressure comes from outside — from new curricula, educational theories, concern with standards, new methods and learning approaches, new technology, new legislation, local management of schools, as well as community education. In England and Wales such pressure is now acute — schools are experiencing more change than at any previous time. Yet those involved in managing or teaching have no more time available. So time management really matters.

Time for managers

By managers I am thinking of headteachers, deputies and other senior staff, heads of departments, curriculum coordinators, heads of house and year, heads of community education and other staff with a specific management role, e.g. in charge of careers guidance or learning resources, as well as some non-teaching staff such as bursars. (In addition all teachers have an important classroom management role but that is dealt with in a later section.)

Many of the suggestions below may seem obvious to experienced managers but are included to assist those who are building their careers.

Analysis

COLLECTING DATA

If as a manager you are unhappy about your time management and seriously wish to do something about it, the first step is to assess the present position. That means keeping a log for a week of how time is spent. It is essential to make an actual log — memory can be very deceptive.

A simple system is to prepare sheets, perhaps headed as in Table 11.1.

Fill in columns 1 – 2 as you go if you can. It's a nuisance but is worthwhile. As long as columns 1 and 2 are complete, 3 and 4 can be finished at the end of the day or week. For column 4 you need to decide on a classification. An example shown in Table 11.1 would be:

A = assembly; T = teaching; PR = preparation; MA = marking; PH = phoning; W = writing; M = monitoring and touring school; TS = talking with individual staff; TP = talking with individual pupils; D = discipline; C = committee meetings; R = relaxation/ recreation, and so on.

You can keep time logs in other forms, as suggested by Craig (1987: 56) or Dean (1987: 220), or invent your own.

USING THIS DATA

At the end of the seven days, tot up the time for each classification and work out its percentage of the total time spent on school activity.

Table 11.1   An example of a time log

1. Time	2. Activity	3. Time spent on activity	4. Classification of activity*		
8.40	Prepared for day	10	PR	T	A
8.50	Saw Mr Brown and Mr Smith	10	TS	W	S/O
9.00	Assembly	20	A	T	T
9.20	Around School	15	M	T	A
9.35	Drafting school day report	15	W	N	P
9.50	Spoke to Tony Bloggs	15	D	T	A
10.05	Continued report	10	W	N	P
10.15	Phone call from Education Office	5	PH	M	O

Note: * for codes etc. see text. The second and third columns are optional extras, explained in text.

Or you may prefer to build up a simple bar chart. Questions then arise:

1.   Is this a typical week?
      Of course it won't be — but is it close enough for the data
      to be useful? If it's quite untypical you may wish to log another
      week.
2.   Look in more detail at the percentages. Do some seem high or
      low? Are there jobs which you should have done in the week,
      and didn't?
3.   Look again at the activities. You could regroup or reclassify
      them. For example, try T = today's business; W = this week's
      (i.e. preparing for an event later this week); M = this month's;
      Y = this academic year's; N = next academic year's business.
      Or you could try P = planning; O = organising; T = teaching;
      A = administration and day to day matters; E = monitoring
      and evaluation; S = staff and personnel matters, etc. (The
      example in Table 11.1 shows both approaches in the second
      and third sub columns of column 4).
4.   Is the balance and range of activities right?
      You can't answer this question unless you have a clear idea
      of your objectives. What is your 'core mission'? Or, a term I find
      more helpful, what are your 'key tasks'? Sometimes job
      descriptions are undiscriminating and just list a number of
      objectives and tasks. Which are your key ones — that small
      number of tasks which if you do them well, you will do your
      job well? Once you have identified them, you can ask the most
      important question...
5.   Did I spend enough time on my key tasks?
      The important thing here is not just to look at the proportion
      of the week spent on key tasks, but also at the balance between
      one type of activity and another. Most managers find the
      demands of the present squeeze out the needs of the future.
      Time logs usually show too much time on administration and
      day-to-day affairs, too little on the strategic management
      functions of long term planning and organisation, team-building
      and evaluation. But it's important not to swing completely and
      sacrifice the present for the future. A colleague of mine used
      to remind me 'The heel of the squire dungs the sod'! In other
      words, the tread of the headteacher prowling the school has its
      own value. Too much time cooped in the office on strategic
      planning can be counter productive. So the right balance is hard
      to find, but important.
6.   What about your *annual* work pattern?
      Obviously you can't log a whole year, but you could think
      your school year through, month by month, and identify the

peaks and troughs and the cycle of different tasks. You could make a simple analysis of this using questions 2 – 5 again.

7. What about long-term investment — reflection and evaluation, training, research and development?

Do you manage to find enough time in the year to reflect on what you are doing and evaluate it?

Do you receive enough training for your job? IBM provides its managers with 20 days training a year. How many do you receive? – and should you receive? And how can this be fitted in without squeezing out time from your other tasks?

And what about R & D? The term isn't even used in education, but it should be. Any industry should be concerned about applying research. Do you set aside any time for serious educational reading, or for simple applied research? Could you? And if so, how could you share ideas with your colleagues?

8. Finally, can you foresee any new tasks which will need to be taken on? A good example here is the devolution of financial and other responsibilities to English and Welsh secondary and larger primary schools as a result of the 1988 Education Reform Act. Whatever else this may imply, it certainly means an extra task for some people in the school. If you are going to be involved, how will this extra commitment affect your weekly and annual use of time?

This analysis stage is crucial. The better the analysis, the more likelihood of improved time management. Possibly it could be linked to an appraisal process, and in this case the comments of an appraiser could be valuable. If not, it would still be useful to discuss it with a colleague.

Action

Probably you have found that you have insufficient time to cover your key tasks effectively. There are only three things you can do:

1. Increase the time available.
2. Decrease the work to be done.
3. Make more effective use of the time that you have.

INCREASE THE TOTAL TIME AVAILABLE

This may not be as difficult as it sounds. You may possibly have pockets of time which could reasonably be made available — at odd times of the week or in the school holiday periods. It's worth asking the question — but with care for the consequences! You might be able to increase the total time available for the team with which you work. It may be possible to increase non-teaching support staff time.

Some staff with management responsibilities may be able to mobilise

voluntary help, from parents or people in the community —
particularly in primary schools and other schools close to their
communities. It may be possible to use senior students for routine
chores. It may also be possible to use student-teachers to assist in
particular tasks — a good example would be in management of careers
guidance or learning resources — or to enlist help from teachers whose
normal load is lightened by a student teacher.

At the end of the day there may be no more time available, but
it is worth thinking through all the possibilities, however wild they
appear at first.

REDUCE THE WORK TO BE DONE
Delay it, ditch it, delegate it or do it!

Delaying tasks isn't easy if you are an energetic manager. But it
may be realistic. Obviously you can't delay regular weekly or annual
tasks, but you can delay an innovation. The problem is that you may
find this more interesting than routine tasks and be reluctant to defer
it — or you may find it disturbing and be over-eager to postpone it!
Innovations are much more time consuming the first time round, much
less if they are repeated regularly. So good candidates for deferral
will be innovations of a one-off variety. But it's obviously a matter of
judgement, since delay may simply build up pressure next year.

Ditching tasks may be easier. Are there jobs you do which do not
need to be done, or do not need to be done in this way or this detail?
Go back to your time log and ask 'What would happen if I did not
do this task?' Is it essential that you take, or attend, school assembly,
for example? What would be lost? And how valuable in practice would
be the time gained? And so on.

The prime candidate for ditching is classroom teaching. In most
countries headteachers do not teach. In some other countries they
do — though even here the position is patchy. In England and Wales
heads of small primary schools normally have a class. In larger primary
schools the head will commonly have no class commitment, although
his or her deputy will have a class and so often has little administrative
time. In most secondary schools heads teach, sometimes to a
considerable extent. (The volume of teaching does not seem closely
related to the size of school.)

Any headteacher with time management problems and a classroom
commitment has to ask whether the latter can be justified. Is it a key
task? It may be argued that it establishes credibility, strengthens staff
morale, brings the head into contact with children and parents. But
it is still hard to argue that it is a key task and that it does not conflict
with effective achievement of the real key tasks.

This issue was brought home to me after fifteen years of headship
with an appreciable teaching commitment in a large school. The school

suddenly acquired both a second site and community education activities, and I decided reluctantly that I would give up all teaching. I found overnight that I became infinitely more effective (or at least, less ineffective). I have to live with the knowledge that I could have done my job much better if I had taken this step earlier. So if you are a headteacher with a teaching commitment, I suggest you drop it for one year. You should find that you have more time to plan, to manage...and to think. Also your staff will respect you more for that than for trying to run the business from the shop floor.

Teachers with a management commitment other than heads are in a different position. They will normally have a substantial teaching load, and dropping it may not be an option. But there may be other options. It may be possible to reduce it, or alter it so that it is less demanding in terms of preparation or marking. There are difficult issues to face here. A school manager does not *ipso facto* require time in school. He or she will be paid more and so can be expected to devote more time at home or in holidays. However it is likely that some management tasks have to be done in school, and this relief may then be essential.

Delegation is a more difficult option, although with greater potential in many schools. It certainly isn't off-loading unpleasant tasks onto someone else. It can and should often be a planned decision to extend a subordinate's responsibilities, enabling him or her to grow as a person, develop new skills and experience and often obtain more satisfaction. Mortimore et al. (1988) found that in ILEA primary schools a substantial proportion of deputy heads desired greater involvement in the school, and that this involvement was one of the key factors identified for school effectiveness. But delegation can go far beyond deputies. Many younger teachers are ready for it, and older teachers can sometimes be revitalised by it. Delegation is a complex business however. It needs considerable thought in defining roles and responsibilities. For example, it is important to distinguish between delegation of decisions which (a) need no report-back (b) need report-back or (c) need referral to you before final decision. And initially it may actually take more time, not less.

MAKING MORE EFFECTIVE USE OF THE TIME AVAILABLE

Some people are naturally expeditious and methodical. Many of us aren't, and changing the habits of a lifetime isn't easy. There are three main areas where gains can be achieved: planning the use of your time and managing your office and meetings more efficiently.

Planning the use of your time

Establishing priorities for your work is crucial. The main priorities will be what is urgent and what is important. The two often conflict.

Today's business is always urgent, next year's planning never is. So today tends to drive out tomorrow. This takes us to the problem often exposed by time logs, where key strategic tasks are starved of time by day to day business. So somehow you need to establish priorities both for today's business and for future planning. This may mean that some of today's business has to be cut or skimped.

So, you need to plan your time. The ideal is to have an outline plan for the week, perhaps sketched out over the weekend with the aid of your diary. It only need take five or ten minutes. You certainly need a plan for the day, ideally drafted the evening before. This enables you to turn over some of the business in your mind before you reach school and to start immediately you arrive. If you leave planning the day to your arrival, inevitably an interruption will disturb it.

Obviously planning involves a diary or filofax and also perhaps a wallchart. You will need to say no to certain engagements or jobs — not always easy. You may find it useful to block in periods for your own work which are not normally to be used for other engagements, even though it isn't always possible to protect them. Visits out of school, to other schools or the education office, etc. can consume a lot of time. You may wish to weigh up their value.

Longer term planning is easier. A useful device is a prompt file, kept by your secretary or yourself if you don't have one. The file can have divisions for each month, this year and next year. All recurring events can have simple prompt sheets for action needed.

Example

An annual parents meeting in July might need three prompt sheets:

May: Advise parents and governors of annual meeting.
June: Prepare reports for annual meeting.
July: Organise public meeting.

The prompts ensure that entries are made in appropriate diaries, and when each month is over they can be carried forward to the next year. This does cut out management by astonishment. Events which are not annual can be planned through a diary, by entering not just the date of the event but also dates for prior action.

However good your plans, they will be blown aside by interruptions, overruns and emergencies. But you can do something to reduce these. If you are a headteacher you may be able to control interruptions as suggested in the next section. Overruns can be reduced if you can shorten telephone conversations or interviews without being abrupt or inconsiderate. For emergencies it's best to think over the main types that occur — say pupil theft or timetable hiccups — and then consider whether these could be prevented or reduced, or whether they could reasonably be routed elsewhere.

It is a mistake to be too clinical about time management. As a manager you do need to be accessible, even if by appointment. Unplanned events and interruptions, or time consuming visits out of school, can bring contacts and ideas which may be a valuable long-term investment. Striking the right balance in using your time is never easy. The important thing is that you plan your time, not just make it available.

If you tend to procrastinate, this may be because you do not establish clear priorities and a firm plan. But it may suggest that you lack confidence and need additional training or support.

Efficient office management

Most teachers have no training or experience in office organisation, so it may be worth your visiting a local firm to see how their office is organised. But you can probably think out improvements for yourself.

First, premises. Is the layout of your office and any supporting rooms as efficient as possible? What do you mainly want to use the space for? Is the furniture suitable? Is the position of phone, files, and office materials convenient? Do you have adequate privacy? (Of course it may not be possible to improve arrangements, but it's surprising how often people accept an unsatisfactory layout just because they are used to it.) The same applies to your secretary's room — saving time for her saves time for you.

Second, equipment like phones with connections, extensions and intercom, wordprocessor, micro-computer, filing. Are improvements possible? Again, think first of what you, or your secretary, need to *do*. Then it is easier to see whether different equipment could save you time.

Third, staff. Could you help your secretary or other colleague to make better use of time — by improving conditions? Altering working hours? Providing training? Could your secretary become more of a personal assistant?

Fourth, procedures. What are the current procedures? House style for correspondence, for example, could a more time saving format be adopted? How about opening, screening and distributing mail? Filing and records? Other office procedures? Many procedures aren't recognised as such and are really just habits. They may be worth re-examining.

Finally, interviews and appointments. Do staff and children have open access? If headteachers allow this they may find that interruptions make work on long-term tasks difficult. It may be quite reasonable to say to staff that you wish to plan your time better and would prefer interviews by appointment, but will accept these without if necessary. Arrangements for children's access can also be made. One doesn't have to be remote and inaccessible to be more efficient. However, deputies and other managers will find this sort of screening much more difficult and perhaps undesirable.

Meetings
Encounters with others can range from casual corridor chat (often the most productive kind of meeting), one-to-one interviews, informal small meetings to formal committees. Each of these can be very effective time wasters. If you are in control of a meeting you need to decide what its main purpose is and plan the agenda so that important items are considered early. You should budget time for each agenda item and try to keep to this. Ideally work should be done in advance for meetings, on paper or at least in thought. For the latter, questions need to go on the agenda or an attached paper. Presentation of minutes is also important. There is much to be said for including a 'person to take action' column.

Evaluation
If you take up some of the suggestions for analysing your use of time and acting to improve it, it is also important to evaluate the success of your efforts. You could make an entry in your diary say six months ahead to check what effect, if any, your action has had. Ideally log another week and compare with the original. If you now feel you make better use of your time, is further improvement possible? If not, why did you fail? Could improvements be made this time?

The foregoing is only an outline of possible action which can be taken to improve your effective use of time. For further practical ideas I would strongly recommend you to read one of the specialist books on time management. John Adair (1987) has some very useful practical chapters on planning the day, office management, handling meetings and the technicalities of delegation. Although not written specifically for schools much of what he suggests is useful. Joan Dean (1987) has some brief but wise advice for primary heads (of interest to others) on identifying main tasks and matching to personal strengths, working with a deputy head, interruptions and office efficiency. Ian Craig (1987: 67) has a useful bibliography. A list of publications and training materials, including some specific to schools, can be produced from the database of the National Development Centre for School Management Training, 35 Berkeley Square, Bristol.

Time for classroom teachers
The same rules apply for classroom teachers as for school managers. Time is a scarce and limited resource, and planned effective

management of it is still important. The same kind of analysis and action can be useful.

Analysis

COLLECTING DATA

The classroom teacher's professional time is spent as much outside the classroom as within it. The two aspects are quite distinct and it may be desirable to work on one and not the other.

Time outside the classroom can be analysed with the same type of log as in Table 11.1. Obviously your classification of activities will be different and could include: marking; lesson and materials preparation; background reading; out-of-school activities; administration; supervision, pastoral tutorial activities; discussion with staff/parents/children; meetings; INSET, etc. The same totting of time for each code and production of percentages or bar charts for the seven days will be useful.

Analysing time within the classroom is much more difficult. Here the teacher is too engaged to keep a log, and research shows that memory of time allocation is treacherous. A good solution is to persuade a colleague, student teacher, or other adult to act as an observer. This may seem threatening but is very worthwhile. Even if they can only observe a couple of hours, some data is still better than none.

You may prefer to design your own instrument for classroom analysis. It should then meet your own needs. A good source of ideas would be Wragg (1987) which discusses in a practical way various approaches to classroom observation for the purpose of teacher appraisal. A useful US example of a classroom log is given in the appendix of 'Time on Task' (American Association of School Administrators, 1982).

There are also good research examples of classroom observation which you may like to look at before you start, although you probably won't want to use anything so elaborate. Hilsum & Cane (1971) and Hilsum & Strong (1978) analysed the teacher's day in English primary and secondary schools. Within classroom time they used a refined breakdown as follows:

- lesson instruction
- organising pupils for work
- supervision (including assemblies)
- physical chores (e.g. sharpening tools, preparing paper)
- clerical tasks
- consultation with other staff
- lesson planning and marking
- pastoral work
- discipline

- emergencies and interruptions
- notices and messages

Mortimore et al. (1988) used an approach more linked to the learning process in primary schools (for example, assessing the amount of teacher communication with (a) the whole class (b) groups as groups (c) individuals (even if working in a group), and the proportion of this communication which was related to the work in hand, and to other matters). Research instruments can also be found in Galton, Simon & Croll (1980 : 171). These are too complex for classroom teachers to use easily, but give ideas, along with other suggestions for monitoring classroom practice.

Whatever system you use however, you still need to tot up the totals and present them in percentage or bar chart form. You might find it interesting to compare your findings with some of the data in the research mentioned above.

USING THE DATA

Out of class data can be approached with the same eight questions used for managers earlier in this chapter. Question four needs a little re-stating. It is helpful to put the 'core mission' for a classroom teacher in a child-centred form, for example 'assist students to learn effectively', even though key tasks may still include lesson preparation etc.

For question five, the balance of time is still important across the range of tasks. Too much marking means too little preparation, and vice versa. But the balance between present and future is also still important. Classroom teaching involves more day to day activity than a management role, but it has an important management element: planning and organising classroom work, future as well as present. So again it is important that this longer view does not get squeezed out.

For question seven, the long term investment of reflection and evaluation, training and research and development are still important. They too are prone to being squeezed out. For question eight, classroom teachers should consider any new pressures. For example, in England and Wales the National Curriculum and its assessment are likely to prove very time consuming, along with other aspects of the 1988 Education Act.

For classroom time these questions aren't appropriate, although you can still examine the range and balance of activities. It would be more helpful to go back to some of the concepts outlined earlier in the book, particularly in chapters one and eight, or to relate your analysis to the recent research on school effectiveness.

Action

For both out of class and classroom time the same three options are available.

INCREASE THE TOTAL TIME AVAILABLE

There may be a range of possibilities. First, there may be a case for improving the non-teaching support provided by the school, whether classroom aides, clerical, technical, etc. But beyond that there is scope in most schools for more volunteer support. First, pupils are not always used sufficiently although they are often keen to accept responsibility. Second, student-teachers. They are not always present or free to help, but when available can be very helpful for specific tasks and can benefit from them. In one English primary school a team of student teachers from a college of education, with their tutors, regularly take over the school for a week each year. It is excellent training for the students, a lively change for the children and frees the staff for a week's curriculum development. Most promising though are parents and community volunteers. There are problems with using volunteers, but they can be overcome, as suggested in the last chapter, and are much less than the problems of doing without. Volunteers are a much under used resource.

REDUCE THE WORK TO BE DONE

The same advice from the earlier section holds. It is worth examining the tasks you do, whether outside or inside the classroom, to see whether any do not need to be done in this way or this detail — or at all. And if there are acute time pressures, then it may be possible to delay certain activities. Again, it is one-off innovations which may be the best candidates.

MAKING MORE EFFECTIVE USE OF THE TIME AVAILABLE

Planning use of your time

Outside the classroom many of the earlier comments are still relevant — establishing priorities and planning use of time over the year and for the week, not just making it available.

Efficient resource management

First, premises. It is well worth looking at your classroom with a critical eye — yet again. It is so easy to accept the familiar. And what about the place where you do out of classroom work — a corner of the staffroom (many schools' staffrooms are very inefficient workplaces) — or your room at home?

Second, equipment. Are improvements possible? Would a word processor or a better photocopier improve your production of classroom materials? Again the best way is to think of the jobs that you do — and then of the best equipment to do them.

Third, staff. If you are supported by any non-teaching staff, is there any way in which you, or the school, could help them to be more effective?

The foregoing remarks may seem obvious, but most people do become conditioned to their surroundings. So a systematic item by item review may well reveal new possibilities for using time more effectively. Doing this with a colleague is more likely to throw up new ideas.

Evaluation

Will you make a date in a few months time to check the effect of any changes you have made?

Time pools

Time management occurs within the pool of time which an individual manager or teacher is prepared to devote to his or her job. The pool is not fixed in size. It may well swell if the teacher is interested or challenged and if his or her morale is high, shrink if the opposite. But at any one moment there is a finite amount of time which a teacher is prepared to give. The teacher may not recognise this explicitly, but at a certain point when he or she feels that no more personal time should be given to the job, the edge of the pool has been reached. So it is the task of school management to create a climate in which teachers feel willing to enlarge their time pool, and so expand the total time resource available for the school.

Conditions of service

A teacher's time management occurs also within the framework of conditions of service. Most states require a minimum number of teaching and other professional days, with a certain amount of time at school per day and often additional obligations.

An interesting development has recently occurred in England and Wales. Previously there were only skeletal regulations establishing the number and minimum length of school days and little else. However, a protracted industrial dispute led to the Secretary of State imposing new conditions of service in 1987. These require that a teacher 'shall be available for work for 195 days in any year, of which 190 days shall be days on which he may be required to teach pupils'. He or she shall be available for teaching and other professional duties as directed by the headteacher for 1,265 hours in any academic year. This directed time, where time and place is specified, includes: attendance before or after school; teaching; registration; assemblies and movement; supervision during and at the beginning and end of the day; staff development and parents' meetings; and some other directed activities.

It has brought advantages in the management of school time as a whole. It has clarified the teacher's commitment, solved the vexed question of teacher attendance at staff and parents meetings, and strengthened supervisory duties. The five non-teaching days have provided time for inservice training and curriculum development, etc.

However, apart from transitional problems it is creating some less desirable effects. Teachers are now more time conscious. Many schools produce quite complicated balance sheets to show where the 1,265 hours have gone, and although some time is usually held in reserve, problems arise. There can be almost theological disputes over the definition of directed and non-directed time, and particular difficulties over out of school activities at weekends and in holidays and residential activities. Because these are generally not accepted as directed time they are being squeezed out in some schools. More intangibly, 1,265 hours is a fixed quantity which may tend to make each teacher's idea of his or her time pool more rigid. It may also lead headteachers to take up more of the 1,265 hours than are absolutely needed, for example in required before or after school attendance or extra meetings which aren't really necessary. This will drain a teacher's time pool unnecessarily.

Probably a professional, unspecified trusting relationship is the ideal. But when it breaks down under industrial relations pressures, specified conditions of service may be an improvement but with hidden adverse features which take some time to work out.

Time for students

There has been relatively little research into the 'total educational time' of students. It is easy to look at a student's daily timetable — though rather harder to know what it means in terms of engaged and academic learning time — and harder still to have any idea of the impact of homework, out-of-school activities, leisure, television and other learning activities. Yet a central argument of this book is that schools should look at the total learning time used by each student. The time provided by school is limited, and perhaps only 50 per cent of the whole; but the remainder can be encouraged and developed by means suggested in chapters six and nine.

At present we can really only speculate about students' total educational time, and hope that research provides insight in the future. It would be very difficult to construct a proper sample of students, but not too difficult to have all-day time logs kept by a few.

12 School time in the future

This chapter brings together many of the ideas developed earlier and examines likely changes in the future use of school time. First we need to consider the kind of educational environment which is likely to exist. So, an excursion into futurology...

What kind of future for education?

The general scenario

Education is the last major industry yet to have an industrial revolution. To be more accurate, schools do use an industrial model of organisation but mainly retain pre-industrial technology. So the key question is, will this situation broadly continue, or will the industry undergo the kind of revolution which has affected areas such as printing, home entertainment, financial services and retailing?

It seems clear that the developed world is in the midst of massive system change, comparable in complexity and scale to the industrial revolution and often called 'The Third Wave', the 'Post-Industrial Revolution' or the 'Information Society'. At its heart is the new electronic technology, but radiating from it are massive technological, economic, industrial and social changes.

The question then is how far schools will be affected by the information society and in what ways. It seems clear that two separate forces will operate.

NEW DEMANDS

First, the effect of socio-economic changes. Changes in industry and commerce and in society as a whole will make new educational demands. Leading futurologists have already speculated on these. Alvin Toffler (1981: 394) suggests that qualities such as initiative and resourcefulness, ability to learn, ability to work in teams and participate in a community and in a more direct democracy, awareness of how our increasingly complex society operates, together with an all round range of practical, intellectual and social skills, will be needed. He predicts 'More learning will occur outside, rather than inside, the classroom...Instead of rigid age segregation, young and old will mingle.

Education will become more interspersed and interwoven with work, and more spread out over a lifetime.'

Tom Stonier (1983) suggests that:

> The most important input to modern productive systems is no longer land, labour or capital — nor raw materials or energy. The most important input is 'know-how'...Education adds value to people. And people are the most valuable resource a country or a company possesses.

He sees education as preparing the mind for further training life-long and fostering 'information handling techniques, entrepreneurship and general self reliance. It's not *what you know* but *how fast you can find out* that will count in a computer-run information environment where information overload will be the rule rather than the exception.' Also, education must go beyond teaching children how to earn a living. 'Equally important is learning how to live. What befits us as a sound economy, if we end up with a neurotic citizenry? The best way to guard against future shock is with an education system geared up for change.'

So economic and social changes outside schools are likely to affect substantially the demands on schools and so the process and content of learning within them.

NEW TECHNOLOGY

This will operate alongside the new educational demands generated by socio-economic change. The information society seems likely to transform the technology and with it the organisation of education itself. For if the information society is driven by the development of new electronic technology for the transfer, storage and retrieval of information and for communication, and if education is largely (but not solely) concerned with information and communication, then it is difficult to believe that education will not eventually be transformed, just like other information and communication industries.

> The implications of the 'accelerative thrust of technology' are probably more far reaching for education systems than for any other organised aspect of society, for two reasons. First electronic technology is accelerating the processing of information. Knowledge and facts are being exchanged so rapidly that this is increasing the development of new knowledge. Ideas are outdated more quickly. Secondly, universal access to television, microcomputer links, video tapes and computerized learning systems reduces the dependence upon the teacher to impart knowledge.
>
> (Handy & Aitken, 1986: 111)

I have suggested elsewhere (Knight 1986) that the main thrust of the new technology will be to individualise education, tailoring it to the needs of each student. So it will no longer be necessary for education to be age-related or status related (school age or adult, full time or part time). It will not need to be school based — students can learn at home, at other centres or through a wider network. And education will not need to be time ration related; students can take a little or as much time as they need.

In the foreseeable future the new educational technology will not affect all aspects of school. The main impact will be in 'classroom' areas such as English, maths, foreign languages, humanities, theoretical science. It will be used much less extensively in areas of practical or affective activity such as practical science, craft, design and technology, the arts and physical education, personal social and moral education. Even in the classroom areas it will only be used for part of the time. The inappropriateness or lack of technology and its software for particular areas and activities, the limitations of finance and the reservations of teachers will delay its full use. More important, the classroom subjects — and that term is only retained for shorthand convenience — will themselves increasingly be concerned with skills and attitudes which can only be developed in a social context. In any case, men and women are social animals and prefer education in a social setting.

It is important to keep a realistic view. No area will be immune — values for example could possibly be taught by interactive video — but no area will be completely taken over. Probably the actual time spent by students in using the new technology will only be a small proportion of the week. But — and this is the key point — a school cannot be part changed and part unchanged. You only need fit a roller skate to one leg of a horse to change the nature of the horse.

The knock-on effect on the use of school time can be foreseen. Just to take a few examples.

Example 1
If a school invests heavily in new technology and concentrates it in a large resource centre, it should obviously maximise its use. So how is a student freed from normal classes so that he or she can use this centre during the main school day? How does the school arrange for day-long open access and still provide supervision and security? How is time provided to advise and help students and monitor their programme? How is what they learn here related to the time they spend on similar curriculum areas in the classroom?

Example 2
If each student has part of the week where he or she is engaged in individual study, with control over the place and time of study, what are the implications for procedures such as student timetabling and registration, assessment and reporting on progress?

Example 3
If students of all ages can use a classroom equipped with technology
for say science learning on a 'drop in' basis, each spending the time
he or she needs for the work in hand, how do they fit this variable
activity into the normal fixed slot timetable?

In each of these examples the school time implications are
considerable, though certainly not impossible. As the system is affected
by the new technology, change judders through all parts of it, including
all aspects of the use of school time.

The rate of change
Possibly many readers may accept the likelihood of some such system
change in education at some time. The critical question then becomes:
When?

Different elements of change
Attempting to identify the different forces of change and predict when
change is likely to occur is clearly hazardous. However I would argue
that the pace of change deriving from the new demands of society
will be different from that driven by the technology itself.

The former we can expect to develop steadily but with gathering
momentum, thus creating an upward rising exponential curve. It will
be steady, on the whole, because it is made up of demands from a
mass of sets and subsets of educational clients — students, parents,
employers, sectors of the community, local and national government
— each influenced by its own perception of the development of the
information society and the changed needs for education within it.
It will gather momentum because these perceptions will accumulate
and so increasingly overcome adherence to the existing familiar system.

The pace of change generated by the use of new technology within
schools will be different. At present in most schools such technology
is peripheral. It affects the process marginally but not fundamentally.
So we could argue for the same gradual exponential change. However
that does not seem to be the experience in other industries. In printing,
financial services and office automation the experience has been of
a steady and increasing build-up to a critical point — at which the
dam bursts and deluging change occurs.

The critical point seems to depend on an amalgam of factors: the
right technology at the right price; the right software, tried tested and
accepted, with appropriate operating systems; sufficient staff trained
and confident to use it, or at least to train others; favourable economic
conditions for the investment; and confidence among senior managers
to take the plunge (or concern about the consequences if they do not).
So I would argue that the pace of change resulting from the technology

will be an upward exponential curve which steepens sharply at the critical point.

Our problem is that our expectations will not fit either curve. We find it difficult to think exponentially. Instead we prefer to think in terms of a steady rate of change. So we may even overestimate initial changes because we don't appreciate the lag between well publicised change at the frontier and substantial change at the heart of the system. So we are likely to feel initially that change is not occurring as fast as we have been led to expect; but then be overwhelmed by its apparently sudden onset. Change in schools will come slower than we expect but quicker than we realise.

A possible model
Figure 12.1 sets out these assumptions in the form of a model.

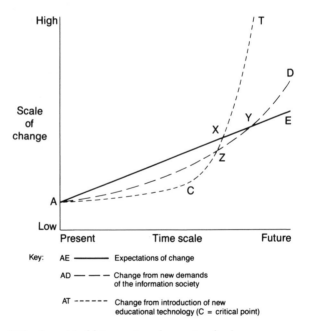

Figure 12.1 – A model of future system changes in schools

Curve AD represents the rate of change in schools arising from new demands from the information society. Curve AT represents changes from the introduction of new educational technology, with C the critical point at which the pace of change accelerates. AE represents our general expectation of change. Initially this is shown as being greater than the actual change, but overtaken by events at points X and Y.

(In practice we should expect the line AE to begin to curve upwards after those points.)

If you accept my main argument then the two change curves and the expectations line are correct in principle, although you may wish to reshape the model by altering the curves or making the expectation line more or less steep. This would change the relationship of points X, Y, Z and C, but would not alter the model fundamentally. (If AE is less steep, then the initial 'disappointment' over the rate of change will be less, but the 'astonishment' greater and slightly earlier; if the AD curve is steepened in relation to AT (or the steepness of the AT curve softened), point Y could arise before (to the left of) X, and point Z be above the AE line.)

Of course the model produces no answer to the 64,000 dollar question: when will points C and X occur? I will rashly hazard a prediction that C, the critical point of technological change, will occur by about the year 2000, with X following soon afterwards. After all, the technology already exists — micro computers, telephone and modem, compact disc, video, satellite communication, together with the technology for networking and interaction. The next ten years will see dramatic changes in capacity and miniaturisation and steady, probably sharp, falls in price. The main delay factor is likely to be the educational software. At present the standard is low overall, and authoring languages and expert systems are still far from allowing learning programmes to be produced as easily as textbooks. Field trialling is an additional cause of delay. However, given another decade with continued technical development linked to advances in desk top publishing, there is no reason why good learning packages should not be developed in quantity. Other delay factors are likely to be the training of teachers and other staff, adaptation of buildings, and most important the development of organisational systems to support the use of new technology.

The prospects for change in the use of school time

If the above scenario is broadly correct, then we can expect initially to see steady and growing demand for changes in school time, particularly in micro-structures and individual patterns of use: longer period lengths; more timetable blocking; wider use of modular approaches; more individualised study and distance learning; extension of activities and use of school premises for the community. Because these changes are driven mainly by the demands of society for altered school outcomes, they are likely to be concentrated at a point closer to the outcomes, i.e. on older pupils and so secondary schools. Primary school time use may be little affected in this period. The growth of local management of schools is likely to lead to more local variations in the school day but not yet to fundamental change.

If this piecemeal change continued long enough it could eventually put pressure on the conventional school day, but it is likely that before then pressure will be extended at the critical point (C) from the second force for change, the needs of the new technology. For if the main thrust of the new technology is to individualise learning, then exactly the same mismatch will arise between the flexible, student-centred and open time structures it needs and the rigid class-based closed structure of the traditional day which was discussed at the beginning of chapter nine. So at that point macro-structures will need radical examination.

However, the conservative forces affecting school time, described in chapter two, will still operate strongly and are likely to resist any radical change. This will be reinforced by the complication that new models and supporting systems can normally only be tested once a year. (Full change can only be implemented at the beginning of the academic year. Trials can be introduced *during* it — but cannot normally be repeated until the following year.) By the time this is printed there will be only ten such change points left this century. So there is a serious risk that change in school time structures will be uncomfortably delayed, so that the technology is in use for some years after point C without the new time system it needs for effective operation.

My conclusion would be that trialling of new systems and supporting sub-systems in advance of the full onset of new technology is essential. The two-part school day described below seems to be a good model and has the additional advantage that it provides an ideal setting for the other, more marginal changes which are currently developing. However, setting up and refining it so that it is widely acceptable and easily copied by schools will take time.

Changes in the use of learning time

In the classroom

In the short term the current interest in teacher effectiveness and the use of classroom time is likely to intensify as concern rises about both the effectiveness of education and the adaptation of its process to fit new demands.

However, if the new technology appears on any scale the scenario changes.

Example

A foreign language department with four classrooms which introduces extensive new technology has four choices:

1. Spread the equipment to equip partially each of the classrooms.
2. Dedicate one room to the new equipment, keep the others as 'normal' classrooms.

3. Extend the equipment (from a bottomless purse?) so that all four rooms are equipped with learning stations for each student, enabling each room to be used for both individualised technology-based learning and conventional classroom instruction at different times.
4. Base the new equipment with technician support within an additional resource centre to maximise use, keep the four classrooms unaltered.

Each of these has quite different implications for the use of time:

- *Choice 1* implies that both group and individualised activities will normally occur simultaneously in each room (otherwise the equipment will be under-used). This puts pressure on teacher time in managing multiple activities and makes allocation of his or her time between students difficult.
- *Choice 2* implies that 25 per cent of each class's time will be spent in the dedicated room. This implies that one class and possibly one teacher will be deprived of a 'normal' classroom base, and therefore will spend one third of their time in each of the other general rooms.
- *Choice 3* is theoretically a good solution, though a very costly one. However there may be time wasted in transition from one mode of learning to another.
- *Choice 4* is also a good solution, but again costly. It does imply that either each teacher spends some time with each class in the centre — and so classrooms will be empty for 25 per cent of the time — or that part-classes of students work in the centre without a language teacher (in which case their learning time becomes unsupported), or that an additional teacher or aide is employed.

These examples illustrate that the new technology can have profound effects upon the use of time in the classroom for class management, school management, management of individual students and of resources and facilities. Unless we are careful it will make the teacher's task more complex and so lead to ineffective time use.

Outside the classroom

In general terms the new technology will mean more individualised learning and less use of the teacher as a fund of knowledge. So learning will tend to move beyond the classroom, either to places where specialised technology or advice is available, like resource centres and public libraries, or to places where learning is more convenient or less subject to distraction (like some but not all homes?) Homework in the traditional extension-of-classwork form may shrink but be replaced by more out of class technology-based assignments.

So, the problems implicit in individualised learning which were discussed in chapter nine will be magnified — particularly the need for an appropriate timetable environment and an effective monitoring and guidance system with the time to service this.

However, the two part day model will be very sympathetic to these out of class learning needs.

Changes in time for community education

We can be reasonably certain that the demand for community education will rise. In developed countries it will be related to demographic changes and particularly the rise in the expectation of life, coupled with some earlier or enforced retirement, a rising level of education and growing realisation of the need for education lifelong. In developing countries it will be more associated with the need to mobilise the strengths of local communities.

In both cases there will be growing demand for school time to be provided for the community — time for learning and time for use of facilities. Both will be accentuated by awareness of the needs of the information society and the educational potential of the new technology. So many schools will come under pressure to make this time available.

Changes in the use of time for the curriculum

Initially we can expect pressure on the curriculum to continue building up. The information explosion, the growing complexity of modern life and the new demands of the information society will ensure this. So we can expect a tendency for governments and administrators to try to increase the total quantity of school time either by lengthening the school day or year or extending the duration of schooling, or to compress the curriculum by use of cross-curricular themes and other devices.

It is possible that curriculum designers may be driven to use a core plus extension approach not for the whole curriculum but for specific subject areas. Pressure on time may lead them to identify an irreducible core for each subject and a desirable but not essential extension. Modular curricula would fit this approach well, particularly as they already offer opportunities both to compress the curriculum and extend the time for it.

The situation is likely to be transformed by the development of new technology. In other industries one of its effects has been to speed up processes, e.g. in hospitals, factories and offices, and so to increase throughput. There is every reason to assume that the same will be true in education. The teachers in our classrooms sweat away with last century's tools, and we have come to accept their slow hand-crafted performance as the norm. Shades of the Luddites! We have hardly a glimpse yet of how much more could be achieved with the human brain. Even a modest increase in productivity — say 20 per cent — would solve most of our curriculum pressure problems.

A new model: the two part school day
In secondary schools
The model is broadly similar in approach to the Oxfordshire day described in chapter three, but with important design improvements and drawing on the experience of compressed and flexible day developments. It has much in common with the day operated in a number of independent boarding schools. It is also similar to the day now functioning in many *Gesamtschulen* (comprehensive schools) in the Federal Republic of Germany — see Appendix, Example 8. None of the features described is untried; all have been used successfully somewhere in the UK. What is new about the model is not its separate features but their combination. Like all models of school day, even minor adjustments will fit it more closely to the needs of individual schools.

DESCRIPTION
The day has two parts (see Fig. 12.2).

A long morning of the traditional type, housing 75 per cent of the curriculum, say 8.30 a.m. – 12.40 p.m. or similar. In the UK context this would allow four hours ten minutes for lessons (three hours 30 minutes e.g. 6 x 35 or similar), registration/assembly (20 minutes) and one break (20 minutes). The early start is preferable, as it brings lunch forward and provides more afternoon time. But a start as late as 8.50 still provides lunch at 1 p.m. The morning could be extended slightly if necessary, say 8.30 a.m. – 1.00 p.m., to provide 80 per cent of the curriculum (say 4 x 55 minutes plus assembly, breaks and circulation).

This part of the day is timetabled in the conventional way, and is identical to the main first part of the normal day. Academic lessons could be packed into it, leaving more recreative lessons for the afternoon, but this would be inadvisable. It unbalances the use of staff and provides a heavy morning diet. It would be preferable just to timetable 75 per cent of each subject.

Given community education development, during the morning some classes could be open to adult enrolment where appropriate, and the library/resource centre/computers, etc, open for community access. Facilities unused during the morning could also be let to the community.

This traditional morning retains the strengths of the conventional day. It is compact and tightly organised. All staff and students are

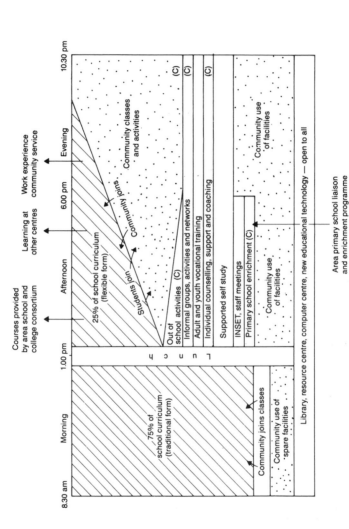

Key: (C) = particularly suitable for community volunteers

Figure 12.2 – A new model: the two-part day for secondary schools

present throughout and so communication and social control are assisted and school corporate identity retained. So it has the effect of reducing the scale of change and reassuring parents, teachers and the community that the bulk of the school day is unaltered.

A flexible afternoon and evening, providing most or all of:

- the remaining 25 per cent of the school curriculum, but in a flexible form within an open timetable, and possibly including short courses of up to ten weeks
- out of school and sports activities
- links with other schools and centres, e.g. for combined arts, sports and other activities
- off-campus activities, e.g. community service, work experience
- community education classes, activities and use of facilities (open where appropriate to school students)
- networks of contacts with people with specific interests
- youth and adult vocational training and retraining
- supported self study (all ages) and distance learning
- individual use by all ages of sports and leisure facilities
- in-service training and staff department meetings.

For timings see Appendix, Example 15.

The atmosphere in this part of the day will be quite different from the morning. Experience from flexible days suggests that the presence of many adults and also younger children, the wider range of activities, the greater voluntary element and the resulting enthusiasm all contribute to provide a less formal, more lively and friendly but very purposeful environment — more like a college than a school.

Transport will be an important factor for rural schools. Contract transport can run after lunch (leaving the second part of the day dependent on private transport arrangements and so voluntary), or mid/late afternoon, or a combination. For heavily bussed schools the key may lie in expanding the number of buses on a dual school-and-community basis, possibly supplemented with a fare-charging service for later buses. Alternatively such schools could adopt a two part week with four conventional and one flexible days.

TIMETABLING CONSIDERATIONS

Open timetabling

Morning timetabling will be conventional. In the afternoons the open timetabling is different — perhaps scheduling would be a better word. It will be the individual departments or faculties and their teachers, plus the community education providers, not the head/principal/timetabler, who determine the range and type of activities, the clientele, and the place and time. For example, activities offered can be adjusted to the specific needs of groups of students and perhaps also teacher enthusiasms. Likewise there can be similar choice of place (activities can be off-campus if required, for example) and time. The timetable will normally be flexible enough to allow teachers to nominate day and time with reasonable chance of securing them, or to lengthen or shorten sessions or establish a less than weekly frequency.

Obviously there has to be overall scheduling to prevent clashes. Co-ordination of faculty/department programmes is needed to ensure broad and balanced provision. Some regulation is necessary. In particular it is essential that lessons are not all allowed to bunch after lunch but are tapered through the afternoon, fading away in the evening. (This is important to maximise flexibility and to free space to build up community activities.) However the greatest concentration will still be in the early afternoon, and classes for younger children will be mainly timetabled then. Some time needs to be earmarked to avoid clashes, e.g. for team games, musical and drama rehearsals, links with other schools or centres, INSET and meetings. Calendar events can still override the timetable, e.g. a sports day or carol service.

But the overall flexibility is great. For example, if the afternoon session begins at 1.30 p.m. it allows seven one-hour sessions with some allowance for circulation between sessions by 9 p.m. This is equivalent to 12 35-minute periods, i.e. twice as many as in the morning but only housing one third as many lessons. Even allowing that school classes will bunch in the afternoons and taper in the evenings there is still great flexibility in the system. It is probably desirable to have a notional time-framework in periods or sessions, although an activity can override these if teacher and taught have no commitment before (or after).

Student commitment

A policy on student commitment is necessary. Possibly students can be required to gain a minimum number of 'credits' for after-lunch activities each year, this varying between year-groups and perhaps individual students. Credits in specific areas could be compulsory for certain groups. There can also be requirements about enrolment in out of school activities, community classes, community service or work experience, and supported self study. This would be an excellent way of effectively extending student learning time without increasing school classroom time and its associated costs. Monitoring of this by tutors and ideally a computerised record system would be important.

Registration in the afternoon and evening is by individual classes and activities, not in the registration groups used in the morning. The older the student the wider the range in place and time of his or her activities, which can include off-campus and non-school activities and distance-learning. Parents will require good information, and it will be parents' responsibility to know the programme of their child during the second part of the day.

Time slots

The two-part day also allows full exploitation of the time slots discussed in chapter six, page 116. The explanation is slightly technical and of most interest to UK readers. If 75 per cent of the curriculum is provided in the morning, and if ten per cent of the normal school week is allocated to a time-slot, the morning time of a school week provides seven and a half time slots and can be supplemented with just five per cent from an afternoon to make eight. Now eight time slots will mount the bulk of the curriculum, sufficient to satisfy all subject-areas' time needs either fully or mainly. For example, a ten per cent slot could be allocated for eight areas: English, maths, humanities, science, first foreign language, craft design and technology, creative arts and physical education. Or they could provide for core and foundation subjects plus some options, totalling eight in all.

Of course not all subject areas would be satisfied with the ten per cent of the school week provided in one time slot — but this can be supplemented with non-time slotted afternoon time. So time slots, with their distinct advantages for blocking the timetable, timetabling teams of teachers and allowing students to break out of the age-related framework can be easily implemented within the two-part day without any of the normal difficulties — and subject areas can still be given their normal allocations of time.

ACTIVITIES

The afternoon and evening possibilities are extensive:

Conventional lessons can be provided in the normal way. Afternoon time would be particularly useful for minority activities like a second foreign language or minority subjects like geology which could build up a viable all-age class. It would also be very sympathetic to activities such as projects, educational visits, field work, oral activities, cross curricular assignments, mini-company schemes. Such a flexible structure is also ideally suited to modular learning approaches. (It would be easier for students to take a module for part of the year only, and modules in the afternoon would not need to be age related.) Lessons could be easily adapted for particular needs — for example, a normal lesson can be 'wound down' and replaced by another giving help just to students finding difficulties with the course.

Short courses can be provided, often spanning year-groups as in flexi-time and electives, (described in chapter three) either recycling staff savings from change elsewhere in the day or from some curriculum reallocation. Just a double period a week from a teacher creates several short courses during the year. Or on a small scale, for example, one period of English for a whole year could be recycled as short courses on poetry, novels, science fiction, etc, giving students a choice. Short courses could include provision for gifted children and others with special needs.

Individual student counselling, educational, vocational and personal, can be provided without withdrawing a student from class — along with medical and dental inspections, vaccinations and similar pull-out activities. Afternoon time can be used for profiling and records of achievement and also for reports to and interviews with parents.

Individual study activities. This type of afternoon and evening is ideal for individual students to take up supported self study, benefit from peer tutoring or coaching, use the library and resources centre, work on projects, use distance learning, computers, word-processors, etc. There is also scope for individual students with work to complete in art or a practical subject to fit into a room where there is space and the teacher agrees. There is scope for individual activities off-campus, for example in local libraries, or assignments in a museum, archives office, local factory, etc.

Full use of new technology. The two-part day makes it possible to maximise use of investment in new technology dawn-to-dusk. However there are time implications — staff are needed throughout for support and supervision.

Informal groups. The second part of the day provides an ideal environment for the growth of informal, ephemeral, lightly supervised groups. Examples would be groups working on a project, preparing a presentation, interviewing members of the community, conducting unsupervised fieldwork, or gathered around a special interest such as a computer programme, a hobby or an enthusiasm generated from classroom activity. Such groups do much to develop interpersonal and cooperative skills.

Out-of-school activities — the traditional range of clubs, teams, arts activities, etc, but perhaps with greater community involvement and possibly strengthened by a minimum commitment for each student.

Links with other schools. This type of day will encourage the growth of school consortia for: minority subjects; leisure or arts activities; TVEI type courses; short courses. These would flourish if the schools of a consortium adopted open afternoon timetables since avoiding timetable clashes and improving transport arrangements would be easier. It also facilitates linked courses with further education colleges, links with and between primary schools, and use of local sports and arts centres.

Charles Handy (1989: 169) goes further. He argues that ultimately schools need to develop into what he calls 'shamrock organisations', where the school provides the core curriculum and guidance for its student clients, but contracts out the remainder of the curriculum to separate specialist agencies ('mini-schools') in the afternoons and evenings. The two-part day would lead to some extent to this kind of federal organisation for education, and could develop more fully in due course. (Handy's idea has a very urban flavour, but could be adapted for deeply rural schools if they set aside say two days of the week for federal activities, to reduce transport problems.)

Community education. Because the school curriculum element in the afternoon is spread more widely, at any time the accommodation is less used by school students and so more available to the community. So we can expect to see strong community education developments, e.g:

- adult classes (but open to school students as well, free or fee-paying)
- jointly sponsored school/community classes (each contributing to the staffing and costs)
- community activities on the school campus including clubs, groups and lettings
- youth activities
- adult and youth training and retraining
- programmes for the unemployed
- adult literacy and numeracy programmes
- advice, counselling and support groups

In addition it is possible to develop supported self study and access to learning resources and new technology for adults.

Volunteers. The second part of the day is ideal for the use of volunteers from both the school student body and the community to help individuals and groups and lead activities. The potential for both groups is enormous, as has been described earlier. Yet it is little tapped in most schools, largely because the conventional day often prevents students being available to be helped or to help, and creates too heavy a school atmosphere to attract the full range of community volunteers.

LOGISTICS

Management. A management system is necessary for the second part of the day. A senior member of staff should have overall responsibility for it, and one nominated member always needs to be in charge of the site at any time for emergencies.

Teaching staff. There are implications for conditions of service. It is important that no attempt is made to increase teachers' workload and there is full consultation. Given care there is no reason why teachers should not find this pattern of day more satisfying and more convenient than its predecessor. Generally speaking working later on one day is felt to be compensated by finishing earlier on another. Moreover the flexibility and the improved atmosphere of the afternoon will be attractive. It is assumed that the pool of teaching time available does not need to be increased, except through the community education programme and supplementation with volunteers.

Non-teaching staff. Some increase will be necessary as resource centres and reception need to be manned for longer hours.

Premises. There will be some increase in wear and tear from extra use, offset by less vandalism because of greater adult presence. Cleaning and caretaking arrangements may need revision, but probably no extra finance is needed until overall use is substantially increased.

Some adaptation of premises may be necessary to reflect new patterns of use. Ideally the opportunity should be taken to improve the general ambience to fit the afternoon atmosphere. However premises still need to be able to house the conventional morning school.

Catering. Lunches can be served as usual. An all-day cafeteria is desirable. The lunch break can be short, staggered if necessary, or long. It can allow both if the first afternoon session allows latitude for classes to start early or late within the time allocated.

Finance. There will be some increased costs for the enhanced non-teaching establishment, some extra heating/lighting costs, and possibly additional transport and premises wear and tear and adaptation. On the other hand, profit on catering should increase and community education should generate more funds. The overall situation would be that sketched in chapter one: total expenditure would rise marginally, but user unit costs would fall and the return on capital invested will be improved.

This new model of day will seem strange to some readers. It will need care in its initial design, and much work to set it up. Some aspects will be unfamiliar and so uncomfortable. Yet every feature of this day already exists successfully somewhere in England. I am absolutely convinced that it is fully workable, acceptable and better than the traditional day. Certainly it would enable a school to do all the things it does now and many other things which it cannot do now, develop welcome timetable flexibility and increase its capability to deliver activities for which there is growing demand. It also enables schools to try out a new system so that it is fully tested when the new technology makes its full impact.

In primary schools

At first sight there is no pressure and little need to adapt the primary school day. It already offers great flexibility. Primary schools will not feel such strong need to adapt their product for the information society and the role of new technology may be less obtrusive (although this is not certain).

However careful scrutiny shows that the present primary day obstructs a number of desirable activities:

- individual tutoring or counselling of students without withdrawal from class
- special activities for the gifted and those with special interests
- a full range of out-of-school activities (many primary schools find it difficult to cater for all needs in the arts, crafts and sports)
- inter-school links and combined activities
- use of additional facilities in the area secondary school and at other centres
- parent-and-child activities, community activities
- use of school facilities by the community during the day
- full use of parental and community volunteers and of senior students from local secondary schools and colleges.

Of course many schools do provide some of these, but often with some difficulty and seldom many of them.

It would be perfectly feasible for a primary school to adopt a modified version of the two part day. It could begin at 8.30 a.m. (but possibly later) with the first part of the day ending at say 12.15 or 12.30. The second part of the day, after lunch, would deliver the remaining one or one and a half hours of schooling in a much more flexible form. Activities could continue to say 4.30 p.m. if necessary, to slim the use of premises in the early afternoon and allow other activities to build up.

Activities would need planning on a weekly timetable, ideally in a consortium of local primary schools linked with secondary school(s) and other centres. So Monday could be an art and craft day, Tuesday music, science, technology, etc. This would allow pooling of the resources of staff and premises from several schools to extend the choice open to children. It should be possible for most if not all of the activities listed for secondary schools earlier to be provided. In addition it would be easier to arrange extended educational visits and to make greater use of computers and other new technology.

For full development the programme would need maximum involvement of parents and the local community, both as volunteers — not just aides but as organisers of activities within a supervised framework — and as providers of transport. Additional transport could be hired, possibly with charges. Schools in very rural areas could limit the change to two or three afternoons, or explore one flexi-day per week of the same pattern, to reduce transport problems.

Transition to such a pattern would not be difficult — there is already a tendency for schools to mount art and crafts, etc, in the afternoons, and out-of-school activities occur in late afternoons anyway. Also primary schools usually already have the links with parents and the community to make this possible.

However, it is not likely to develop widely because the need for it is not pressing. It does require good inter-school cooperation, imaginative raising of parental and community support and some risk of friction with parents initially — probably too much risk for many schools. However this type of day could be well worth trying. Again, most of the individual features already exist in one situation or another in the UK.

In the longer term the impact of new technology on primary schools is difficult to foresee. It may well be greater than we seem to expect. However the present class teacher centred day with its built-in flexibility will probably accommodate quite easily the use of new technology both within the classroom and in an adjoining resource centre. The main reservation is in the dispersal of a teacher's time in a multi-task situation.

Changes in the school year and school week

The logic for operating a school year of four reasonably short and even length terms, spaced by holidays long enough to refresh but not so long to encourage regression, is powerful. However the forces of inertia are more powerful still, so we can expect the spread of the four term year worldwide to be slow.

The six day week however seems likely to fade. The social forces against it, where it exists, seem to be growing and it is more expensive to operate than its five day counterpart. However, it is almost certain to continue in boarding schools where there is good logic for its retention.

Other time implications: training

The system changes discussed above will require time for training. The new demands on schools will transform the role of the teacher. Teachers will need new skills in guiding, monitoring and supporting learners, managing technology and software, working with a much larger number of non-school volunteers and outside agencies and operating a new type of institution — not to mention new attitudes. The training implications are massive, and compounded if I am correct by the relatively short timescale. It will be important that a strategic view of the training is taken by both trainers and teachers, i.e. that skills are not just acquired piecemeal but are seen as part of a complete re-equipping process to fit teachers for work in a different system.

*   *   *   *   *

Some readers will reject this chapter as fantasy. 'It can't happen here'. Or, 'not in my lifetime'. Or, 'not at that rate of change'. There is sense in that response. The changes of the future are often oversold. And even a year is a long time — plenty of time for human beings to come to terms with a specific development. However I would ask readers to confront not the superficial description of likely change but the underlying logic for substantial system change that I have described in the first part of the chapter, particularly the pattern of change set out in Fig. 12.1.

If that logic is accepted, even grudgingly, then the remainder of the chapter needs to be taken seriously. The new two-part model of school day is a logical design for such a situation. It is not an optional extra. It is the central element to facilitate system change. In many ways it is the focal point of this book, since it draws together current developments in the school day examined in chapter three, and needs for new structuring of school time examined in the chapters on the curriculum, classroom and modular time, individual learning and time for the community.

13 Strategies for change

Changing school time systems can be tricky, even hazardous. This chapter draws from the experience of a number of schools and authorities to offer practical advice to those about to venture into the jungle. It begins by suggesting a general plan for change, and then considers specific strategies in each area examined earlier in the book.

A plan of action
General considerations
Most change in school time is pragmatic, amending what already exists. This has virtues — it minimises disruption and builds on the known. But I would argue strongly that a systematic approach is more productive. It is more likely to uncover a wider range of alternatives.

So I would suggest a logical approach following a normal management planning sequence: analysis, objectives, design, resource planning, implementation and evaluation. This is a general planning approach for any school time change. It will obviously need amending for local needs. Experienced managers may find it obvious, but I hope some readers will find it helps systematic thinking.

Obviously the bigger the change the more careful the consideration needed. Time macro-structures — school year, week and day — need particular care because they affect the everyday life of so many individuals and groups and because they can arouse all the conservative forces described in chapter two. In contrast, micro-structures — lesson lengths, timetable, course structures, out-of-school activities — are much easier to change, since they are internal to the school. They can involve technical considerations and so need careful design, but if a mistake is made it can often be put right quite easily. Individual time patterns — the actual use of time by the individual teacher or student — are in contrast deceptively difficult to change. They are too intertwined with personality and habit.

A systematic approach
ANALYSIS
The more searching the analysis, the more likely a good solution. It might be helpful to read through chapters one and two again for general ideas.

(a) What are the defects or disadvantages of the feature under examination? (It is helpful to be as precise and detailed as possible.)
What is their importance — in total and relation to each other?
Which do you most wish to change?

(b) What are its advantages? (particularly those taken for granted.)
Which do you most wish to preserve?

(c) What are the fixed constraints which cannot be altered easily, or at all? Not all those below will be relevant to any one plan:

- any regulations relating to this feature
- time: fixed dates (days/times?)
    fixed transport arrivals/departure times (could these possibly be altered?)
    fixed durations?
    other time considerations?

- staffing: personnel, roles, total establishment, man hours available?
    other staffing considerations?

- premises: spaces and suitability for use?
    duration of use, access, security, other premises considerations?

- resources: furniture and furnishings, equipment; books and materials; other resources considerations?

- finance: for capital? for annual expenditure?

- transport: vehicles? provision for students, community, staff other transport considerations.

(d) What are the tactical considerations for change?
- Decision-makers: Who has sanction or influence over this area? Are there any fixed times at which decisions have to be made?
- Who else needs to be consulted? Or informed?
- What are the people/groups/forces likely to resist change in this area?
- What are the people/groups/forces which are likely to support it?

OBJECTIVES

What exactly are you planning to achieve? The more clearly you can define your objectives, the better the chance of a good scheme. But in school time planning you often can't see all the possible benefits at the start.

It is helpful to keep objectives concise. If there are several, try to put in priority and/or distinguish between essentials and optional extras.

DESIGN
An important stage which often needs considerable time, Three points arise:

1. Who should be involved? Obviously you can't develop a design with a whole staff, but a small working group is helpful for producing ideas, even if these have to go to a larger group later.
2. The range of possibilities. These will often be much wider than you think. Removing one obstacle or changing even a small detail can make a lot of difference. So keep thinking — what are the possibilities I haven't yet thought of?
3. Take care over the details. Once you have decided on a general outline for the new arrangements, it's worth taking a lot of trouble to get the detail right. A slight adjustment can often make a surprising difference to the people whom it affects.

Are there any special design considerations for this feature to bear in mind?

RESOURCE IMPLICATIONS
Do your new arrangements have any implications for existing or additional resources:

-   staff, teaching and non-teaching: deployment, hours, conditions, training and other considerations?
-   premises: modification, maintenance, heat and light? Other considerations?
-   resources: furniture and fittings, equipment; books and materials, other considerations?
-   finance: additional or reduced costs of any of the above?
-   transport arrangements?

Are there any other resource considerations?

IMPLEMENTATION
Is a limited trial of the innovation desirable, possible? If so, when?
When should this change be fully operational?
What actual changes need to be made?
When do these need to be made? (for a major change a flow chart may help).
What sort of problems are likely to arise, and how can they be dealt with?
What consultation needs to take place?
What public relations action is necessary, for parents and other groups and for the media (if appropriate?)
Would it be better to phase any of these actions over a longer period?
What is the first action to be taken?

EVALUATION
For what purpose are you going to evaluate this change?
How should the evaluation be made?
When? By whom, to whom, and in what form?
(You may not necessarily need a formal evaluation. The general 'feel' of the change may be obvious to all. But some more disciplined thinking about the change may be helpful, either to modify arrangements or to point to improvements for future innovation.)

Changing the school day

This is a feature which many schools are interested in improving and over which most schools have some, although not often complete, control. The main thrust of the previous chapter was that altering the school day in time for the possible changes ahead, particularly in secondary schools, is a high priority. However, major change in the school day while perfectly feasible needs very careful planning.

If you only want to consider more limited changes such as lesson lengths or break/lunch arrangements, most of the suggestions below should still be useful, but some of them may not be relevant, e.g. transport arrangements.

Analysis

The check-list above should be helpful. A good first step could be to write down your present day in the form used in the Appendix, and perhaps compare it with other days there. You may find the McREL approach on page 145 useful.

It is particularly important to examine existing transport arrangements for students (and possibly staff), whether by school, public or private transport, and to determine to what extent it is possible to alter them. For example school buses may be linked with other schools or users and so unalterable. Public transport arrivals or departures may be at irregular intervals, and long waiting times will not be welcome! It is also worth looking for any other fixed times, e.g. the range of possible school cafeteria opening times, or the minimum reasonable time to feed students.

It is also worth checking the actual text of any regulations or guidance concerning the school day and not relying on memory!

The other possible fixed elements in the earlier list, like staffing, premises and resources, may not at first seem relevant. However, if you think them through in detail you may well identify elements which must be borne in mind.

Under 'tactical considerations', groups which may need to approve or be consulted may only meet irregularly, and so a flow chart may be necessary to work out the minimum time requirement for the whole process (and allowing for some slippage). For example, for a change of day in September 1992 you might need to start discussions some time in 1991.

Objectives
Definition may not be easy. It's important to remember that there may well be potential benefits in a change which you won't realise at first. People always see problems quicker than possibilities!

Design
A very useful device is a kind of time slide rule to work out all the possible permutations (see Fig. 13.1).

On a piece of graph paper with small squares, rule a vertical line and mark off times at five minute intervals, making a timescale. Write the times on the left of the scale say for every ten minutes (i.e. 8.30, 8.40, etc) beginning at the earliest conceivable start time and finishing at the latest conceivable. Now take a second sheet, cut off the left hand margin and cut out templates for each block of lessons, marking on them the actual lessons as suggested in Fig. 13.1.

You can then move these templates up and down the time scale, trying out the effect of changing forward or back in five minute steps, altering starting or finishing times, changing a lunch length, etc. You may wish to make some alternative templates, e.g. with different lesson lengths or combinations, to test out variations (as in Fig.13.1).

You may also like to refer back to chapter three or four to examine the full range of variations possible or to look at the examples in the Appendix. It is interesting to use the 'slide rule' to edge lessons forward or back until one pattern 'flops' into another (as described on page 210). You may come up with a 'best day', but you may prefer to identify several alternatives and set them out for comparison or comment. Don't be surprised if this throws up further variations you hadn't thought of! The range of possible variations seems inexhaustible.

When you feel the design of your new day or lesson system is complete, it is still worth going over it again to see if any minor improvement is possible. It is surprising how often even five minutes change makes an appreciable improvement.

Resources
The check-list above should be useful. There can often be some additional resource outlay in a change of day, not always expected.

Implementation
If you are making a major change in the school day, there is much to be said for running a limited experiment first without any commitment beyond it. This defuses a lot of opposition and puts fears to the test.

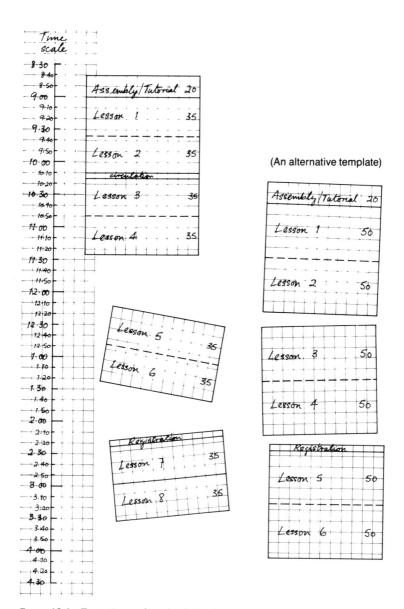

Figure 13.1 – Time planner for school day design

The tricky area is consultation and publicity. I think at the planning stage the safest procedure is to notify relevant groups such as staff, parents, students, etc, as early as possible that a change in the day is being considered (but giving no details) and stating that if any definite suggestions emerge these will be fully circulated with plenty of time for consultation. You can throw the subject open to general debate at the outset, but this may risk arousing unnecessary fears about wild suggestions which would have been killed during the planning stage. After consultation is over and plans have been finally approved there will be a need for a fuller notification to all affected. If the proposals are controversial or unusual it would be wise to consider how they could best be presented to the press or other media.

Evaluation

The list above should help. It will be surprising if some fine tuning is not necessary.

Changing the school week

The same approach as for the school day is necessary. They are linked since changing one will probably change the other.

Changing the school year

Only a few readers will be in a position to alter this. The key factor is the fixed dates in the year, particularly religious or main holidays, external examinations or tests, and changeover times to the next phase of education. Religious holidays are the most difficult as the dates cannot be altered. In Christian countries it is very difficult to plan the year effectively unless either a fixed date Easter can be allotted, or it can be treated as a single or two day holiday within the school term.

Of course there will be a large number of local factors, including traditional variations, climate, finance, etc. Anyone planning a four term year or similar would be well advised to study the Association of County Council's report and the work of the various Australian states described in chapter five.

Changing the use of time for the curriculum and for modular approaches

For both, the check-list above should be helpful with some modification. In particular a much more fundamental analysis will be needed. I would hope that chapter six may be helpful for this for the curriculum, and chapter seven for modules.

Changing the use of classroom time

Strategies for change here need to be quite different. What is required is a sensitive and accurate analysis of how time is actually used in a particular classroom, principally for the benefit of the teacher who works in it. Techniques for this are discussed in the later part of chapter eleven. The McREL package 'Achieving Excellence' could also be of value.

Once that data is established it is possible to ask questions about the use of time and so derive possible objectives for change. The ideas on various levels of time use in chapter eight may be useful here. This needs to push beyond the initial questions if useful suggestions are to emerge. For example, it's little use to suggest that better use of time could come from reducing time spent on transitions and student inattention. We need to go further and ask 'How in this classroom could loss of time from transition and student inattention be reduced?' Also, it is important to formulate objectives which can be assessed, however crudely, e.g. 'to reduce time lost in transition by organising learning materials so that they are set out more conveniently for use and can be easily checked'.

It is then possible to follow the rest of the cycle above: design (the actual measures planned), resources, implementation and evaluation. The last is most important, ideally through a follow-up a few months later.

A self-aware and resourceful teacher can carry through this kind of operation on his or her own. However some teachers will find it much easier to work with a colleague, who will also learn much from the process. Others may need or want to work with a headteacher/principal or an inspector/adviser.

Changing the use of time for individual study

For supported self study Philip Waterhouse, Director of the NCET SSS project, has always recommended 'Start small'. This is good advice. It minimises change, allows developments to grow naturally and avoids the need for grand plans. But if the development grows, the time will come when a broader strategy for change is necessary. If the development is to be central to the school and not peripheral, the issues raised in chapter nine need to be faced. There are three issues in particular: the conflict between the open timetable which self study deserves and the closed timetable in which it is usually expected to operate; the actual provision of time, for students without pulling them out of a class, and for tutors; and time for an effective monitoring and guidance system if student time is not to be misspent.

Implementing self study on any scale therefore needs thoughtful analysis. After that, the sequence in the check-list should be a helpful guide.

Other features of individual study covered in chapter nine such as homework, arrangements for distance learning and peer group tutoring do not need specific suggestions. But each needs planning carefully in its use of time and the checklist should be of use here.

Time for the community and parents

There are limits to how far a school can have a strategy or a policy for developing this. Or at least, a school may have a fine policy on paper, but this provides no guarantee that any development will occur.

The three key factors seem to be:

1. *Time for management.* Unless the school can find time for someone to make community education his or her main task, or at least one of his or her key tasks, then there is little chance of serious development.
2. *Attitude.* Whatever the school says, it is what it does that matters. Only unselfish community-centred attitudes are likely to create the right response from the community so that it feels able to use the resources of the school and willing in return to put time back into it.
3. *Personal contacts.* People will devote time to an activity, whether learning, participating or helping, much more readily if they know someone involved or if they have been invited.

I am probably overstating. A strategy for developing time for the community and parents, and receiving time from them, is needed, and again the check-list should be helpful. But it is the intangibles that will matter most.

Changing personal time management

An outline strategy for change is already provided in chapter eleven. However, anyone seriously interested is certainly advised to look at some of the excellent specialist books and training materials available.

* * * * *

Throughout this book I have tried to suggest that the effective use of school time is important — really important — for good education. Yet often time structures just grow, largely unplanned and unobserved. I have argued that they need to be analysed and designed. In these last chapters I have tried to suggest that change, and radical change, is both necessary and possible. Change will not be easy — it seldom is — but with careful planning it is perfectly feasible, even in the most unlikely places. So I hope that this book may encourage you to look hard at the use of school time in your own country, state, district, school, classroom, community...and in your own professional life. And if it needs changing, change it.

Good luck!

Appendix: Examples of school days world-wide

For key and notes to these examples see p.218

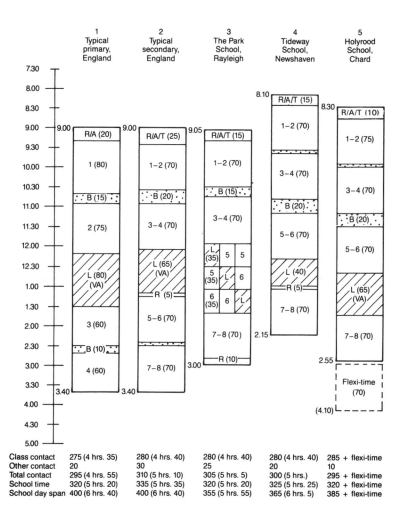

Figure App. – *Examples of school days world-wide*

215

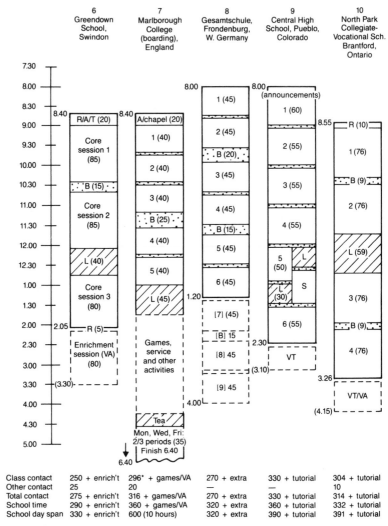

Figure App. — Examples of school days world-wide (contd.)

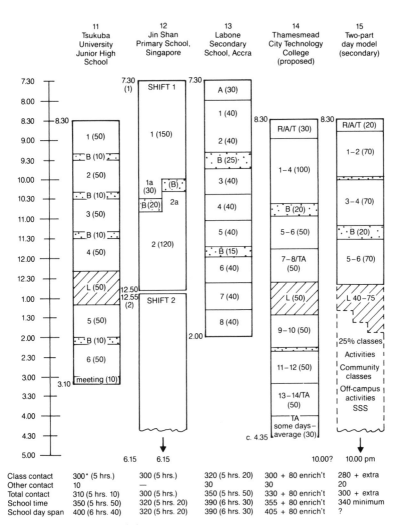

Figure App. — Examples of school days world-wide (contd.)

Key:

R	Registration
A	Assembly
T	Tutorial
VT	Voluntary tutorial
TA	Activities (not lessons) timetabled and compulsory
VA	Voluntary activities
B	Breaks
L	Lunch
1,2,etc	Lessons
(15)	15 minutes, etc.

```
r - - - - -,
!         ! Sessions not attended by all students
L - - - - J
```

⊏=⋅=⋅=⊐ Break or movement of 5 minutes

Notes:

Note that even five minutes difference per day amounts to 25 minutes difference per week)

1. *Typical primary school, England and Wales* (see p 43)
   Longer morning. Long lunch-hour, but tending to shorten.

2. *Typical secondary school, England and Wales* (see p 46)
   Many 35 minute periods paired as doubles. Equal amount of classroom time in morning and afternoon.

3. *The Park School, Rayleigh, Essex, England* (see p 48)
   Staggered three-shift lunch system compresses the day slightly. Learning centred on the morning. Registration at end of day.

4. *Tideway School, Newhaven, Sussex, England* (see p 60)
   First major example of compressed day in England, and probably still the earliest start in the UK. Minimum lunch hour. Learning centred on the morning.

5. *Holyrood School, Chard, Somerset, England* (see p 65)
   Flexi-time only affects some staff and children on the days that it operates. Long lunch-hour retained. Learning centred on the morning.

6. *Greendown School, Swindon, Wiltshire, England* (see p 70)
   Main day of three long core sessions, serviced for each year-group by one of three curriculum schools. Enrichment does not involve every student every day.

7. *Marlborough College, Marlborough, Wiltshire, England* (see p 57)
   A leading boarding public school. Classroom learning centred on morning. Long mid-morning break. Variety of afternoon activities (not every student engaged every day.) Two or three lessons on early

evening on three days. Saturday morning school same as weekdays. Total contact time is high, but reduced by shorter terms.

8. *Gesamtshule, Frondenburg, West Germany* (see p 78)
    Very early start and compressed main day, finishing early. No lunch session. Central European pattern of 45 minute periods separated by breaks or movement time. Most German schools finish at the end of the morning, but many comprehensive schools like Frondenburg have afternoon activities.

9. *Central High School, Pueblo, Colorado, USA* (see p 79)
    Very early start. Traditional US high school pattern of 'hours' (but including five minutes movement time.) Total possible class contact time is high, but not all students are in class for the six hours. Tutorial period obligatory for teachers, voluntary for pupils. Short, staggered lunch; early finish.

10. *North Park Collegiate-Vocational School, Brantford, Ontario, Canada.*
    Unusual timings, not at five minute points. Equal classroom time in morning and afternoon. Tutorial period similar to Example 9.

11. *Tsukuba University Junior High School, Japan* (see p 84)
    Fifty minute period + break pattern (cf. Example 8). Contrary to myth, total contact time and school day span are little different from the English examples 1-6.

12. *Jin Shan Primary School, Singapore* (see p 85)
    Very early start and very compressed day (short break, no lunch) make possible a two shift system. The two main learning sessions are divided into periods.

13. *Labone Secondary School, Accra* (see p 217)
    Very early start to avoid heat. Opening assembly and 40 minute periods probably originate from British influence. The highest total contact time of any of the examples.

14. *Thamesmead City Technology College, Bexley, England* — draft proposals (see p 71)
    Reflects thinking of City Technology Colleges: slightly higher class contact than in most English schools (20 minutes per day) plus obligatory enrichment sessions. Timetable in 25 minute units. Different days have different patterns and finishing time.

15. *Two part day model, secondary* (see page 195)
    Classroom learning centred on morning (cf. Examples 4 and 5). Remaining classroom time spread through rest of day with wide range of additional activities. Flexible lunch-hour.

References

Adair, J, 1987 *How to Manage your Time* Talbot Adair Press, Guildford (ISBN 0 9511835 08).

American Association of School Administrators, 1982 *Time on Task* 1801 North Moore Street, Arlington, Virginia 22209 USA.

Anderson, L, 1983 *Time and School Learning* Croom Helm, Beckenham, Kent.

Association of County Councils, 1986 *Education in Even Terms* London (ISBN 0 901783 315).

Audit Commission, 1985 *Obtaining Better Value from Further Education* HMSO, London.

Audit Commission, 1986 *Towards Better Management of Secondary Education* HMSO, London.

Ballinger, C, Kirschenbaum, N, and Poimbeauf, R, 1987 *The Year-Round School : Where Learning Never Stops* Phi Delta Kappa Educational Foundation, Bloomington, Indiana.

Berliner, D, 1979 'Tempus Educare'. In Peterson, P, and Walberg, H, *Research on Teaching: Concepts Findings and Implications* McCutchan, Berkeley, California.

Blake, M, 1967 'Time of day effects on a range of tasks'. *Psychonomic Science* 9 (349).

Bloom, B, 1968 'Learning for Mastery'. *Evaluation Comment* 1 (2) (reprinted in Anderson 1983).

Bond, G, 1974 *Voluntary Helpers in Schools* Home and School Publications, Sheffield (ISBN 0 901181 16).

Bray, M, 1989 *Multiple-Shift Schooling: Design and Operation for Cost-Effectiveness* Commonwealth Secretariat, Marlborough House, Pall Mall, London SW1Y 5HX (ISBN 0 85092 332 8)

Brown, B, and Saks, D, 1975 'The production and distribution of cognitive skills within schools'. *Journal of Political Economy* 83 (3).

Brown, B, and Saks, D, 'Production technologies and resource allocations within classrooms and schools'. In Dreeben, R, and Thomas, J, (Eds) *The analysis of Educational Production I. Issues in microanalysis* Ballinger, Lexington USA

Brown, B, and Saks, D, 1986 'Measuring the effects of Instructional Time on teacher learning'. *American Journal of Education* 94 (4) August 1986.

Bullock, A, 1975 *A Language for Life* Report of Committee of Inquiry, HMSO, London.

Burns, R, and Kojimoto, C, 1988 *The Practice of Mastery Learning in School* Far West Laboratory for Educational Research and Development, San Francisco, USA.

Carroll, J, 1963 'A Model of School Learning'. *Teachers College Record* 64 (8) (reprinted in Anderson 1983).

Carroll, J, 1989 'The Carroll Model of School Learning: A 25-Year Retrospective-Prospective View' *Educational Researcher* 18 (1) pp 26 – 31.

CIPFA, 1988 *Education Estimates 1988 – 89* Chartered Institute of Public Finance and Accountancy, 3 Robert Street, London WC2N 6BH.

Coventry LEA, 1981 *Comprehensive Education for Life* Coventry.

Coulter, F, 1979 'Homework — a neglected research area', *British Educational Research Journal* 5 (1) pp 21-33.

Craig, I, (Ed), 1987 *Primary School Management in Action*, Longman.

Davis, Z, 1987 'Effects of Time-of-Day of Instruction on Beginning Reading Achievement'. *Journal of Educational Research* 80 (3).

Dean, J, 1987 *Managing The Primary School*, Croom Helm, Beckenham, Kent.

Fisher, C, and Berliner, D, 1985 *Perspectives in Instructional Time* Longman, USA.

Fitz-Gibbon, C, 1988 'Peer Tutoring as a Teaching Strategy'. *Educational Management and Administration* 16 (3).

Folkard, S, 1975 'Diurnal Variation in Logical Reasoning'. *British Journal of Psychology* 66 (1).

Folkard S, et al, 1977 'Time of Day Effects on Schoolchildren's Immediate and Delayed Recall of Meaningful Material', *British Journal of Psychology* 68 (45).

Frederick, W, and Walberg, H, 1980 'Learning as a Function of Time'. *Journal of Educational Research* 73.

Freeman, G, and Hovland, C, 1934 'Diurnal Variations in Performance and Related Physiological Processes'. *Psychology Bulletin* 31.

Further Education Unit, 1979 *A Basis for Choice* Department of Education and Science, London.

Galton, M, and Simon, B, (Eds), 1980 *Progress and Performance in the Primary Classroom* Routledge & Kegan Paul, London.

Galton, M, Simon, B, and Croll, P, 1980 *Inside the Primary Classroom* Routledge & Kegan Paul, London.

Gates, A, 1916 'Diurnal Variations in Memory and Association'. *University of California Publ. Psychol.1*.

Gilbert, R, and Price, A, 1981 *The School Day: Is It Long Enough?* from Professor R Gilbert, Northwestern State University, Natchitoches, Louisiana.

Glass, G, Cahen, L, Smith, M, Filby, N, 1980 *School Class Size: Research and Policy* Sage, Beverly Hills, California.

Handy, C, and Aitken, R, 1986 *Understanding Schools as Organisations* Penguin Books, England

Handy, C, 1989 *The Age of Unreason* Century Hutchinson, London.

Hargreaves, D, 1983 'The Teaching of Art and the Art of Teaching: towards an Alternative View of Aesthetic Learning'. In Hammersley, M, and Hargreaves, A, *Curricular Practice — Some Sociological Case Studies* Falmer Press, Lewes.

Hargreaves, D, 1984 *Improving Secondary Schools* Inner London Education Authority.

Hilsum, S, and Cane, B, 1971 *The Teacher's Day* NFER, Windsor.

Hilsum, S, and Strong, C, 1978 *The Secondary Teacher's Day* NFER, Windsor.

HMI, 1978 *Primary Education in England* HMSO, London.

Holsinger, D, 1982 *Time, Content and Expectations as Predictors of School Achievement in the USA and Other Countries : A Review of the IEA Evidence* Department of Education, Washington, USA.

Husen,T, (Ed), 1967 *International Study of Achievement in Mathematics* (IEA) Almqvist & Wiksell, Stockholm.

Husen, T, and Postlethwaite, T, 1988 *The International Encyclopedia of Education* Pergamon, Oxford.

IEA, 1976a *The National Case Study: an Empirical Study of Twenty One Educational Systems* John Wiley, New York, USA.

IEA, 1976b *The IEA Six Subject Survey: An Empirical Study of Education in Twenty One Countries* John Wiley, New York.

Johnson, K, 1980 *Timetabling* Hutchinson, London.

Knight, B, 1983 *Managing School Finance* Heinemann Educational Books, London.

Knight, B, 1986 'The Industrial Revolution'. *Education 168* (18) 31 October 1986.

Levin, H, et al, 1984 *Cost-effectiveness of Four Educational Interventions* Stanford University Institute for Research of Educational Finance and Governance — a report (IFG PR 84 A11).

Mid-Continent Regional Educational Laboratory, 1988 *Achieving Excellence: A Site-based Management System for Efficiency, Effectiveness, Excellence* McREL, 12500 E Illiff Avenue, Suite 201, Aurora Colorado 80014, USA.

Mortimore, P, Scammons, P, Stoll, L, Lewis, D, and Ecob, R, 1988 *School Matters: the Junior Years* Open Books, Wells.

National Commission on Excellence in Education, 1983 *A Nation at Risk*, US Government Printing Office, Washington D.C.

Newsom, J, 1963 *Half our Future* Central Advisory Council for Education (England) HMSO, London.

Northern Territory Department of Education, 1986 *Information Statement 1. The Curriculum* Darwin, Australia.

NUT, 1987 *Pupils Teachers and Parents* National Union of Teachers, London.

Odden, A, 1983 *School Finance Reform: Past Present and Future* Issuegram 26, Education Commission of the States, Denver, USA.

Osborne, A, 1986 'A Comprehensive Approach to the Management of Time?' *School Organisation* 6 (2).

Oxfordshire LEA, 1982 *A Change in the Oxfordshire School Day.*

Palmer, K, and Carter, C, 1984 *Stepping Stones* from 'Gatesgarth', 47 High Street, Bodicote, Oxon, OX15 4BP.

Palmer, K, 1987 *Stepping-Stones at Larkrise* from 'Gatesgarth', 47 High Street, Bodicote, Oxon, OX15 4BP.

Parker, G, 1986, Year Round Schools *Programme on Educational Building: Long Term Perspectives* Organisation for Economic Cooperation and Development, Paris.

Plowden, B, 1967 *Children and their Primary Schools* Central Advisory Council for Education (England), HMSO, London.

Power, C, 1980 'Ab Initio Ad Finem: Dr. Who and Alternative Ways of Organising Time in Education.' In *Alternative Ways of Organising Education* Australian Council for Educational Administration.

Richburg, W, and Sjogren, D, 1982 'The Four-Day School Week'. *Phi Delta Kappan* May 1982.

Rutter, M, Maughan, B, Mortimore, P, Ouston, J, 1979 *Fifteen Thousand Hours* Open Books, London.

Scottish Education Department, 1983 *16 – 18s in Scotland, An Action Plan,* Scottish Education Department, Edinburgh.

Sharp, C, 1981 *The Economics of Time* Martin Robertson, London.

Simkins, T, 1987 'Economics and the Management of Schools'. In Thomas, H, and Simkins, T, (Eds) *Economics and the Management of Education: Emerging Themes* Falmer Press, Lewes.

South Australia Education Department, 1984 *Time Allocation and the Curriculum* (ISBN 0 7243 7342X).

Stonier, T, 1986 'The Wealth of Information'. *School Technology* September 1986.

Tizard, J, Schofield, N, and Hewison, J, 1982 'Collaboration between Teachers and Parents in Assisting Children's Reading'. *British Journal of Educational Psychology* 52 (1).

Toffler, A, 1981 *The Third Wave* Pan Books, London (first published Collins 1980).

Turner, E, 1970 'The Effects of Long Summer Holidays on Children's Literacy'. *Educational Research* 14 (3) June 1972.

UNESCO International Bureau of Education, 1986 *International Yearbook of Education* 38.

Walberg, H, 1988 'Synthesis of Research on Time and Learning'. *Educational Leadership* March 1988.

Watkins, P, 1987 *Modular Approaches to the Secondary Curriculum* Longman (for the School Curriculum Development Committee).

Wragg, E, 1987 *Teacher Appraisal — a practical guide* McMillan Education.

Index